RAMADAN 2023

Qur'anic Reading Journal & Historical Digest

Ramadan Qur'anic Reading Journal & Historical Digest

ResearchMinister.Com

873 Vance Ave.

Memphis, TN 38126

Ordering Information:

Quantity sales. Special discounts are available on quantity purchases by corporations, associations, and others. For details, contact the publisher at the address above.

Printed in the Nation of Islam

ISBN: 978-1-7375613-4-7

"The book that the so-called American Negroes (Tribe of Shabazz) should own and read, the book that the slave masters have, but have not represented it to their slaves, is a book that will heal their sin-sick souls that were made sick and sorrowful by the slave masters. The book will open their blinded eyes and open their deaf ears. The book that will purify them, the book that makes a distinction between the God of righteous and the God of evil, the book of guidance, the book of light and truth, the book of wisdom and judgment."

- Hon. Elijah Muhammad, September 29, 1956 Pittsburgh Courier Newspaper

"The Bible is my poor people's graveyard. The Holy Qur'an will resurrect them if they would make a study of its teachings, along with someone to teach its meanings."

-Hon. Elijah Muhammad, July 5, 1958 Pittsburgh Courier Newspaper

Table of Contents

Introduction: "A Nation the Qur'an Produced"

As-Salaam-Alaikum,

Ramadan Mubarak!

I have listened to my teacher, the Honorable Minister Louis Farrakhan, discuss many times that during the founding of the Nation of Islam in America it was the Great Mahdi, Master W. Fard Muhammad who identified a curriculum of study for his principal student the Honorable Elijah Muhammad. This curriculum was made up of 104 books that were to be found in the Library of Congress. Minister Farrakhan said that all of those books had one thing in common; each one was devoted to a subject or topic that discussed or explained the life and history of Prophet Muhammad ibn Abdullah of Arabia(pbuh/saw).

Minister Farrakhan said that his teacher, the Most Honorable Elijah Muhammad, said to him that the best of those 104 books that he studied was the Holy Qur'an. In fact, the official photo of the founder of the Nation of Islam, Master W. Fard Muhammad is a picture of him reading the Holy Qur'an.

This history is very, very significant for us to reflect upon. It is an especially important set of historical facts to ponder and reflect upon during the holy month of Ramadan, which is widely known as "the month of the Holy Qur'an."

From this early history we can see how, contrary to popular belief, the Nation of Islam in America is the product of the presence of the Holy Qur'an in America. Specifically, it is the product of the Most Honorable Elijah Muhammad's study of the Holy Qur'an and his sincere work to apply the teachings and principles of the Holy Qur'an inside of America-a Judeo/Christian society.

Before the popularization of the Holy Qur'an in America by the Nation of Islam, it was a rare book and was the exclusive possession of academic institutions, religious scholars, Moslem Shriners and certain highly placed individuals. But it is the Nation of Islam that freed the Qur'anic text so that it could, at long last, establish a presence in America by becoming a familiar and popular book among the poor and oppressed Black people of America.

The critics of the Nation of Islam often fail to appreciate that the history of the Nation of Islam in America is simultaneously the history of the Holy Qur'an in America. This is no doubt rooted in, on the one hand, these critics' inability to conceive what kind of reality and what kind of community that the Qur'an would give birth to if it could be freely read, studied and utilized as a guidebook inside of America, amidst all of America's myriad of social ills. It is an entirely different experience that one has with a sacred text when one seeks to go beyond simply reading and interpreting it to begin applying and implementing it inside an actual society of people.

Secondarily, the Nation of Islam's critics are frequently too ignorant of the factual history of the Nation of Islam to draw appropriate conclusions where we are concerned. I have experienced that most critics base their opinions on the media generated "propagandized" coverage of the Nation's leadership, membership, events and activities.

The current volume is therefore conceived as a historical digest that focuses on the history of the Nation of Islam in its relationship with the Religion of Islam and its leaders, rituals, traditions and global community of adherents. It will introduce the reader to brief episodes of history both familiar and not familiar so that the reader gets a closer look at the Nation of Islam as a community that the presence of the Holy Qur'an has given birth to.

It is also a space and place for what Islam has described as the "sacred use of the pen." In Islam, writing is a very important companion skill to reading and teaching. There are many traditions in classical Islam that highlight the divine creation of the pen. The pen is referenced in the very first of the revelations of the Holy Qur'an that is found in Surah 96. And the pen is referenced again in Allah's defense of Prophet Muhammad in Surah 68.

To appreciate how reading, writing and teaching are conceived as being integrated and sacred in Islam consider the Arabic morphology of the triliteral root "**ktb**". From this Arabic root system, we are able to morph the word **kitab**. The Holy Qur'an is referred to affectionately as **al-kitab**, which means **"the book."** Other common words that morph out of the "ktb" root are **khutbah(sermon/lecture**) and **khatib(teacher**). The idea then is that these are related concepts and they are woven together and seamlessly so through the grammatic rules of the Arabic language that are not capricious or arbitrary, but the morphology clearly proves them to be very significant.

The believer is then invited to use this volume as a companion to their study and daily reading of the Holy Qur'an during the month of Ramadan. Each section is arranged with space to take notes based upon the daily reading of the Holy Qur'an. Each 'Juz or part to be read for the day is listed above each notes' page and each pair of notes pages is followed by daily hadiths and episodic histories of the Nation of Islam.

The Prophet Muhammad(pbuh) was initially commanded "iqra" which means "read and proclaim." In other words, "read and teach to others what you have read and now understand". And in between reading and teaching is writing. It is my sincere prayer and desire that the believer will be greatly benefitted by this work and that it will aid us in reading Allah's word; writing our thoughts and understanding of his word; learning the history of our beloved community-the Nation of Islam and that all of this leads us to being more confident and proficient in the teaching and proclaiming the message of Islam among our people across America and the world.

Your Brother in Islam,

Demetric Muhammad

The Reward of History

Excerpted from Most Hon. Elijah Muhammad's Letter to the Ministry Class

First: History is above all our studies the most attractive and best qualified to reward our research. As it develops the springs and motives of human actions and displays the consequence of circumstances which operates most powerfully on the destinies of the human being.

Second: It stands true that we the Lost Found NATION, of ISLAM, in the wilderness of North America, have not applied ourselves to the study of History, but rather to folly. Having a lot of the bread of idleness, and when an effort was made to the above effect of History study, it was to our detriment by not knowing what History that was more valuable, to aid us in the knowledge of our own NATION.

THE WISE MAN is the one who has made a careful study of the PAST events of ANCIENT and MODERN HISTORY. The KNOWLEDGE of the FUTURE is JUDGED by the KNOWLEDGE of the PAST. There are MEN born with a gift of PROPHECY. While some are trained into the KNOWLEDGE by intense studies of the PAST EVENTS OF HISTORY

What Does Ramadan Fasting Mean?

Arabic root word definitions on the etymology of Ramadan and Fasting excerpted from the Dictionary of the Holy Qur'an by Abdul Manan Omar

The month of Ramadan is that in which the Qur'an was revealed, a guidance to men and clear proofs of the guidance and the Criterion. So, whoever of you is present in the month, he shall fast therein, and whoever is sick or on a journey, (he shall fast) a (like) number of other days. Allah desires ease for you, and He desires not hardship for you, and (He desires) that you should complete the number and that you should exalt the greatness of Allah for having guided you and that you may give thanks. -Holy Qur'an 2:185

Ramidza رَمِضَ

رَمَضاً :يرمَض. يرمُض

To be burning, heat, be blasted by the sun. *Ramadza* رَمَضَ: To sharpen (a spear) between stones, roast, pasture on a burning ground, burn. *Ramdzâ'* رَمْضا: Scorching heat; Burning hot (ground) *Ramadzân* رمضان: The ninth month of Islamic calendar, the month of Fast.

Ramadzân رَمضان (*n.*): The month of Fasting. (2:185). (L; T; R; LL)

Sâma صام

صِياماً. صَوماً : يَصُوم

To fast. *Sâma 'an*: To abstain from. *Sau* صَوا and *Siyâm* صيام: Act of fasting; Fast. *Sâimun* صائم: One who fasts.

Li Yasum لِيَصم (*imp. 3rd. p.m.*): He should fast. ***Tasûmû*** تَصُومُوا (*imp. 2nd. p. m. plu. acc.*): You fast. ***Sâ'imât*** صائمات (*act. pic. f. plu.*): Fasting women. ***Sâ'imîna*** صائمين (*act. pic. m. plu.*): Fasting men. *Sauman* صوم (*n. acc.*): A fast. ***Siyâmun/ Siyâman*** صيامٌ / صياماً (*nom./ acc.n.*); ***Siyâmin*** صيامٍ (*gen. n.*): Fasting.(L; T; R; LL)

The root with its above forms has been used in the Holy Qur'ân about 14 times.

The Power of Taking Notes

In the name of Allah, the Beneficent, the Merciful. 96:1Read in the name of thy Lord who creates —Creates man from a clot, Read and thy Lord is most Generous, Who taught by the pen, Taught man what he knew not.
-Holy Qur'an 96: 1-5

Excerpted from An Invincible Truth: Pittsburgh Courier Articles Collection

Then when he said, "oh Brother you don't have to study, you just stand up and let God speak through you." **This is after I would take a week to write a half hour broadcast. I would search every word and then economize on words to see if I could say a sentence better and sharper by using different words. This is the truth. I did this for 3 years.**

I went in a studio that I made in my garage at 2311 97th Street in East Elmhurst which was the home that Brother Malcolm lived in. I had the garage soundproofed. I took my Nagra recorder, which was the best in the world at that time. I went in that studio with my script. Nobody in there but me and a microphone and the spirit of God and my love for Him. I didn't need an audience. I just dealt and I've got this down to a science where if you said to me, you got 20 seconds, I could develop my point in 20 seconds and be off. I mean that's how refined it got. ... I remember as a little child I would look up and it said from Bacon. "Writing maketh a man exact." So, the more I wrote the more exact my language became. **-Hon. Min. Louis Farrakhan**

Excerpted from Writing to Read: Evidence for How Writing Can Improve Reading, by Steve Graham and Michael Hebert

Ariel and Will Durant were right when they said, "Education is the transmission of civilization." Putting our current challenges into historical context, it is obvious that if today's youngsters cannot read with understanding, think about and analyze what they've read, and then write clearly and effectively about what they've learned and what they think, then they may never be able to do justice to their talents and their potential. (In that regard, the etymology of the word education, which is "to draw out and draw forth"—from oneself, for example—is certainly evocative.) Indeed, young people who do not have the ability to transform thoughts, experiences, and ideas into written words are in danger of losing touch with the joy of inquiry, the sense of intellectual curiosity, and the inestimable satisfaction of acquiring wisdom that are the touchstones of humanity. What that means for all of us is that the essential educative transmissions that have been passed along century after century, generation after generation, are in danger of fading away, or even falling silent.

In a recent report, the National Commission on Writing also addresses this concern. They say, "If students are to make knowledge their own, they must struggle with the details, wrestle with the facts, and rework raw information and dimly understood concepts into language they can communicate to someone else. In short, if students are to learn, they must write."

Comprehending a text involves actively creating meaning by building relationships among ideas in text, and between the text and one's knowledge, beliefs, and experiences (Wittrock, 1990). Having students write about a text should enhance reading comprehension because it affords greater opportunities to think about ideas in a text, requires them to organize and integrate those ideas into a coherent whole, fosters explicitness, facilitates reflection, encourages personal involvement with texts, and involves students transforming ideas into their own words (Applebee, 1984; Emig, 1977; Klein, 1999; Smith, 1988; Stotsky, 1982). In short, writing about a text should enhance comprehension because it provides students with a tool for visibly and permanently recording, connecting, analyzing, personalizing, and manipulating key ideas in text. The evidence shows that having students write about the material they read does enhance their reading abilities.... Writing about a text proved to be better than just reading it, reading and rereading it, reading and studying it, reading and discussing it, and receiving reading instruction.

Response Note Taking
Writing an extended response to material involves either a personal reaction to the text or analysis and interpretation of it. The former includes writing a personal response to narrative material read or writing about a personal experience related to it.

Summary Note Taking
Transforming a mental summary of text into writing requires additional thought about the essence of the material, and the permanence of writing creates an external record of this synopsis that can be readily critiqued and reworked. As a result, summary writing seems likely to improve comprehension of the material being summarized.

Note Taking in General
The act of taking written notes about text material should enhance comprehension (Kiewra, 1989; Peverly et al., 2007). This writing practice involves sifting through a text to determine what is most relevant and transforming and reducing the substance of these ideas into written phrases or key words. Intentionally or unintentionally, note takers organize the abstracted material in some way, connecting one idea to another, while blending new information with their own knowledge, resulting in new understandings of texts

Holy Qur'an Journaling:
How To Start Using the SOAP Method

(Courtesy of Momentora.Com)

Have you ever felt like you weren't sure how to connect with the Qur'an on a personal level? Or how to delve into an ayah and get as much out of it in a short amount of time? As a mother of a busy toddler, I've felt this way and despite the many Qur'an courses and lectures happening, I still needed a way to connect with the Qur'an on my own. I was thinking to myself how I can make the Qur'an a part of my daily self-care while also doing what I love - writing in my planner! It's one thing to read ayats and reflect on them on a surface level, but I noticed when I dig into each ayah using the SOAP method in my planner, I find so much more meaning and connection throughout my day.

So, what does SOAP stand for?

Subject / Ayah: Write down the Qur'anic ayah you wish to study that day. Focus on each word as you write it down. I prefer to write the translation of the ayah and pick out Arabic words that I want to understand further if they are new to me.

Observation: Using any of the prompts below, journal your observations of the ayah.

- What stands out to you in this ayah?
- Are there any new words?
- What is one thing you didn't notice before?
- Is there repetition, contrast, or comparison?
- Look into the context in the tafseer (explanation) and reasons for revelation if available.
- Look into any particular virtues of that ayah or surah and note them down. (Ex.: Reciting Surah Al Mulk provides protection in the grave)

Application: Now ask yourself how the ayah applies to your own life. What are the key lessons for you? Is there an instruction, warning or encouragement? What can you change in your heart, mind, worship, choices, temperament, or relationships, after learning about this ayah?

Prayer: Thank Allah Almighty for opening your heart to the Qur'an and ask for increased love for the Qur'an, wisdom, and strength to apply what you learn. Write down specific reminders for du'as / prayers to make that remind you of this ayah.

Why does the SOAP method work for Qur'an study and journaling?

I've found is that it helps you interact with the Qur'an one ayah at a time and it's all about applying Allah's directives in one's life. It's also one that can take as little less time as 10 minutes to write out or as long as you'd like depending on the research you do.

What do you need to start?

To start this process, all you need is your planner, a Qur'an, as well as a translation you can easily understand. You can use Quran.com, or my personal favorites - The M.A.S Abdel Haleem Translation by Oxford Press and Mufti Taqi Usmani's Tafseer. To look up the root letters of an Arabic word that is new to me, I use Project Root Word. Also have with you a couple of pens and highlighters - I recommend using finer tip pens to help you write more details. I always use black ink for writing and colored ink for acronyms or quotes.

As you write each section, simply add the acronym letter S O A P where it corresponds on the left side of your planning page. Get creative and write short quotes in different fonts as your BIG take-away so they stand out to you as you scan your page.

If you don't already have the Seeking Jannah Planner, the planner shop is currently on pause due to the recent outbreak but I'll be sure to share when they are back on the storefront. You can certainly start using this method in any vertical format worksheet as well, though this method fits perfectly in the Seeking Jannah Planners' vertical undated layout.

For the 'weeks' focus' section, you can write down which surah you are focusing on. And in the daily date boxes, I usually put in the numerical surah and ayah number for that day. I personally don't do consecutive ayats for my journaling. For example, if I studied ayah 7 of a surah, I may not do ayah 8 next as it's possible the context was easily understandable or the subject was the same, so in that case, I will skip to ayah 12 or 18.

What are the benefits of Qur'an journaling consistently?

- Expression of your personal connection with the Qur'an and expressing any deeper thoughts in a private writing space.
- Expression of thoughts and reactions towards Allah's words and examples, towards yourself, and others.
- An opportunity to reflect & sort out your experience (past, present, or future) as it relates to the Qur'an.
- Finding themes that emerge which point to personal challenges, resilience or strengths
- Finding self-compassion or compassion for others
- More wise and Allah-centric decision-making going forward
- Seeking Allah's pleasure through giving time and attention to His words.

This is not an exhaustive list, but I encourage you to give this simple method a try and you'll be surprised at how great it feels Insha'Allah for your heart, mind, and soul.

"Islam is the True Religion; the Sun of Law and Truth; the help of the helpless poor. It brought the White Race up out of the dark caves of Europe.... Islam built their homes; carpeted their floors; alighted their homes with lamps; put clothes on their naked bodies and cooked their food, and put pure drinks in their stomachs; taught them the manners of society; gave them the Scriptures of God for their guidance and taught them true language of mathematics that they may build a kingdom of wonders and ascend above the clouds."

-Hon. Elijah Muhammad, April 5, 1958 New Amsterdam News

The Muslim Program

Annotated With Supporting Ayats From The Holy Qur'an

What the Muslims Want

1. We want freedom. We want a full and complete freedom.

Surah 90:11-17 And what will make thee comprehend what the uphill road is? It is to free a slave, Or to feed in a day of hunger, An orphan nearly related, Or the poor man lying in the dust, Then he is of those who believe and exhort one another to patience, and exhort one another to mercy.

Surah 2:177 - It is not righteousness that you turn your faces towards the East and the West, but righteous is the one who believes in Allah, and the Last Day, and the angels and the Book and the prophets, and gives away wealth out of love for Him to the near of kin and the orphans and the needy and the wayfarer and to those who ask and to set slaves free and keeps up prayer and pays the poor-rate; and the performers of their promise when they make a promise, and the patient in distress and affliction and in the time of conflict. These are they who are truthful; and these are they who keep their duty.

2. We want justice. Equal justice under the law. We want justice applied equally to all regardless of creed, class, or color.

Surah 3: 108 - These are the messages of Allah which We recite to thee with truth. And Allah desires no injustice to (His) creatures.

Surah 4: 135 - O you who believe, be maintainers of justice, bearers of witness for Allah, even though it be against your own selves or (your) parents or near relatives — whether he be rich or poor, Allah has a better right over them both. So follow not (your) low desires, lest you deviate. And if you distort or turn away from (truth), surely Allah is ever Aware of what you do.

Surah 5: 8 - O you who believe, be upright for Allah, bearers of witness with justice; and let not hatred of a people incite you not to act equitably. Be just; that is nearer to observance of duty. And keep your duty to Allah. Surely Allah is Aware of what you do.

Surah 16:90 - Surely Allah enjoins justice and the doing of good (to others) and the giving to the kindred, and He forbids indecency and evil and rebellion. He admonishes you that you may be mindful.

Surah 60: 8 - Allah forbids you not respecting those who fight you not for religion, nor drive you forth from your homes, that you show them kindness and deal with them justly. Surely Allah loves the doers of justice.

3. We want equality of opportunity. We want equal membership in society with the best in civilized society.

Surah 8:58 - And if thou fear treachery on the part of a people, throw back to them (their treaty) on terms of equality. Surely Allah loves not the treacherous.

Surah 33:35 - Surely the men who submit and the women who submit, and the believing men and the believing women, and the truthful men and the truthful women, and the patient men and the patient women, and the humble men and the humble women, and the charitable men and the charitable women, and the fasting men and the fasting women, and the men who guard their chastity and the women who guard, and the men who remember Allah much and the women who remember — Allah has prepared for them forgiveness and a mighty reward.

Surah 28:77 - And seek the abode of the Hereafter by means of what Allah has given thee, and neglect not thy portion of the world, and do good (to others) as Allah has done good to thee, and seek not to make mischief in the land. Surely Allah loves not the mischief-makers.

4. We want our people in America whose parents or grandparents were descendants from slaves to be allowed, to establish separate state or territory of their own -- either on this continent or elsewhere. We believe that our former slave-masters are obligated to provide such land and that the area must be fertile and minerally rich. We believe that our former slave-masters are obligated to maintain and supply our needs in this separate territory for the next 20 or 25 years until we are able to produce and supply our own needs. Since we cannot get along with them in peace and equality after giving them 400 years of our sweat and blood and receiving in return some of the worst treatment human beings have ever experienced, we believe our contributions to this land and the suffering forced upon us by white America justifies our demand for complete separation in a state or territory of our own.

Surah 7:10 - And certainly We established you in the earth and made therein means of livelihood for you; little it is that you give thanks!

Surah 24: 41 - Those who, if We establish them in the land, will keep up prayer and pay the poor-rate and enjoin good and forbid evil. And Allah's is the end of affairs.

Surah 7:74 - And remember when He made you successors after 'Ad and settled you in the land — you make mansions on its plains and hew out houses in the mountains. So remember Allah's bounties and act not corruptly in the land, making mischief.

Surah 14:6 - And when Moses said to his people: Call to mind Allah's favour to you, when He delivered you from Pharaoh's people, who subjected you to severe torment, and slew your sons and spared your women. And therein was a great trial from your Lord.

Surah 4:75 - And what reason have you not to fight in the way of Allah, and of the weak among the men and the women and the children, who say: Our Lord, take us out of this town, whose people are oppressors, and grant us from Thee a friend, and grant us from Thee a helper!

5. We want freedom for all Believers of Islam now held in federal prisons. We want freedom for all black men and women now under death sentence in innumerable prisons in the North as well as the south.

Surah 39:53 - Say: O My servants who have been prodigal regarding their souls, despair not of the mercy of Allah; surely Allah forgives sins altogether. He is indeed the Forgiving, the Merciful.

Surah 3:16 - Those who say: Our Lord, we believe, so forgive our sins and save us from the chastisement of the fire.

Surah 46:31 - O our people, accept the Inviter to Allah and believe in Him. He will forgive you some of your sins and protect you from a painful chastisement

6. We want every black man and woman to have the freedom to accept or reject being separated from the slave-masters' children and establish a land of their own. We know that the above plan for the solution of the black and white conflict is the best and only answer to the problem between two people.

Surah 6: 165 And He it is Who has made you successors in the land and exalted some of you in rank above others, that He may try you by what He has given you. Surely thy Lord is Quick in requiting (evil), and He is surely the Forgiving, the Merciful.

Surah 17:70 - And surely We have honoured the children of Adam, and We carry them in the land and the sea, and We provide them with good things, and We have made them to excel highly most of those whom We have created.

Surah 21: 105 - And certainly We wrote in the Book after the remainder that My righteous servants will inherit the land.

7. We want an immediate end to the police brutality and mob attacks against the so-called Negro throughout the United States. We believe that the Federal government should intercede to see that black men and women tried in white courts receive justice in accordance with the laws of the land, or allow us to build a new nation for ourselves, dedicated to justice, freedom and liberty. As long as we are not allowed to establish a state or territory of our own, we demand not only equal justice under the laws of the United States but equal employment opportunities -- NOW! We do not believe that after 400 years of free or nearly free labor, sweat and blood, which has helped America become rich and powerful, so many thousands of black people should have to subsist on relief or charity or live in poor houses.

Surah 42:42 - The way (of blame) is only against those who oppress men and revolt in the earth unjustly. For such there is a painful chastisement.

Surah 42:41 - And whoever defends himself after his being oppressed, these it is against whom there is no way (of blame).

Surah 22:60 - That (is so). And whoever retaliates with the like of that with which he is afflicted and he is oppressed, Allah will certainly help him. Surely Allah is Pardoning, Forgiving.

Surah 22:39 - Permission (to fight) is given to those on whom war is made, because they are oppressed. And surely Allah is Able to assist them —

8. We want the government of the United States to exempt our people from ALL taxation as long as we are deprived of equal justice under the laws of the land.

Surah 90:2 - And thou wilt be made free from obligation in this City

9. We want equal education -- but separate schools up to 16 for boys and 18 for girls on the conditions that the girls be sent to women's' colleges and universities. We want all black children educated, taught and trained by their own teacher. Under such school system we believe we will make a better nation of people. The United States government should provide free all necessary text books and equipment, schools and college buildings. The Muslim teachers shall be left free to teach and train their people in the way of righteousness, decency and self-respect.

Surah 2:255- Allah — there is no god but He, the Ever-living, the Self-subsisting by Whom all subsist. Slumber overtakes Him not, nor sleep. To Him belongs whatever is in the heavens and whatever is in the earth. Who is he that can intercede with Him but by His permission? He knows what is before them and what is behind them. And they encompass nothing of His knowledge except what He pleases. His knowledge extends over the heavens and the earth, and the preservation of them both tires Him not. And He is the Most High, the Great.

Surah 3: 36 - And when she brought it forth, she said: My Lord, I have brought it forth a female — and Allah knew best what she brought forth — and the male is not like the female, and I have named it Mary, and I commend her and her offspring into Thy protection from the accursed devil.

Surah 3:79 - It is not meet for a mortal that Allah should give him the Book and the judgement and the prophethood, then he should say to men: Be my servants besides Allah's; but (he would say): Be worshippers of the Lord because you teach the Book and because you study (it);

Surah 7:169 - Then after them came an evil posterity who inherited the Book, taking the trail goods of this low life and saying: It will be forgiven us. And if the like good came to them, they would take it (too). Was not a promise taken from them in the Book that they would not speak anything about Allah but the truth? And they study what is in it. And the abode of the Hereafter is better for those who keep their duty. Do you not then understand?

Surah 20:52 - He said: The knowledge thereof is with my Lord in a book; my Lord neither errs nor forgets —

Surah 96: 1-5: Read in the name of thy Lord who creates — Creates man from a clot, Read and thy Lord is most Generous, Who taught by the pen, Taught man what he knew not.

10. We believe that intermarriage or race mixing should be prohibited. We want the religion Islam taught without hindrance or suppression.

Surah 4:1 - O people, keep your duty to your Lord, Who created you from a single being and created its mate of the same (kind), and spread from these two many men and women. And keep your duty to Allah, by Whom you demand one of another (your rights), and (to) the ties of relationship. Surely Allah is ever a Watcher over you.

Surah 5:57 – O you who believe, take not for friends those who take your religion as a mockery and a sport, from among those who were given the Book before you and the disbelievers; and keep your duty to Allah if you are believers.

Surah 24:3 The adulterer cannot have sexual relations with any but an adulteress or an idolatress, and the adulteress, none can have sexual relations with her but an adulterer or an idolater; and it is forbidden to believers.

Surah 49:13 - O mankind, surely We have created you from a male and a female, and made you tribes and families that you may know each other. Surely the noblest of you with Allah is the most dutiful of you. Surely Allah is Knowing, Aware.

Surah 60: 1 – O you who believe, take not My enemy and your enemy for friends. Would you offer them love, while they deny the Truth that has come to you, driving out the Messenger and yourselves because you believe in Allah, your Lord? If you have come forth to strive in My way and to seek My pleasure, would you love them in secret? And I know what you conceal and what you manifest. And whoever of you does this, he indeed strays from the straight path.

What The Muslims Believe

1. We believe in the One God Whose proper name is Allah.

Surah 2:163 - And your God is one God; there is no God but He! He is the Beneficent, the Merciful.

Surah 16:51- Allah has commanded: "Do not take two gods; or He is but One God. So fear Me alone.

Surah 17: 110 - Say: Call on Allah or call on the Beneficent. By whatever (name) you call on Him, He has the best names. And utter not thy prayer loudly nor be silent in it, and seek a way between these.

Surah 41:6 - Say, 'O Prophet,' "I am only a man like you, 'but' it has been revealed to me that your God is only One God. So take the Straight Way towards Him, and seek His forgiveness. And woe to the polytheists

Surah 112 " Say He Allah is One. Allah is He on Whom all depend. He begets not, nor is He begotten. And none is like Him.

2. We believe in the Holy Quran and the Scriptures of all the Prophets of God.

Surah 2: 2 - This Book, there is no doubt in it, is a guide to those who keep their duty.

Surah 6: 82 And this is a Blessed Book We have revealed, verifying that which is before it, and that thou mayest warn the mother of the towns and those around her. And those who believe in the Hereafter believe in it, and they keep a watch over their prayers.

Surah 6: 155 - And this is a Book We have revealed, full of blessings; so follow it and keep your duty that mercy may be shown to you.

Surah 13:1 And this is a Book We have revealed, full of blessings; so follow it and keep your duty that mercy may be shown to you.

Surah 18:1 Praise be to Allah! Who revealed the Book to His servant, and allowed not therein any crookedness.

Surah 2: 136 - Say: We believe in Allah and (in) that which has been revealed to us, and (in) that which was revealed to Abraham, and Ishmael and Isaac and Jacob and the tribes, and (in) that which was given to Moses and Jesus, and (in) that which was given to the prophets from their Lord, we do not make any distinction between any of them and to Him do we submit

Surah 3:84- Say: We believe in Allah and that which is revealed to us, and that which was revealed to Abraham and Ishmael and Isaac and Jacob and the tribes, and that which was given to Moses and Jesus and to the prophets from their Lord; we make no distinction between any of them, and to Him we submit.

Surah 4: 150 - Those who disbelieve in Allah and His messengers and desire to make a distinction between Allah and His messengers and say: We believe in some and disbelieve in others; and desire to take a course in between--

Surah 4: 152 - And those who believe in Allah and His messengers and make no distinction between any of them, to them He will grant their rewards. And Allah is ever Forgiving, Merciful

Surah 29: 47 - And thus have We revealed the Book to thee. So those whom We have given the Book believe in it, and of these there are those who believe in it; and none deny Our messages except the disbelievers.

3. We believe in the truth of the Bible, but we believe that it has been tampered with and must be reinterpreted so that mankind will not be snared by the falsehoods that have been added to it.

Surah 5:46 - And We sent after them in their footsteps Jesus, son of Mary, verifying that which was before him of the Torah; and We gave him the Gospel containing guidance and light, and verifying that which was before it of the Torah, and a guidance and an admonition for the dutiful

Surah 5: 47 - And let the People of the Gospel judge by that which Allah has revealed in it. And whoever judges not by what Allah has revealed, those are the transgressors.

Surah 5: 66 - And if they had observed the Torah and the Gospel and that which is revealed to them from their Lord, they would certainly have eaten from above them and from beneath their feet. There is a party of them keeping to the moderate course, and most of them — evil is that which they do.

Surah 5: 68 - Say: O People of the Book, you follow no good till you observe the Torah and the Gospel and that which is revealed to you from your Lord. And surely that which has been revealed to thee from thy Lord will make many of them increase in inordinacy and disbelief: so grieve not for the disbelieving people.

4. We believe in Allah's Prophets and the Scriptures they brought to the people.

Surah 2:285 - The Messenger believes in what has been revealed to him from his Lord, and (so do) the believers. They all believe in Allah and His angels and His Books and His messengers. We make no difference between any of His messengers. And they say: We hear and obey; our Lord, Thy forgiveness (do we crave), and to Thee is the eventual course.

Surah 5: 15 - O People of the Book, indeed Our Messenger has come to you, making clear to you much of that which you concealed of the Book and passing over much. Indeed, there has come to you from Allah, a Light, and a clear Book.

5. We believe in the resurrection of the dead -- not in physical resurrection but mental resurrection. We believe that the so-called Negroes are most in need of mental resurrection; therefore, they will be resurrected first.

Furthermore, we believe we are the people of God's choice as it has been written that God would choose the rejected and the despised. We can find no other persons fitting this description in these last days more than the so-called Negroes in America. We believe in the resurrection of the righteous.

Surah 2:85 - Yet you it is who would slay your people and turn a party from among you out of their homes, backing each other up against them unlawfully and exceeding the limits. And if they should come to you as captives you would ransom them, whereas their turning out itself was unlawful for you. Do you then believe in a part of the Book and disbelieve in the other? What then is the reward of such among you as do this but disgrace in the life of this world, and on the day of Resurrection they shall be sent back to the most grievous chastisement. And Allah is not heedless of what you do.

Surah 2:113 - And the Jews say, The Christians follow nothing (good), and the Christians say, The Jews following nothing (good), while they recite the (same) Book. Even thus say those who have no knowledge, like what they say. So Allah will judge between them on the day of Resurrection in that wherein they differ.

Surah 3:27 - Thou makest the night to pass into the day and Thou makest the day to pass into the night; and Thou bringest forth the living from the dead and Thou bringest forth the dead from the living; and Thou givest sustenance to whom Thou pleasest without measure.

Surah 22:5 - O people, if you are in doubt about the Resurrection, then surely We created you from dust, then from a small life-germ, then from a clot, then from a lump of flesh, complete in make and incomplete, that We may make clear to you. And We cause what We please to remain in the wombs till an appointed time, then We bring you forth as babies, then that you may attain your maturity. And of you is he who is caused to die, and of you is he who is brought back to the worst part of life, so that after knowledge he knows nothing. And thou seest the earth barren, but when We send down thereon water, it stirs and swells and brings forth a beautiful (growth) of every kind.

Surah 22: 6 - That is because Allah, He is the Truth, and He gives life to the dead, and He is Possessor of power over all things

Surah 22:7 And the Hour is coming, there is no doubt about it, and Allah will raise up those who are in the graves.

Surah 36: 51 - And the trumpet is blown, when lo! from their graves they will hasten on to their Lord.

Surah 70: 43 - The day when they come forth from the graves in haste, as hastening on to a goal

6. We further believe in the judgment. We believe this first judgment will take place, as God revealed, in America.

Surah 6:62 - Then are they sent back to Allah, their Master, the True One. Now surely His is the judgment and He is Swiftest in taking account.

Surah 51: 6 - And the Judgment will surely come to pass

Surah 20:102- The day when the trumpet is blown; and We shall gather the guilty, blue-eyed, on that day,

Surah 22: 1-3 O people, keep your duty to your Lord; surely the shock of the Hour is a grievous thing. The day you see it, every woman giving suck will forget her suckling and every pregnant one will lay down her burden, and thou wilt see men as drunken, yet they will not be drunken, but the chastisement of Allah will be severe. And among men is he who disputes about Allah without knowledge, and follows every rebellious devil.

7. We believe this is the time in history for the separation of the so-called Negroes and the so-called white Americans. We believe the black man should be freed in name as well as in fact. By this, we mean that he should be freed from names imposed upon him by his former slave masters. Names which identified him as being the slave of the slave-master. We believe that if we are free indeed, we should go in our own people's names -- the black peoples of the earth.

Surah 4: 75 - And what reason have you not to fight in the way of Allah, and of the weak among the men and the women and the children, who say: Our Lord, take us out of this town, whose people are oppressors, and grant us from Thee a friend, and grant us from Thee a helper!

Surah 7: 137 And We made the people who were deemed weak to inherit the eastern lands and the western ones which We had blessed. And the good word of thy Lord was fulfilled in the Children of Israel — because of their patience. And We destroyed what Pharaoh and his people had wrought and what they had built

Surah 7: 141 And when We delivered you from Pharaoh's people, who subjected you to severe torment, killing your sons and sparing your women. And therein was a great trial from your Lord

8. We believe in justice for all whether in God or not. We believe as others that we are due equal justice as human beings. We believe in equality - as a nation -of equals. We do not believe that we are equal with our slave-masters in the status of Freed slaves. We recognize and respect American citizens as independent peoples, and we respect their laws which govern this nation.

Surah 3: 108 - These are the messages of Allah which We recite to thee with truth. And Allah desires no injustice to (His) creatures.

Surah 4: 135 - O you who believe, be maintainers of justice, bearers of witness for Allah, even though it be against your own selves or (your) parents or near relatives — whether he be rich or poor, Allah has a better right over them both. So follow not (your) low desires, lest you deviate. And if you distort or turn away from (truth), surely Allah is ever Aware of what you do.

Surah 5: 8 - O you who believe, be upright for Allah, bearers of witness with justice; and let not hatred of a people incite you not to act equitably. Be just; that is nearer to observance of duty. And keep your duty to Allah. Surely Allah is Aware of what you do.

Surah 16:90 - Surely Allah enjoins justice and the doing of good (to others) and the giving to the kindred, and He forbids indecency and evil and rebellion. He admonishes you that you may be mindful.

Surah 60: 8 - Allah forbids you not respecting those who fight you not for religion, nor drive you forth from your homes, that you show them kindness and deal with them justly. Surely Allah loves the doers of justice.

9. We believe that the offer of integration is hypocritical and is made by those who are trying to deceive the black peoples into believing that their 400-year-old open enemies of freedom, justice, and equality are, all of a sudden, their friends. Furthermore, we believe that such deception is intended to prevent black people from realizing that the time in history has arrived for the separation from the whites of this nation. If the white people are truthful about their professed friendship toward the so-called Negro, they can prove it by dividing up America with their slaves. We do not believe that America will ever be able to furnish enough jobs for her own millions of unemployed in addition to jobs for the 20,000,000 black people.

Surah 4:120 - He promises them and excites vain desires in them. And the devil promises them only to deceive.

Surah 7:113-114 - And the enchanters came to Pharaoh, saying: We must surely have a reward if we prevail. He said: Yes, and you shall certainly be of those who are near (to me).

10. We believe that we who declared ourselves to be righteous Muslims should not participate in wars which take the lives of humans. We do not believe this nation should force us to take part in such wars, for we have nothing to gain from it unless America agrees to give us the necessary territory wherein we may have something to fight for.

Surah 5:32 - For this reason, We prescribed for the Children of Israel that whoever kills a person, unless it be for manslaughter or for mischief in the land, it is as though he had killed all men. And whoever saves a life, it is as though he had saved the lives of all men. And certainly, Our messengers came to them with clear arguments, but even after that many of them commit excesses in the land.

11. We believe our women should be respected and protected as the women of other nationalities are respected and protected.

Surah 4:19- O you who believe, it is not lawful for you to take women as heritage against (their) will. Nor should you straiten them by taking part of what you have given them unless they are guilty of manifest indecency. And treat them kindly. Then if you hate them, it may be that you dislike a thing while Allah has placed abundant good in it.

Surah 3:36 - So when she brought it forth, she said: My Lord, I have brought it forth a female — and Allah knew best what she brought forth — and the male is not like the female, and I have named it Mary, and I commend her and her offspring into Thy protection from the accursed devil.

Surah 33:59 - O Prophet, tell thy wives and thy daughters and the women of believers to let down upon them their over-garments. This is more proper, so that they may be known, and not be given trouble. And Allah is ever Forgiving, Merciful.

12. We believe that Allah (God) appeared in the Person of Master W. Fard Muhammad, July 1930 -- the long-awaited Messiah of the Christians and the Mahdi of the Muslims. We believe further and lastly that Allah is God and besides HIM there is no God and He will bring about a universal government of peace wherein we can live in peace together.

Surah 2:210 - They wait for naught but that Allah should come to them in the shadows of the clouds with angels, and the matter has (already) been decided. And to Allah are (all) matters returned.

Surah 89:22 - And thy Lord comes with the angels, ranks on ranks

Surah 59:2 - He it is Who caused those who disbelieved of the People of the Book to go forth from their homes at the first banishment. You deemed not that they would go forth, while they thought that their fortresses would defend them against Allah. But Allah came to them from place they expected not and cast terror into their hearts — they demolished their houses with their own hands and the hands of the believers. So take a lesson, O you who have eyes!

Surah 16:33 - Await they aught but that the angels should come to them or that thy Lord's command should come to pass. Thus did those before them. And Allah wronged them not, but they wronged themselves

Surah 16:102-103: Say: The Holy Spirit has revealed it from thy Lord with truth, that it may establish those who believe, and as a guidance and good news for those who submit. And indeed We know that they say: Only a mortal teaches him. The tongue of him whom they hint at is foreign, and this is clear Arabic language.

Surah 19:17 - So she screened herself from them. Then We sent to her Our spirit and it appeared to her as a well-made man.

The Vindication Of
The Most Honorable Elijah Muhammad's Theology
Day 1

Allah Is A Man

Wesley Muhammad

"The ignorant belief of the Orthodox Muslims that Allah (God) is some formless something and yet He has an Interest in our affairs, can be condemned in no limit of time. I would not give two cents for that kind of God in which they believe. God is a man and we just cannot *make Him other than a man, lest we make Him an inferior one."*

- The Honorable Elijah Muhammad

Those Muslims who take issue with the Honorable Elijah Muhammad on this point usually cite the first verse of Surat al-Nisa' [4] which reads:

> O People (*Yā ayyuha al-nās*)! Reverence your Lord Who created you from a single Person/Soul (*nafs*) and created, of like nature, his mate and from these two scattered many men (*rijālan*) and women.

It is apparently assumed that this verse is a "proof" that Allah is not a man because here it is affirmed that Allah created *rijālan* (men) and *nās* (people). This is a very shallow engagement of the Qur'an that takes no account of its philological context.

These Muslim nay-sayers of the Hon. Elijah Muhammad are apparently unaware of the distinct connotations of the different words in Arabic for 'man'. To illustrate the relevance of this philological fact to our subject, allow me to cite the Biblical Hebrew example. Hebrew has five words (plus their derivatives) for man: *'īsh*, *geber*, *'ādhām*, *'enôš* and *mt*. The last two terms (*'enôš* and *mt*) connote human frailty and weakness and as such are never applied to God. It is a different story, however, with *'īsh* and *geber*. These two terms connote strength, kingship, and spirituality and the Hebrew Bible declares that God is this sort of man: Yahweh is an *'īsh* and *geber* or rather *gibbôr*, mighty man. The Book of Exodus states emphatically *YHWH 'īsh milhāmāh*, "Yahweh is a man (*'īsh*) of war (15:3).

We find the same linguistic circumstance with Arabic. There are several terms for "man" or "human," each with distinct connotations. The general term for "mankind" or "human being" is *bashar*. This term derives from the verb *bashara* which means "to peal, scrap, shave off; to grate, shred." It also means "peal the hide or skin off". The noun *bashara* means external skin closest to the flesh (epidermis). It is thus a cognate of the Hebrew word *bāsār* "flesh". The Arabic term *bashar* thus indicates that human beings are 'fleshy' and it associates them with "scrapes". It also hints at humans as sexual beings: Form III of the verb means "to touch; to have sex with". We can understand why this term is never associated with God. In the Hebrew, God is a kingly, spiritual man (*'īsh/ gibbôr*) but He is emphatically disassociated from *bāsār* corruptible "flesh."

For related reasons the common term for man, *rajul*, would be disassociated from Allah, the Most High as well. The lexicons tell us that a *rajul* is specifically an adult male from among *bashar* or human beings (See Lane s.v.). The "lowness" of this designation is inherent, as it is related to "feet". The verb *rajala* means "to go on foot" and *rijl* is foot or (lower) leg. Those familiar with Arabic culture and the taboo associated with feet therein understand immediately why this term would be inappropriate as a designation for God. The term *nās* may be derived from *nāsa, yanūsu*, "to hang down; to be in a state of commotion." Like *rajul*, the term *nās* is applied to both humans and jinn, which alone makes them inapplicable to Allah. That *nās* implies creaturely weakness is indicated by its derivative, *insān*, "human, man, person". In the same Surat al-Nisa' [4]: 28 it is written: "Allah wishes to lighten your (difficulties), for He created man (*al-insān*) weak (*da'if*)." So these Muslims are right on this point: It is inappropriate to call Allah a *rajul* or *insān*: He is not *that* type of man. What *type* of man is He then?

The Qur'an does not explicitly affirm or deny that Allah is man. Such clarification was left to Allah's Prophet, Muhammad ibn Abd Allah, who did just that. According to *hadith al-shābb* which was authenticated by Imam Ahmad b. Hanbal and many others (see my book, ***Take Another Look***), Allah appeared to Muhammad as a *shābb*, which is a young man between the ages of sixteen and thirty-two. But the term has more connotations. The verb *shabba* means "he was raised or elevated", thus connoting height and elevation. *Shabba* means also "to kindle a burning fire" and "to appear bright and beautiful". All of these are appropriate for God and consistent with what we otherwise know of Allah.

Al-Bukhari and Muslim report a hadith from the Prophet on the authority of the Companion Al-Mughira b. Shu'ba:

> No *shakhṣ* is more jealous (*aghyar*) than Allah; no *shakhṣ* is more pleased to grant pardon than He; no *shakhṣ* loves praiseworthy conduct more than He.[i]

A *shakhṣ* is a corporeal person, a man.[ii] The term connotes "the bodily or corporeal form or figure or substance (*suwād*) of a man," or "something possessing height (*irtifā'*) and visibility (*ẓuhūr*)," Ibn Manzūr informs us in his *Lisān al- 'Arab* (7, 45, 4-11).[iii] Ibn al-Jawzī, in his *Kitāb Akhbār al-Sifāt* 53-4 (Ar.), admits as well that "the term *shakhṣ* implies the existence of a body (*jism*) composed of parts, for one terms something a *shakhṣ* because it possesses corporeality (*shukhūs*) and height." A *shakhs* is thus literally a man with a body and height. It too implies elevation, which is fitting for the Most High. The verb *shakhasa* means "He rose or became elevated."

The Arabic syntax of the sentence of this hadith suggests that God is a man/person with a physical body, but an elevated man. This is a sentence with a superlative (e.g. *aghyar*). In such a sentence, attention is drawn to one from a whole that is greatest at something that is characteristic of the whole. The noun described by the superlative (i.e. Allah) is one of the whole or genus (i.e. *shakhṣ*), though a remarkable one. The sentence could thus be re-written: "Allah is the most jealous *shakhṣ*." This is because the apparent meaning (*ẓāhir*) of the text presents us with an *istithnā' al-muttaṣil* or "joined exception", i.e. an exception from among likes. The excepted noun is joined to or of the same kind as the genus from which it is excepted.

- Genus = شخص *shakhṣ*
- Excepted Noun = Allah

Allah is thus an exceptional *shakhṣ*. However, those with an anti-anthropomorphist theology like Ibn al-Jawzi chose to read this as an example of *istithnā' al-munqaṭi#* or the "severed exception," in which the excepted noun (i.e. Allah) is severed from or of a wholly different kind than the genus.[iv] But Ibn al-Jawzi confirms that the Traditionalist Sunni (Hanbalī) scholars against whom he was writing – that is to say the *orthodox* Hanbalīs - read the hadith according to its apparent meaning with an *istithnā' al-mutta**ṣil***, thus acknowledging Allah as a man.[v] He says of them: "These anthropomorphists are persons who describe the Divine Attributes in terms required by sense experience...and they represent Him as a physical man (*shakhṣ*) whose beauty exceeds all beauty..."vi No less of an authority than the leading orthodox Hanbalī, al-Qadi Abu Ya'la', affirms this in his ***Kitab al-Mu'tamad fi Usul al-Din***:

> If it is said, "He is a person (*shakhṣ*) or form (*ṣūra*)," it (should be) said: The report from different routes on the night of the *mi'raj* mentioned, "I saw my Lord in the most beautiful form"...And the application of that is not to be refused. Just as "soul" (*nafs*) not like souls and essence (*dhāt*) not like essences weren't denied Him. Likewise form unlike forms, for the *shari'a* (uses it in this manner).vii

It was thus well within Sunni orthodoxy as represented and championed by the Hanbalīs, the school of the paradigmatic Sunni scholar himself Imam Ahmad, to refer to Allah as a man (*shakhṣ*) because according to the apparent meaning of a prophetic hadith the Prophet himself referred to Allah as man. Thus, *contra* what many Muslims claim, Surat al-Nisa' [4]:1 in no way "proves" that Allah is not a man: it only suggests that He is not a *rajul* or *insane*. According to the Prophet, Allah is a *shakhṣ* and *shābb.*

We learn from Shams-i Tabrizi (d. 1248) about a *wāʿiz* or popular Islamic preacher in the Old Iranian city of Hamadan who sermonized on Allah's human-like form. As he preached, the Qur'an-reciters (*qurrāʾ*) would recite the verses affirming Allah's anthropomorphism, such as Q 20:5 "Al-Rahmān sat upon the Throne" and Q 89:22, "Your Lord and the Angels will come, rank upon rank." The wāʿiz supplemented and interpreted these Qur'anic proofs with hadiths from the Prophet Muhammad (PBUH), such as:

> 1.] Jarir ibn 'Abd-Allah said: "We were sitting with the Prophet (peace and blessings of Allah be upon him), looking at the moon on the night of the fourteenth (of the month). He said, 'You will see your Lord with your own eyes just as you are looking at this (moon), without any doubt that you are seeing Him.'" (al-Bukhaari, 6883; Muslim, 1002)
>
> 2.] "Narrated Abu Hurairah: The Prophet said: 'Allah created Adam according to His Form/Image (*ṣūra*)'". (Al-Bukhari, vol. 8, # 246; Muslim, #4731]
>
> 3.] Ibn Abbas narrated:"The Messenger of God said: 'I saw my Lord under the form of a young man (*shābb*) beardless (*amrad*) with curly hair (*jaʿd*) and clothed in a red garment (*ḥulla*)." (Ibn Adī, *al-Kāmil*, 2:677)

The wāʿiz then declared: "Woe to anyone who does not declare Allah's resemblance in these Attributes (*ṣifāt*) and who does not know His Form (*ṣūra*)! His outcome will be Hell, even if he performs the worship, for he would have denied the Form of God. How can his obedience be accepted?" People then stood up and questioned the wāʿiz about this, citing verses such as Q 42:11, "Nothing is Like Him (sic)". But the learned wāʿiz explained that such verses are to be understood in the context of God's anthropomorphism or human-like form that is yet different from the corruptible human form in ways. The audience was convinced, and the men went home and declared to their wives and children:

> You must know that God is on the Throne, in a beautiful form, His two feet hanging down and placed on the Footstool, with the angels all around the Throne! The wāʿiz said, "If anyone negates these forms, his faith is negated. Woe upon his death! Woe upon his grave! Woe upon his outcome!"

This is hard core Old School Islam!

<u>Article Footnotes:</u>

1 Bukhari, ***Sahih***, *tawhid*, 20:512; Muslim, ***Sahih***, *li'an*, 17; Ibn Hanbal, ***Musnad*** IV:248; Nisa'i, ***al-Sunan***, *nikah*, 37, 3.

1 *Al-Mawrid*, 664

1 See also Lane, ***Arabic Lexicon***, 2:1517.

1 Ibn al-Jawzī, *Kitāb Akhbār al-Sifāt*, 190-191 (Eng.). On *istithnā' al-muttasil* and *istithnā' al-munqaāi#* see W. Wright, ***A Grammar of the Arabic Language*** 2vols. (3rd edition; Beirut: Librairie du Liban, 1996 [1974]) II, 335D-336A.

1 Ibn al-Jawzī, *Kitāb Akhbār al-Sifāt*, 189-191 (Eng.)

1 *Talbis Iblis*, 87.

1 al-Qadi Abu Ya'la, *Kit§b al-M'#tammad fi usul al-din*. 58. Cf. 85.

Ramadan Day 1-The Believer's Notes

Surah 1:1 – Surah 2:141

Ramadan Day 1-The Believer's Notes

Surah 1:1 – Surah 2:141

Hadith Wisdom For Ramadan Fasting

Narrated Abu Huraira:

Allah's Messenger (peace be upon him) said, "Fasting is a shield (or a screen or a shelter). So, the person observing fasting should avoid sexual relation with his wife and should not behave foolishly and impudently, and if somebody fights with him or abuses him, he should tell him twice, 'I am fasting." The Prophet (peace be upon him) added, "By Him in Whose Hands my soul is, the smell coming out from the mouth of a fasting person is better in the sight of Allah than the smell of musk. (Allah says about the fasting person), 'He has left his food, drink and desires for My sake. The fast is for Me. So I will reward (the fasting person) for it and the reward of good deeds is multiplied ten times."

Day 1	NOI	Regional	Cities	Prayer	Times	2023
City	Fajr	Sunrise	Dhuhr	Asr	Maghrib	Isha
Atlanta	06:30 AM	07:38 AM	01:45 PM	05:13 PM	07:51 PM	09:00 PM
Chicago	05:31 AM	06:48 AM	12:58 PM	04:25 PM	07:06 PM	08:24 PM
Houston	06:17 AM	07:22 AM	01:29 PM	04:58 PM	07:36 PM	08:42 PM
London	04:14 AM	05:49 AM	12:12 PM	03:31 PM	06:25 PM	07:43 PM
Los Angeles	05:45 AM	06:54 AM	01:00 PM	04:29 PM	07:07 PM	08:16 PM
Miami	06:20 AM	07:22 AM	01:28 PM	04:55 PM	07:33 PM	08:37 PM
New York	05:40 AM	06:56 AM	01:03 PM	04:30 PM	07:10 PM	08:27 PM
Philadelphia	05:46 AM	07:01 AM	01:08 PM	04:35 PM	07:15 PM	08:30 PM
Washington DC	05:55 AM	07:08 AM	01:16 PM	04:43 PM	07:22 PM	08:36 PM

The Vindication Of The Most Honorable Elijah Muhammad's Theology Day 2

"God is a man and we just cannot make Him other than man, lest we make him an inferior one; for man's intelligence has no equal in other than man. His wisdom is infinite; capable of accomplishing anything that his brain can conceive. A spirit is subjected to us and not we to the spirit. Habakkuk uses the pronoun "He" in reference to God. This pronoun "He" is only used in the case when we refer to a man or boy or something of the male sex."

-Most Hon. Elijah Muhammad, Is God A Man or Spirit

Below is a sample of some of the "anthropomorphic" hadiths. The word anthropomorphic means: **"the attribution of human form or behavior to a deity, animal, etc".** Allah (God) is frequently described in Islamic sacred literature in anthropomorphic ways.

Allah has a Face/Person:

Translation of Sahih Bukhari, Volume 9, Book 93, Number 503: Narrated Jabir bin 'Abdullah: The Prophet said, "I take refuge with Your Face..."

Allah has a Shin/Leg:

Translation of Sahih Bukhari, Volume 9, Book 93, Number 532s: Narrated Abu Sa'id Al Khudri: Then the Almighty will come to them in a shape other than the one which they saw the first time, and He will say, 'I am your Lord,' and they will say, 'You are not our Lord.' And none will speak: to Him then but the Prophets, and then it will be said to them, 'Do you know any sign by which you can recognize Him?' They will say. 'The Shin,' and so Allah will then uncover His Shin whereupon every believer will prostrate before Him...

Allah has a Foot:

Translation of Sahih Bukhari, Volume 6, Book 60, Number 373: Narrated Abu Huraira: The Prophet said, ...Then Allah said to the (Hell) Fire, 'You are my (means of) punishment by which I punish whoever I wish of my slaves. And each of you will have its fill.' As for the Fire (Hell), it will not be filled till Allah puts His Foot over it whereupon it will say, 'Qati! Qati!'...

Translation of Sahih Bukhari, Volume 9, Book 93, Number 481: Narrated Anas: The Prophet said, "(The people will be thrown into Hell (Fire) and it will keep on saying, 'Is there any more?' till the Lord of the worlds puts His Foot over it, whereupon its different sides will come close to each other, and it will say, 'Qad! Qad! (enough! enough!) By Your 'Izzat (Honor and Power) and YOUR KARAM (Generosity)!...

Allah has Hands:

Translation of Sahih Bukhari, Volume 9, Book 93, Number 509: Narrated Ibn 'Umar: Allah's Apostle said, "On the Day of Resurrection, Allah will grasp the whole Earth by His Hand, and all the Heavens in His Right, and then He will say, 'I am the King." Abu Huraira said, "Allah's Apostle said," Allah will grasp the Earth...' "

Translation of Sahih Bukhari, Volume 9, Book 93, Number 515: Narrated Abu Huraira: The Prophet said, "The Right (Hand) of Allah Is full, and (Its fullness) is not affected by the continuous spending night and day. Do you see what He has spent since He created the Heavens and the Earth? Yet all that has not decreased what is in His Right Hand. His Throne is over the water and in His other Hand is the Bounty or the Power to bring about death, and He raises some people and brings others down."

.

Surely, We give life to the dead, and We write down that which they send before and their footprints, and We record everything in a clear writing. And set out to them a parable of the people of the town, when apostles came to it. When We sent to them two, they rejected them both; then We strengthened (them) with a third, so they said: Surely, we are sent to you. They said: You are only mortals like ourselves, nor has the Beneficent revealed anything — you only lie. They said: Our Lord knows that we are surely sent to you. And our duty is only a clear deliverance (of the message). They said: Surely, we augur evil from you. If you desist not, we will surely stone you, and a painful chastisement from us will certainly afflict you. They said: Your evil fortune is with you. What! If you are reminded! Nay, you are an extravagant people. And from the remote part of the city there came a man running. He said: O my people, follow the apostles.

Holy Qur'an 36:12-20

Ramadan Day 2-The Believer's Notes

Surah 2:142 – Surah 2:252

Ramadan Day 2-The Believer's Notes

Surah 2:142 – Surah 2:252

Hadith Wisdom For Ramadan Fasting

Narrated by Sahl:

The Prophet (peace be upon him) said, "There is a gate in Paradise called Ar-Raiyan, and those who observe fasts will enter through it on the Day of Resurrection and none except them will enter through it. It will be said, 'Where are those who used to observe fasts?' They will get up, and none except them will enter through it. After their entry the gate will be closed and nobody will enter through it."

Day 2	NOI	Regional	Cities	Prayer	Times	2023
City	Fajr	Sunrise	Dhuhr	Asr	Maghrib	Isha
Atlanta	06:28 AM	07:37 AM	01:45 PM	05:13 PM	07:52 PM	09:01 PM
Chicago	05:29 AM	06:47 AM	12:57 PM	04:26 PM	07:08 PM	08:25 PM
Houston	06:15 AM	07:21 AM	01:29 PM	04:58 PM	07:36 PM	08:42 PM
London	04:13 AM	05:47 AM	12:11 PM	03:32 PM	06:27 PM	07:45 PM
Los Angeles	05:43 AM	06:52 AM	01:00 PM	04:29 PM	07:07 PM	08:17 PM
Miami	06:18 AM	07:21 AM	01:28 PM	04:55 PM	07:34 PM	08:37 PM
New York	05:38 AM	06:54 AM	01:03 PM	04:31 PM	07:11 PM	08:28 PM
Philadelphia	05:44 AM	06:59 AM	01:08 PM	04:36 PM	07:16 PM	08:31 PM
Washington DC	05:53 AM	07:07 AM	01:15 PM	04:44 PM	07:23 PM	08:37 PM

The Vindication Of The Most Honorable Elijah Muhammad's Theology Day 3

"They teach that God sees, hears, talks, walks, stands, sits, rides, and flies; that He grieves or sorrows; and that He is interested in the affairs of human beings. They also teach that once upon a time He made the first man like Himself in the image and likeness of Himself, but yet they believe that He, Himself, is not a man or human. They preach and prophesy of His coming and that He will be seen on the Judgment Day but is not man. They cannot tell us what He looks like, yet man is made like Him and in the image of God, and yet they still say that He is a mystery (unknown)."

-Most Hon. Elijah Muhammad, Who Is That Mystery God

Below is a section of more "anthropomorphic" hadiths. The word anthropomorphic means: **"the attribution of human form or behavior to a deity, animal, etc".** Allah (God) is frequently described in Islamic sacred literature in anthropomorphic ways. The presence of anthropomorphism throughout Islam's primary sources are key and important evidences of the truth of the theological position of the Most Hon. Elijah Muhammad and the Hon. Min. Louis Farrakhan

Allah has a Finger: Translation of Sahih Bukhari, Volume 9, Book 93, Number 510: Narrated 'Abdullah: A Jew came to the Prophet and said, "O Muhammad! Allah will hold the heavens on a Finger, and the mountains on a Finger, and the trees on a Finger, and all the creation on a Finger, and then He will say, 'I am the King.' " On that Allah's Apostle smiled till his premolar teeth became visible, and then recited:– 'No just estimate have they made of Allah such as due to him....(39.67) 'Abdullah added: Allah's Apostle smiled (at the Jew's statement) expressing his wonder and believe in what was said.

Translation of Sahih Bukhari, Volume 9, Book 93, Number 511: Narrated 'Abdullah: A man from the people of the scripture came to the Prophet and said, "O Abal-Qasim! Allah will hold the Heavens upon a Finger, and the Earth on a Finger and the land on a Finger, and all the creation on a Finger, and will say, 'I am the King! I am the King!' " I saw the Prophet (after hearing that), smiling till his premolar teeth became visible, and he then recited:

— 'No just estimate have they made of Allah such as due to him... (39:67).

Allah Writes: Translation of Sahih Bukhari, Volume 9, Book 93, Number 501: Narrated Abu Huraira: The Prophet said, "When Allah created the Creation, He wrote in His Book–and He wrote (that) about Himself, and it is placed with Him on the Throne–'Verily My Mercy overcomes My Anger."

Allah has a Throne: Translation of Sahih Bukhari, Volume 3, Book 41, Number 595: Narrated Abu Said Al- Khudri: ...for on the Day of Resurrection all the people will fall unconscious and

I will be the first to emerge from the earth, and will see Moses standing and holding one of the legs of the Throne...

Allah Laughs: Translation of Sahih Bukhari, Volume 9, Book 93, Number 532c: Narrated 'Ata' bin Yazid Al-Laithi:

...Allah will laugh because of his sayings...

Translation of Sahih Bukhari, Volume 1, Book 12, Number 770: Narrated Abu Huraira: ...So Allah will laugh and allow

Allah's Form: Translation of Sahih Bukhari, Volume 9, Book 93, Number 529: Narrated Jarir: We were sitting with the Prophet and he looked at the moon on the night of the full-moon and said, ..."You people will see your Lord as you see this full moon, and you will have no trouble in seeing Him,... so if you can avoid missing (through sleep or business, etc.) a prayer before sunrise (Fajr) and a prayer before sunset (Asr) you must do so."

Sahih Bukhari, Volume 9, Book 93, Number 532s: Narrated Abu Sa'id Al- Khudri: ...Then the Almighty will come to them in a shape other than the one which they saw the first time, and He will say, 'I am your Lord,' and they will say, 'You are not our Lord.' And none will speak: to Him then but the Prophets, and then it will be said to them, 'Do you know any sign by which you can recognize Him?' They will say. 'The Shin,' and so Allah will then uncover His Shin whereupon every believer will prostrate before Him and there will remain those who used to prostrate before Him just for showing off and for gaining good reputation...

Sahih Bukhari, Volume 6, Book 60, Number 105: ...The Prophet said, "(Similarly) you will have no difficulty in seeing Allah on the Day of Resurrection as you have no difficulty in seeing either of them.... ....Then (Allah) the Lord of the worlds will come to them in a shape nearest to the picture they had in their minds about Him...

Sahih Bukhari, Volume 8, Book 76, Number 577: Narrated Abu Huraira: Some people said, "O Allah's Apostle! Shall we see our Lord on the Day of Resurrection?" He said, "... Allah will come to them in a shape other than they know and will say, 'I am your Lord.' They will say, 'We seek refuge with Allah from you. This is our place; (we will not follow you) till our Lord comes to us, and when our Lord comes to us, we will recognize Him... Then Allah will come to them in a shape they know and will say, "I am your Lord..."

From The Dictionary of Islam by T.P. Hughes

“Al-Mahdi”

foundation of a building, commencing a journey, &c.; but more frequently by the Persians and Turks. The Prophet pronounced Astrology to be a branch of magic. Another branch of Kihaneh is Geomancy, called "Darb er Ramal" (*Ẕarbu Raml*); a mode of divination from certain marks made on sand (whence its appellation), or on paper; and said to be chiefly founded on astrology. The science called "ez Zijr," or "el Eyafeh" (*al-'Iyāfah*), is a third branch of Kihaneh, being divination or auguration, chiefly from the motions and positions, or postures, of birds, or of gazelles and other beasts of the chase. Thus what was termed a "Saneh" (*Sāniḥ*), that is, such an animal standing or passing with its right side towards the spectator, was esteemed among the Arabs as of good omen; and a "Bareh" (*Bāriḥ*), or an animal of this kind, with its left side towards the spectator, was held as inauspicious. "El Kiyafeh" (*al-Qiyāfah*), under which term are included Chiromancy and its kindred sciences, is a fourth branch of Kihaneh, "El Tefaul" (*at-Tafawwul*), or the taking an omen, particularly a good one, from a name or words accidentally heard or seen, or chosen from a book belonging to the same science. The taking a "fál," or omen, from the Kurán, is generally held to be lawful. Various trifling events are considered as ominous. For instance, a Sultan quitting his palace with his troops, a standard happened to strike a "thureiya" (*ṡurayyā*, a cluster of lamps so called from resembling the Pleiades), and broke them: he drew from this an evil omen, and would have relinquished the expedition; but one of his chief officers said to him, "O our Lord, thy standard has reached the Pleiades," and being relieved by this remark, he proceeded, and returned victorious.

(See *The Thousand and One Nights*, a new translation, with copious notes, by Edward W. Lane; new ed. by E. S. Poole, vol. i. p. 60.)

MAGISTRATES. [QAZI.]

MAGPIE. Arabic *'aq'aq* (عقعق). According to Abū Ḥanīfah, the flesh of the magpie is *mubāḥ*, or indifferent; but the Imām Yūsuf held it to be *makrūh*, or reprobated, because it frequently feeds on dead bodies. (*Hidāyah*, vol. iv. p. 74.)

AL-MAHDĪ (المهدى). *Lit.* "The Directed One," hence, "who is fit to direct others, Guide, Leader." A ruler who shall in the last days appear upon the earth. According to the Shī'ahs, he has already appeared in the person of Muḥammad Abu 'l-Qāsim, the twelfth Imām, who is believed to be concealed in some secret place until the day of his manifestation before the end of the world. But the Sunnis say he has not yet appeared. In the history of Muḥammadanism, there are numerous instances of impostors having assumed the character of this mysterious personage, amongst others, Saiyid Aḥmad, who fought against the Sikhs on the North-West frontier of the Panjāb, A.D. 1826, and still more recently, the Muḥammadan who has claimed to be *al-Mahdi* in the Sudān in Egypt.

The sayings of the Prophet on the subject, according to al-Bukhārī, and other traditionists, are as follows:—

"The world will not come to an end until a man of my tribe and of my name shall be master of Arabia."

"When you see black ensigns coming from the direction of Khorosān, then join them, for the Imām of God will be with the standards, whose name is *al-Mahdi*."

"The *Mahdi* will be descended from me, he will be a man with an open countenance and with a high nose. He will fill the earth with equity and justice, even as it has been filled with tyranny and oppression, and he will reign over the earth seven years."

"Quarrelling and disputation shall exist amongst men, and then shall a man of the people of al-Madīnah come forth, and shall go from al-Madīnah to Makkah, and the people of Makkah shall make him Imām. Then shall the ruler of Syria send an army against the *Mahdi*, but the Syrian army shall perish by an earthquake near Badā', between al-Madinah and Makkah. And when the people shall see this, the Abdāl [ABDAL] will come from Syria, and also a multitude from al-'Irāq. After this an enemy to the *Mahdi* shall arise from the Quraish tribe, whose uncles shall be of the tribe of Kalb, and this man shall send an army against the *Mahdi*. The *Mahdi* shall rule according to the example of your Prophet, and shall give strength and stability to Islām. He shall reign for seven years, and then die."

"There shall be much rain in the days of the *Mahdi* and the inhabitants both of heaven and earth shall be pleased with him. Men's lives shall pass so pleasantly, that they will wish even the dead were alive again." (*Mishkātu 'l-Maṣābiḥ*, book xxiii. ch. 3.)

According to Shī'ah traditions, Muḥammad is related to have said: "O ye people! I am the Prophet and 'Alī is my heir, and from us will descend *al-Mahdi*, the seal (*i.e.* the last) of the Imāms, who will conquer all religions and take vengeance on the wicked. He will take fortresses and will destroy them, and slay every tribe of idolaters, and he will avenge the deaths of the martyrs of God. He will be the champion of the Faith, and a drawer of water at the fountain of divine knowledge. He will reward merit and requite every fool according to his folly. He will be the approved and chosen of God, and the heir of all knowledge. He will be the valiant in doing right, and one to whom the Most High has entrusted Islām. . . . O ye people, I have explained to you, and 'Alī also will make you understand it." (*Ḥiyātu 'l-Qulūb*, Merrick's ed., p. 342.)

It is probable that it is from these traditions that the opinion became current amongst the Christians that the Muḥammadans expected their Prophet would rise again.

MAHJŪR (مهجور). A slave inhibited by the ruler from exercising any office or agency. (*Hidāyah*, vol. iii. 5.)

Ramadan Day 3-The Believer's Notes

Surah 2:253 – Surah 3:92

Ramadan Day 3-The Believer's Notes

Surah 2:253 – Surah 3:92

Hadith Wisdom For Ramadan Fasting

Narrated by Abu Huraira:

Allah's Messenger (peace be upon him) said, "When the month of Ramadan starts, the gates of the heaven are opened and the gates of Hell are closed and the devils are chained."

Narrated by Ibn `Umar:

I heard Allah's Messenger (peace be upon him) saying, "When you see the crescent (of the month of Ramadan), start fasting, and when you see the crescent (of the month of Shawwal), stop fasting; and if the sky is overcast (and you can't see it) then regard the month of Ramadan as of 30 days."

Day 3	NOI	Regional	Cities	Prayer	Times	2023
City	Fajr	Sunrise	Dhuhr	Asr	Maghrib	Isha
Atlanta	06:27 AM	07:35 AM	01:44 PM	05:14 PM	07:53 PM	09:02 PM
Chicago	05:27 AM	06:45 AM	12:57 PM	04:26 PM	07:09 PM	08:26 PM
Houston	06:14 AM	07:20 AM	01:28 PM	04:58 PM	07:37 PM	08:43 PM
London	05:11 AM	06:45 AM	01:11 PM	04:33 PM	07:28 PM	08:46 PM
Los Angeles	05:42 AM	06:51 AM	01:00 PM	04:29 PM	07:08 PM	08:18 PM
Miami	06:17 AM	07:20 AM	01:28 PM	04:55 PM	07:34 PM	08:38 PM
New York	05:36 AM	06:52 AM	01:03 PM	04:31 PM	07:12 PM	08:29 PM
Philadelphia	05:42 AM	06:57 AM	01:07 PM	04:36 PM	07:17 PM	08:32 PM
Washington DC	05:51 AM	07:05 AM	01:15 PM	04:44 PM	07:24 PM	08:38 PM

The Vindication Of
The Most Honorable Elijah Muhammad's Theology
Day 4

Important Qur'anic Anthropomorphisms

Allah sent His spirit in the form of a Well-Made Man ...Then We sent unto her Our Spirit and it assumed for her the likeness of a perfect man... (Qur'an 19:16-22).

How can a spirit be located on the Throne of Power (`arsh) unless that spirit was contained in a body (57:4)? He it is Who created the heavens and the earth in Six Days, and is moreover firmly established on the Throne (of Authority). (57:4).

How can the Angels surround something that doesn't have a geographical location? (39:75) Allah Himself is established upon His throne (57:4). How can Allah have a book with Him if he is an everywhere-type spirit? Allah doth blot out or confirm what He pleaseth: with Him is the Mother of the Book [Umm- ul-Kitab] (Holy Qur'an 13: 39).

If Allah is closer to man than man's own life vein, then Allah must be within man! We created man and We [even] know the promptings of his mind. We are closer to him than his life vein. (50:16)

Allah teaches us about Himself through His writing and by way of the Manifest/Clear Leader (Imam al- Mubeen) in Surah 36:12. Most Qur'anic translators improperly write it as a manifest/clear book although it clearly refers to a person.

Allah will come from where & how? And thy Lord comes with the angels, ranks on ranks; (Quran 89:22)

Allah's Person/Face will endure: But will abide (forever) the Person/Face of thy Lord,- full of Majesty, Bounty and Honour. (55:27).

Allah has eyes: Al-Qur'an 096:014: "Knows he not that Allah does see (what he does)?"

Al-Qur'an 052:048: "So wait patiently (O Muhammad SAW) for the Decision of your Lord, for verily, you are under Our Eyes , and glorify the Praises of your Lord when you get up from sleep."

Al-Qur'an 020:039: "Saying: Put him (the child) into the Taboot (a box or a case or a chest) and put it into the river (Nile), then the river shall cast it up on the bank, and there, an enemy of Mine and an enemy of his shall take him. And I endued you with love from Me, in order that you may be brought up under My Eye,"

Al-Qur'an 054:014: "Floating under Our Eyes, a reward for him who had been rejected!"

Allah has a Shin/Leg: Translation of Al- Qur'an 068:042: "(Remember) the Day when the Shin shall be laid bare (i.e. the Day of Resurrection) and they shall be called to prostrate (to Allah), but they (hypocrites) shall not be able to do so,"

Allah has Hands: Translation of Al-Qur'an 039:067: "They made not a just estimate of Allah such as is due to Him. And on the Day of Resurrection the whole of the earth will be grasped by His Hand and the heavens will be rolled up in His Right Hand. Glorified is He, and High is He above all that they associate as partners with Him!" Translation of Al-Qur'an 048:010: "Verily, those who give Baia (pledge) to you (O Muhammad SAW) they are giving Baia (pledge) to Allah. The Hand of Allah is over their hands. Then whosoever breaks his pledge, breaks only to his own harm, and whosoever fulfills what he has covenanted with Allah, He will bestow on him a great reward."

Allah Writes: Al-Qur'an 007:145: "And We wrote for him on the Tablets the lesson to be drawn from all things and the explanation of all things (and said): Hold unto these with firmness, and enjoin your people to take the better therein. I shall show you the home of Al-Fasiqoon (the rebellious, disobedient to Allah)."

Allah has a Throne: Al-Qur'an 007:054 Your Guardian-Lord is Allah, Who created the heavens and the earth in six days, and is firmly established on the throne (of power): (Al-istiwa 'ala al-'Arsh).

Al-Qur'an 0069:017: "And the angels will be on its sides, and eight angels will, that Day, bear the Throne of your Lord above them." Al-Qur'an 0057:004: (Allah) Most Gracious is firmly established on the throne (of authority).

Allah can be Seen: Translation of Al- Qur'an 075:022-025: "Some faces that Day shall be Nadirah (shining and radiant). Looking at their Lord (Allah);... And some faces, that Day, will be Basirah (dark, gloomy, frowning, and sad), Thinking that some calamity was about to fall on them;"

"Only A Mortal Teaches Him"

16:101 وَإِذَا بَدَّلْنَآ ءَايَةً مَّكَانَ ءَايَةٍ ۙ وَٱللَّهُ أَعْلَمُ بِمَا يُنَزِّلُ قَالُوٓا۟ إِنَّمَآ أَنتَ مُفْتَرٍۭ ۚ بَلْ أَكْثَرُهُمْ لَا يَعْلَمُونَ

And when We change a message for a message – and Allah knows best what He reveals – they say: Thou art only a forger. Nay, most of them know not.

16:102 قُلْ نَزَّلَهُۥ رُوحُ ٱلْقُدُسِ مِن رَّبِّكَ بِٱلْحَقِّ لِيُثَبِّتَ ٱلَّذِينَ ءَامَنُوا۟ وَهُدًى وَبُشْرَىٰ لِلْمُسْلِمِينَ

Say: The Holy Spirit has revealed it from thy Lord with truth, that it may establish those who believe, and as a guidance and good news for those who submit.

16:103 وَلَقَدْ نَعْلَمُ أَنَّهُمْ يَقُولُونَ إِنَّمَا يُعَلِّمُهُۥ بَشَرٌ ۗ لِّسَانُ ٱلَّذِى يُلْحِدُونَ إِلَيْهِ أَعْجَمِىٌّ وَهَٰذَا لِسَانٌ عَرَبِىٌّ مُّبِينٌ

And indeed We know that they say: Only a mortal teaches him. The tongue of him whom they hint at is foreign, and this is clear Arabic language.

The above criticism of Prophet Muhammad found within the 16th Surah of the Holy Qur'an serves as a fascinating allusion to the criticism faced by the Most Honorable Elijah Muhammad. The Holy Qur'an maintains that the Holy Spirit revealed the Qur'anic reveltions to the Prophet (peace be upon him). The Most Honorable Elijah Muhammad declared that Allah's Holy Spirit appeared in the person of a real live man (i.e. "mortal") , His Teacher, Master W. Fard Muhammad

Ramadan Day 4-The Believer's Notes

Surah 3:93 – Surah 4:23

Ramadan Day 4-The Believer's Notes

Surah 3:93 – Surah 4:23

Hadith Wisdom For Ramadan Fasting

Narrated by Abu Huraira:

The Prophet (peace be upon him) said, "Whoever established prayers on the night of Qadr out of sincere faith and hoping for a reward from Allah, then all his previous sins will be forgiven; and whoever fasts in the month of Ramadan out of sincere faith, and hoping for a reward from Allah, then all his previous sins will be forgiven."

Day 4	NOI	Regional	Cities	Prayer	Times	2023
City	Fajr	Sunrise	Dhuhr	Asr	Maghrib	Isha
Atlanta	06:25 AM	07:34 AM	01:44 PM	05:14 PM	07:53 PM	09:02 PM
Chicago	05:26 AM	06:43 AM	12:57 PM	04:27 PM	07:10 PM	08:28 PM
Houston	06:13 AM	07:18 AM	01:28 PM	04:58 PM	07:37 PM	08:44 PM
London	05:09 AM	06:42 AM	01:11 PM	04:34 PM	07:30 PM	08:48 PM
Los Angeles	05:40 AM	06:49 AM	12:59 PM	04:30 PM	07:09 PM	08:18 PM
Miami	06:16 AM	07:19 AM	01:27 PM	04:55 PM	07:35 PM	08:38 PM
New York	05:34 AM	06:51 AM	01:02 PM	04:32 PM	07:14 PM	08:30 PM
Philadelphia	05:41 AM	06:56 AM	01:07 PM	04:37 PM	07:18 PM	08:34 PM
Washington DC	05:50 AM	07:04 AM	01:15 PM	04:45 PM	07:25 PM	08:40 PM

Notes On The Theme of Theology

The Vindication Of
The Most Honorable Elijah Muhammad's Theology
Day 5

The Most Honorable Elijah Muhammad teaches that Allah (God) is a man. And in point no. 12 of What The Muslim Believe he states that Allah (God) "appeared in the person of Master W. Fard Muhammad." The Ramadan Journal, while not seeking to point the reader in the direction of too much Biblical materials during the month of the Holy Qur'an-Ramadan- does include the key word "theophany" and its definition/explanation below. This is because, Prophet Muhammad, peace be upon him, believed in the same God as the Prophets who came before him. The Prophets and their scriptures comprise the Torah and the Gospel. Muslims believe in the Holy Qur'an and the scriptures revealed before the Holy Qur'an. And this makes it vitally important to examine how Allah (God) is described in those previous revelations of divine truth. The Torah and Gospel are replete with the theological phenomenon of Allah (God) appearing as a human being to select ones of His servants. This phenomenon is called "theophany."

"The meaning of the word theophany is **"appearance or personal manifestation of a god to a person."** The basic postulate here is that to see God could be fatal. "He said, 'You cannot see My face, for no one can see Me and live!'" (Exod. 33:20 HCSB; cp. Gen. 16:13; Exod. 3:2-6; 19:20-21; Judg. 6:22-23; 13:20-22). Yet the record is unmistakable that people did see God, such as Moses and others at Sinai (Exod. 24:9-10); the Lord's rebuke of Aaron and Miriam (Num. 12:4-8); and the majestic vision to Isaiah (Isa. 6:1,5). Customarily, God is not revealed to ordinary sight, but at times chooses to reveal Himself in theophanies.

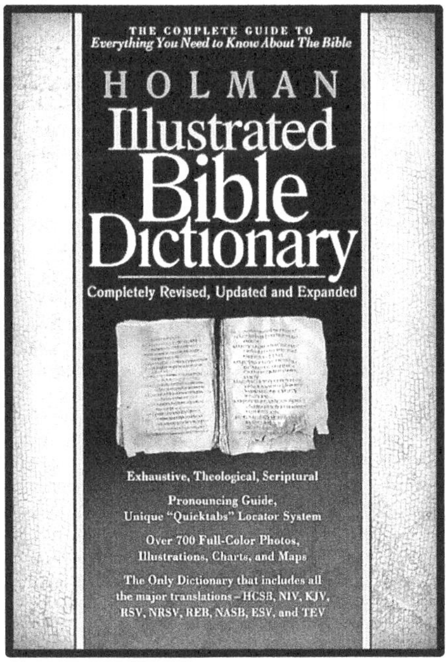

In human form Without question the theophany in Exod. 24:10 involved the appearance of a human being, for the text clearly states that a pavement of sapphire appeared "under His feet." At Peniel, Jacob testified that he had seen God face to face (Gen. 32:30). On Mount Horeb it was the experience of Moses to speak to God "face to face, just as a man speaks with his friend" (Exod. 33:11 HCSB). In the same passage when Moses begged God to show him His glory (v.18), the Lord graciously granted Moses a vision of Himself, saying, "I will take My hand away, and you will see My back, but My face will not be seen" (v. 23). If it is protested that the subject is enveloped in mystery, it needs to be remembered that theology without mystery is sheer nonsense. God in His wisdom does not restrict Himself to one method of self-revelation. Notice God's pronouncement in Num. 12:6-8, which was quite unlike that of Deut. 4:12-15 where only a voice was granted."

Ramadan Day 5-The Believer's Notes

Surah 4:24 – Surah 4:147

Ramadan Day 5-The Believer's Notes

Surah 4:24 – Surah 4:147

Hadith Wisdom For Ramadan Fasting

The Prophet (peace be upon him) was the most generous amongst the people, and he used to be more so in the month of Ramadan when Gabriel visited him, and Gabriel used to meet him on every night of Ramadan till the end of the month. The Prophet (peace be upon him) used to recite the Holy Qur'an to Gabriel, and when Gabriel met him, he used to be more generous than a fast wind (which causes rain and welfare).

Narrated by Abu Huraira:

The Prophet (peace be upon him) said, "Whoever does not give up forged speech and evil actions, Allah is not in need of his leaving his food and drink"

Day 5	NOI	Regional	Cities	Prayer	Times	2023
City	Fajr	Sunrise	Dhuhr	Asr	Maghrib	Isha
Atlanta	06:24 AM	07:33 AM	01:44 PM	05:14 PM	07:54 PM	09:03 PM
Chicago	05:24 AM	06:42 AM	12:56 PM	04:27 PM	07:11 PM	08:29 PM
Houston	06:11 AM	07:17 AM	01:28 PM	04:58 PM	07:38 PM	08:44 PM
London	05:07 AM	06:40 AM	01:10 PM	04:35 PM	07:32 PM	08:49 PM
Los Angeles	05:39 AM	06:48 AM	12:59 PM	04:30 PM	07:10 PM	08:19 PM
Miami	06:15 AM	07:18 AM	01:27 PM	04:55 PM	07:35 PM	08:39 PM
New York	05:33 AM	06:49 AM	01:02 PM	04:32 PM	07:15 PM	08:31 PM
Philadelphia	05:39 AM	06:54 AM	01:07 PM	04:37 PM	07:19 PM	08:35 PM
Washington DC	05:48 AM	07:02 AM	01:14 PM	04:45 PM	07:26 PM	08:41 PM

The Vindication Of
The Most Honorable Elijah Muhammad's Theology
Day 6

This hadith points to the ultimate goal of a Muslim; it is achieved when he or she has submitted so fully and so completely to Allah, that Allah will act through and in the person of the righteous believer. The oneness of Allah and the true believer may be thusly considered "ultimate tauheed."

On the authority of Abu Hurayrah (may Allah be pleased with him), who said that the Messenger of Allah (ﷺ) said:

"Allah (mighty and sublime be He) said: Whosoever shows enmity to someone devoted to Me, I shall be at war with him. My servant draws not near to Me with anything more loved by Me than the religious duties I have enjoined upon him, and My servant continues to draw near to Me with supererogatory works so that I shall love him. **When I love him I am his hearing with which he hears, his seeing with which he sees, his hand with which he strikes and his foot with which he walks.** Were he to ask [something] of Me, I would surely give it to him, and were he to ask Me for refuge, I would surely grant him it. I do not hesitate about anything as much as I hesitate about [seizing] the soul of My faithful servant: he hates death and I hate hurting him. It was related by al-Bukhari."

Ramadan Day 6-The Believer's Notes

Surah 4:148 - Surah5:81

Ramadan Day 6-The Believer's Notes

Surah 4:148 - Surah5:81

Hadith Wisdom For Ramadan Fasting

Narrated by Abu Huraira:

Allah's Messenger (ﷺ) said, "Allah said, 'All the deeds of Adam's sons (people) are for them, except fasting which is for Me, and I will give the reward for it.' Fasting is a shield or protection from the fire and from committing sins. If one of you is fasting, he should avoid sexual relation with his wife and quarreling, and if somebody should fight or quarrel with him, he should say, 'I am fasting.' By Him in Whose Hands my soul is' The unpleasant smell coming out from the mouth of a fasting person is better in the sight of Allah than the smell of musk. There are two pleasures for the fasting person, one at the time of breaking his fast, and the other at the time when he will meet his Lord; then he will be pleased because of his fasting."

Day 6	NOI	Regional	Cities	Prayer	Times	2023
City	Fajr	Sunrise	Dhuhr	Asr	Maghrib	Isha
Atlanta	06:22 AM	07:31 AM	01:43 PM	05:14 PM	07:55 PM	09:04 PM
Chicago	05:22 AM	06:40 AM	12:56 PM	04:28 PM	07:12 PM	08:30 PM
Houston	06:10 AM	07:16 AM	01:28 PM	04:58 PM	07:39 PM	08:45 PM
London	05:05 AM	06:38 AM	01:10 PM	04:36 PM	07:33 PM	08:50 PM
Los Angeles	05:38 AM	06:47 AM	12:59 PM	04:30 PM	07:10 PM	08:20 PM
Miami	06:14 AM	07:17 AM	01:27 PM	04:55 PM	07:36 PM	08:39 PM
New York	05:31 AM	06:47 AM	01:02 PM	04:33 PM	07:16 PM	08:32 PM
Philadelphia	05:37 AM	06:53 AM	01:06 PM	04:38 PM	07:20 PM	08:36 PM
Washington DC	05:46 AM	07:00 AM	01:14 PM	04:45 PM	07:27 PM	08:42 PM

The Vindication Of
The Most Honorable Elijah Muhammad's Theology
Day 7

A.S. Tritton, in his Islam, observes:

"The Koran and tradition (sayings of the Prophet and his companions) often speak of God as if He were a man; to take two examples only, 'When God created the world He wrote with His Hand for Himself, 'My mercy precedes My anger, ' and, 'He opens the gates of heaven in the last third of the night, stretches out His hand and says, 'Is there none to ask of me that I may give?' He stays like this till dawn.' In consequence many thought of God as (having) a body; they asked if the throne supported Him and did He fill it. He had the limbs of a man, He was a .. .light in the form of a man and His hair was black light; He was a body but not like other bodies."

-p.36

Ramadan Day 7-The Believer's Notes

Surah 5:82 – Surah 6:110

Ramadan Day 7-The Believer's Notes

Surah 5:82 – Surah 6:110

Hadith Wisdom For Ramadan Fasting

Narrated by 'Alqama:

While I was walking with `Abdullah he said, "We were in the company of the Prophet (peace be upon him) and he said, 'He who can afford to marry should marry, because it will help him refrain from looking at other women, and save his private parts from committing illegal sexual relation; and he who cannot afford to marry is advised to fast, as fasting will diminish his sexual power."

Day 7	NOI	Regional	Cities	Prayer	Times	2023
City	Fajr	Sunrise	Dhuhr	Asr	Maghrib	Isha
Atlanta	06:21 AM	07:30 AM	01:43 PM	05:15 PM	07:56 PM	09:05 PM
Chicago	05:20 AM	06:38 AM	12:56 PM	04:28 PM	07:13 PM	08:32 PM
Houston	06:09 AM	07:15 AM	01:27 PM	04:58 PM	07:39 PM	08:46 PM
London	05:04 AM	06:36 AM	01:10 PM	04:37 PM	07:35 PM	08:52 PM
Los Angeles	05:36 AM	06:45 AM	12:59 PM	04:30 PM	07:11 PM	08:21 PM
Miami	06:13 AM	07:16 AM	01:26 PM	04:55 PM	07:36 PM	08:40 PM
New York	05:29 AM	06:46 AM	01:01 PM	04:33 PM	07:17 PM	08:34 PM
Philadelphia	05:35 AM	06:51 AM	01:06 PM	04:38 PM	07:21 PM	08:37 PM
Washington DC	05:45 AM	06:59 AM	01:14 PM	04:46 PM	07:28 PM	08:43 PM

The Vindication Of
The Most Honorable Elijah Muhammad's Theology
Day 8

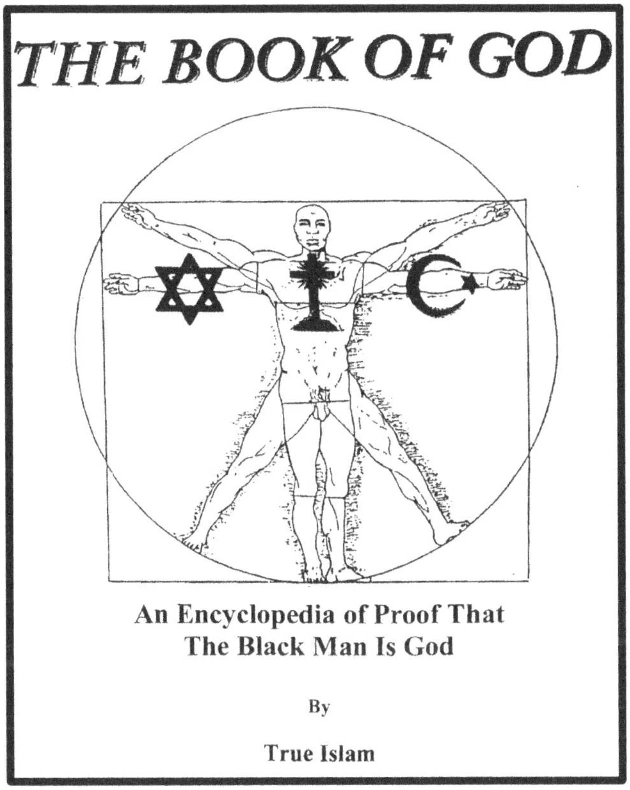

"But of all that we have above stated, the most convincing saying of the Prophet that Allah manifests Himself in human form is that tradition in which the Prophet says:

"Allah created Adam in His form" (inna Allah 'azza wajalla khalaqa Adam 'ala suratihi). "

In case there was any confusion of whose "form" is actually meant here, the tradition is repeated except it states even more explicitly that Adam was created in the form of al-Rahman, The Beneficent.

This tradition clearly shows that Allah has a human form after which Adam was created. This is why the Qur'an states that Adam was created by Allah in **"the best of forms (95:4)."** Adam was fashioned from Black mud into the "best of forms" because he was fashioned after the make or form of Allah."

-Dr. Wesley Muhammad, The Book of God, p. 99

Ramadan Day 8-The Believer's Notes

Surah 6:111 -Surah 7:87

Ramadan Day 8-The Believer's Notes

Surah 6:111 -Surah 7:87

Hadith Wisdom For Ramadan Fasting

Narrated by Abu Huraira:

The Prophet (peace be upon him) said, "None of you should fast a day or two before the month of Ramadan unless he has the habit of fasting (Nawafil) (and if his fasting coincides with that day) then he can fast that day."

Day 8	NOI	Regional	Cities	Prayer	Times	2023
City	Fajr	Sunrise	Dhuhr	Asr	Maghrib	Isha
Atlanta	06:20 AM	07:29 AM	01:43 PM	05:15 PM	07:56 PM	09:06 PM
Chicago	05:18 AM	06:37 AM	12:55 PM	04:29 PM	07:14 PM	08:33 PM
Houston	06:08 AM	07:14 AM	01:27 PM	04:58 PM	07:40 PM	08:46 PM
London	05:01 AM	06:33 AM	01:10 PM	04:38 PM	07:37 PM	08:54 PM
Los Angeles	05:35 AM	06:44 AM	12:58 PM	04:30 PM	07:12 PM	08:22 PM
Miami	06:12 AM	07:15 AM	01:26 PM	04:55 PM	07:37 PM	08:40 PM
New York	05:27 AM	06:44 AM	01:01 PM	04:34 PM	07:18 PM	08:35 PM
Philadelphia	05:34 AM	06:49 AM	01:06 PM	04:39 PM	07:22 PM	08:38 PM
Washington DC	05:43 AM	06:57 AM	01:13 PM	04:46 PM	07:29 PM	08:44 PM

The Vindication Of The Most Honorable Elijah Muhammad's Theology Day 9

Hadith Sayings of Prophet Muhammad:

Believers Will See Allah (God) On The Day of Judgment

Sa'id ibn Jubayr reported: Ibn Abbas, may Allah be pleased with him, used to say, "**O Allah, I ask You by the light of Your Face**, which shines over the heavens and the earth, that you place me within Your fortress, Your protection, Your guardianship, and under Your shadow."

Source: Muṣannaf Ibn Abī Shaybah 29539

Abu Huraira reported: The Messenger of Allah, peace and blessings be upon him, said, "Do you overlook a crowd to see the full moon? Do you overlook a crowd to see the sun?" They said no. The Prophet said, "Verily, **you will see your Lord** just as you see the full moon and you will not need to overlook a crowd to see Him."

Source: Sunan al-Tirmidhī 2554

Suhayb reported: The Prophet, peace and blessings be upon him, said, "When the people of Paradise enter it, Allah Almighty will say: Would you like anything more? They will say: Have You not brightened our faces? Have You not admitted us into Paradise and saved us from Hellfire? Then, **Allah will lift the veil and nothing they are given will be more beloved to them than looking at their Lord Almighty**." The Prophet recited the verse, "For those who do good is even more." (10:26)

Source: Ṣaḥīḥ Muslim 181

Jarir ibn Abdullah reported: We were with the Prophet, peace and blessings be upon him, and he looked at the full moon one night. The Prophet said, "**Verily, you will see your Lord just as you see this moon.** There will be no crowd to block your sight. Thus, if you can avoid missing prayer before the rising of the sun and its setting, then do so." Then, the Prophet recited the verse, "Glorify your Lord with praises before the rising of the sun and its setting." (50:39)

Source: Ṣaḥīḥ al-Bukhārī 554, Ṣaḥīḥ Muslim 633

"It is reported by Ahmad ibn Nasru'l-Khuza'i that the Prophet said again, "**Ye shall see your Lord in the day of judgment, as ye see the moon.**

An-Nawawi, author of the **Forty Hadith**, says, "The position of the PEOPLE OF THE SUNNAH is that seeing Allah is possible and not absurd...". "The people of the Sunnah" are the original followers of the Prophet who transmitted his teachings. It is thus made clear that the faithful will see Allah as one sees a full moon at night or bright sun on a cloudless day."

-Dr. Wesley Muhammad, The Book of God p. 103

The Holy Qur'an's making the believer aware of visions from Allah provide important context for the popular Biblical passage in Ezekiel chapter 1 and its relationship to the Most Honorable Elijah Muhammad's claim that Allah (God) appeared in the person of Master W. Fard Muhammad on July 4, 1930.

"Ezekiel's Vision & Master W. Fard Muhammad"

17:60 وَإِذْ قُلْنَا لَكَ إِنَّ رَبَّكَ أَحَاطَ بِٱلنَّاسِ ۚ وَمَا جَعَلْنَا ٱلرُّءْيَا ٱلَّتِىٓ أَرَيْنَـٰكَ إِلَّا فِتْنَةً لِّلنَّاسِ
وَٱلشَّجَرَةَ ٱلْمَلْعُونَةَ فِى ٱلْقُرْءَانِ ۚ وَنُخَوِّفُهُمْ فَمَا يَزِيدُهُمْ إِلَّا طُغْيَـٰنًا كَبِيرًا

And when We said to thee: **Surely thy Lord encompasses men. And We made not the vision which We showed thee but a trial for men,** as also the tree cursed in the Qur'an. And We warn them, but it only adds to their great inordinacy.

"Now it came to pass in the thirtieth year, in the fourth month, on the fifth day of the month, as I was among the captives by the River Chebar, that the heavens were opened and I saw visions of God."
-Ezekiel 1:1

42:51 وَمَا كَانَ لِبَشَرٍ أَن يُكَلِّمَهُ ٱللَّهُ إِلَّا وَحْيًا أَوْ مِن وَرَآئِ حِجَابٍ أَوْ يُرْسِلَ رَسُولًا فَيُوحِىَ
بِإِذْنِهِۦ مَا يَشَآءُ ۚ إِنَّهُۥ عَلِىٌّ حَكِيمٌ

And it is not vouchsafed to a mortal that Allah should speak to him, except by revelation or from behind a veil, or by sending a messenger and revealing by His permission what He pleases. Surely He is High, Wise.

30th YEAR-In Ezekiel 1:1 the reference to the "30th year" is related to the year 1930 when Master W. Fard Muhammad began His work among the southern "Negro" migrants of Detroit's Black Bottom and Paradise Valley communities.

4TH MONTH-The reference to the "fourth month" is related to the month of Master W. Fard Muhammad's inaugural ministry, the month of July. According to the Library of Congress "This holiday dedicated to tomfoolery can be traced to a very important event. In 1582, Pope Gregory XIII replaced the Julian calendar created by Julius Caesar in 46 B.C. with what is now called the Gregorian calendar. Until this change occurred, New Year's Day was celebrated on April 1, around the time of the vernal equinox, when the hours of day and night are nearly equal." This means that when April was the first month, July was the 4th month.

5TH DAY-The reference to the 5th Day in the above passage is related to the coming of Master W. Fard Muhammad on the 4th of July in Detroit, Michigan for astronomical reasons. In Astronomy we learn that the so-called "rising of the sun" begins in the Eastern Hemisphere. This means that when it is already the 5th day in the East, it is still the 4th day in the Western Hemisphere.

CAPTIVES-The above passage makes a reference to being "among the captives." This is related to the coming of Allah (God) in the person of Master W. Fard Muhammad on July 4, 1930 to Black people in Detroit. The Black people in Detroit were either direct descendants of America's enslaved Blacks, or may have themselves actually been chattel slaves or served in peonage as share croppers. Either way, Master W. Muhammad was for sure "among the captives."

Ramadan Day 9-The Believer's Notes

Surah 7:88 – Surah 8:40

Ramadan Day 9-The Believer's Notes

Surah 7:88 – Surah 8:40

Hadith Wisdom For Ramadan Fasting

Narrated by Al-Bara:

It was the custom among the companions of Muhammad that if any of them was fasting and the food was presented (for breaking his fast), but he slept before eating, he would not eat that night and the following day till sunset. Qais bin Sirma-al-Ansari was fasting and came to his wife at the time of Iftar (breaking one's fast) and asked her whether she had anything to eat. She replied, "No, but I would go and bring some for you." He used to do hard work during the day, so he was overwhelmed by sleep and slept. When his wife came and saw him, she said, "Disappointment for you." When it was midday on the following day, he fainted and the Prophet (peace be upon him) was informed about the whole matter and the following verses were revealed: "You are permitted To go to your wives (for sexual relation) At the night of fasting." So, they were overjoyed by it. And then Allah also revealed: "And eat and drink Until the white thread Of dawn appears to you Distinct from the black thread (of the night)." (2.187)

Day 9	NOI	Regional	Cities	Prayer	Times	2023
City	Fajr	Sunrise	Dhuhr	Asr	Maghrib	Isha
Atlanta	06:18 AM	07:27 AM	01:42 PM	05:15 PM	07:57 PM	09:07 PM
Chicago	05:16 AM	06:35 AM	12:55 PM	04:29 PM	07:15 PM	08:34 PM
Houston	06:06 AM	07:12 AM	01:27 PM	04:58 PM	07:40 PM	08:47 PM
London	04:59 AM	06:31 AM	01:09 PM	04:38 PM	07:38 PM	08:55 PM
Los Angeles	05:33 AM	06:43 AM	12:58 PM	04:30 PM	07:13 PM	08:23 PM
Miami	06:11 AM	07:14 AM	01:26 PM	04:54 PM	07:37 PM	08:41 PM
New York	05:25 AM	06:42 AM	01:01 PM	04:34 PM	07:19 PM	08:36 PM
Philadelphia	05:32 AM	06:48 AM	01:06 PM	04:39 PM	07:23 PM	08:39 PM
Washington DC	05:41 AM	06:56 AM	01:13 PM	04:46 PM	07:30 PM	08:45 PM

The Vindication Of The Most Honorable Elijah Muhammad's Theology
Day 10

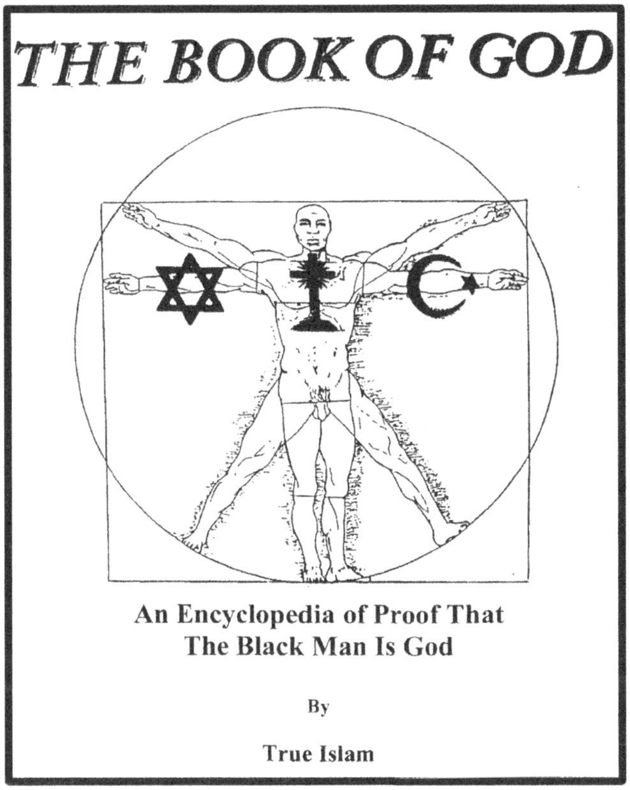

"The verse that the modem orthodox [*conforming to what is generally or traditionally accepted as right or true; established and approved.*], those who were originally heterodox [*not conforming with accepted or orthodox standards or beliefs.*], quote in their attempt to make Allah an immaterial being that is invisible is Surah 2:3 ("Those who believe in the unseen")were Allah is referred to as **Al-Ghaib**."

"The Muslim writers of today deceptively translate that word as "Unseen." However, that word does not mean "unseen" in Arabic. **It means "absent" or "to withdraw ones presence from."** This word is similar to the Greek aoratos and does not mean physical invisibility but unseen due to location or distance-absent from view. Allah is not here described by the Qur'an as an invisible being, but as one who has made Himself absent until the Day of Judgment at which time He will make His presence known again. This is why the faithful have to wait until that Day before they could "see their Lord." The above cited Quranic passages were read by the early Muslims as literal representations of Allah. The Encyclopedia of Islam notes that "the ancient traditionalists took these verses on their face value."

"A.J. Arberry, in **Revelation And Reason In Islam**, observes:

> "From earliest Islam there had been a strong preference to take these descriptions literally. It was said that God when he grows angry, grows heavier and the throne groans under his weight like a camel saddle. Others explained that it was the throne that grew heavier, not God."

George F. Moor, in his History of Religion agrees:

> '**The common idea of God was crudely anthropomorphic**. Taking the words of the Koran in their natural sense, men imagined God sitting upon a throne in heaven, a being with hands and feet, eyes and ears; a body, therefore, **and some doctors of repute did not hesitate to say a body of flesh and blood."**

Indeed, the people of the "Sunna," the original orthodox of Islam which included the companions of the Prophet, armed with the words of the Prophet himself, understood these anthropomorphic verses of the Holy Qur'an literally and thus conceived of Allah in that same way. They are referred to as Ashab-Al-Hadith, or "People of the Tradition." This group later came to be anathematized and called Al-Hashwiyya. The exact meaning of Hashwiyya is unknown but it is clearly used in a derogatory way. Writers today refer to the Hashwiyya as a "sect" within Islam. But A.S. Halkin has shown that, far from being a sect, it represented the orthodox majority. In his article, "The Hashwiyya," he states:

"We learn also that the name is by no means applicable to a well-defined group, including as it does virtually the whole community."

Today the Orthodox Muslim world wants to disown the ashab al-hadith and make it appear that it was an insignificant sect. But Halkin has convincingly shown, as well as the writings of their enemies, that they represented the orthodox majority. Armstrong notes,

"Muslims often spoke about God anthropomorphically, making him a larger-than-life man ..."

They are today anathematized because they believed in the God of Religion. In the polemic of Jahiz (772-872) against the Nabita, which is another name for the Hashwiyya, he says of them:

> "But the Nabita insisted: He is a body; and it ascribed form to Him and declared anyone who believes in the beatific vision (seeing Allah in Paradise) without 'Tajsim' (acknowledging God has a body) to be a heretic. Again most maintain that God's word is excellent and clear, evidence and proof that if He wished to add to it, He could; and subtract from it, He could. The acts of disobedience of this community had never exceeded sin and error until the Nabita and their followers, THE MASSES, appeared Now the PREVAILING trend of this generation is Kufr, that is anthropomorphism and determinism."

Jahiz, who was an enemy of the Hashwiyya, here acknowledges that they represented the masses and their view of anthropomorphism was the "prevailing" view.

-Dr. Wesley Muhammad, The Book of God, p. 103-104

The Nation of Islam in America is the only community of Muslims that is widely known to process new Muslims into the community of the faithful using what is known as a "Saviour's Letter." It is like a written "declaration of faith." In most Islamic communities the first pillar of Islam, known as the "shahadah", is a verbal declaration of faith uttered by new believers in the presence of witnesses. This Saviour's Letter, in the Nation of Islam, creates a written record and document of all who comprise the "register" of believers in what Master W. Fard Muhammad revealed to the Most Honorable Elijah Muhammad. I find it fascinating that the Saviour's Letter of the Nation of Islam perfectly resembles the "shahadah on a card" discussed in the hadith of Prophet Muhammad cited below.

"The Saviour's Letter & Hadith of Shahadah On A Card"

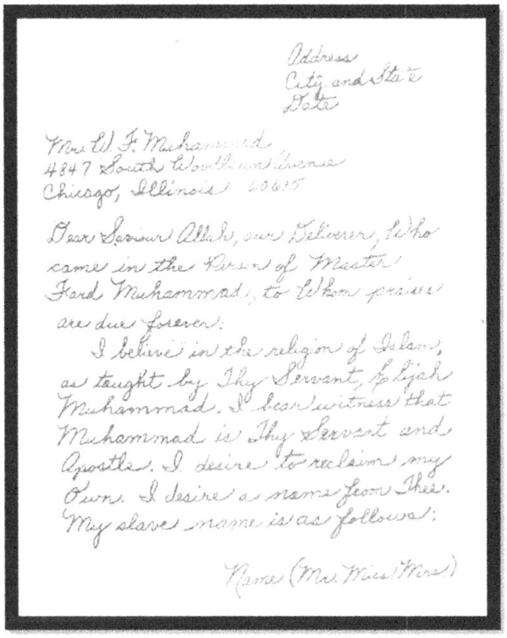

Address
City and State
Date

Mr. W. F. Muhammad
4847 South Woodlawn Avenue
Chicago, Illinois 60615

Dear Saviour Allah, our Deliverer, Who came in the Person of Master Fard Muhammad, to Whom praises are due forever:
I believe in the religion of Islam, as taught by Thy Servant, Elijah Muhammad. I bear witness that Muhammad is Thy Servant and Apostle. I desire to reclaim my Own. I desire a name from Thee. My slave name is as follows:

Name (Mr. Miss Mrs.)

Abdullah lbn 'Amr Ibnul- 'As, may Allah be satisfied with him, narrated, "The Messenger of Allah (PBUH) said, 'Allah will select a man from my Ummah before creatures on the Day of Resurrection, and He will display to him ninety-nine records each of which will be as (long and wide as) the sight can reach. Then He will say, 'Do you deny anything from this? Were My guardian scribes unjust to you?' He will say, 'No, Oh my Lord.' Allah will say, 'Do you have any excuse?' He will say, 'No, Oh my Lord.' Allah will say, 'Yes you have, for there is a good deed for you with Us, and on this Day you will not suffer from any injustice.' **Then a card containing, 'I testify that there is no god but Allah, and I testify that Muhammad is His servant and Messenger,' will appear.** Then Allah will say, 'Witness your scales.' He will say, 'Oh my Lord, what is this card (supposed to do) with these records?' Allah will say, 'No injustice will be done to you'.' **He (the Prophet) continued, 'Then the records will be put on a scale and the card on the other scale, and the records will become light and the card heavy, as nothing is heavy (when compared) with the Name of Allah."'**

(At-Tirmidhi, Ahmad, and Ibn Majah)

Ramadan Day 10-The Believer's Notes

Surah 8:41 – Surah 9:92

Ramadan Day 10-The Believer's Notes

Surah 8:41 – Surah 9:92

Hadith Wisdom For Ramadan Fasting

Narrated by `Adi bin Hatim:

When the above verses were revealed: 'Until the white thread appears to you, distinct from the black thread,' I took two (hair) strings, one black and the other white, and kept them under my pillow and went on looking at them throughout the night but could not make anything out of it. So, the next morning I went to Allah's Messenger (peace be upon him) and told him the whole story. He explained to me, "That verse means the darkness of the night and the whiteness of the dawn."

Day 10	NOI	Regional	Cities	Prayer	Times	2023
City	Fajr	Sunrise	Dhuhr	Asr	Maghrib	Isha
Atlanta	06:17 AM	07:26 AM	01:42 PM	05:15 PM	07:58 PM	09:08 PM
Chicago	05:14 AM	06:33 AM	12:55 PM	04:30 PM	07:16 PM	08:35 PM
Houston	06:05 AM	07:11 AM	01:26 PM	04:58 PM	07:41 PM	08:48 PM
London	04:57 AM	06:29 AM	01:09 PM	04:39 PM	07:40 PM	08:56 PM
Los Angeles	05:32 AM	06:41 AM	12:58 PM	04:31 PM	07:13 PM	08:24 PM
Miami	06:09 AM	07:13 AM	01:25 PM	04:54 PM	07:38 PM	08:41 PM
New York	05:24 AM	06:41 AM	01:00 PM	04:35 PM	07:20 PM	08:37 PM
Philadelphia	05:30 AM	06:46 AM	01:05 PM	04:39 PM	07:24 PM	08:40 PM
Washington DC	05:39 AM	06:54 AM	01:13 PM	04:47 PM	07:31 PM	08:46 PM

Notes On The Theme of Theology

The Vindication Of
The Most Honorable Elijah Muhammad's Theology
Day 11

Allah Is Producing A New Islam Out Of The Black People Of America

"This black people of America, who have been swallowed symbolically by the white slave-master and his children, must now be brought out of this race of people and be taught the knowledge of their own. Allah is holding the affair in person in the name of Master Fard Muhammad. He has chosen us today to be His people and establish forever a people of righteousness and a people with unlimited knowledge of the Divine Supreme Being. The very last of one of these will become greater than the greatest of this world. The Orthodox Muslims will have to bow to the choice of Allah. Allah will bring about a new Islam. As for the Principles of Belief, they remain the same. There will be no more signs to be watched for the coming of God and the setting up of a new world of Islam. We are seeing this change now and entering into it. The devils oppose this change, and the Orthodox join them in opposing us because of their desire to carry on the old way of Islam.

Allah will place those of His choice in authority in the making of the new world, and others must obey whomever He puts in authority or find themselves fighting against the power of whomever they hold to be on their side and in their favor. We must have a new world. We accept for a new nation completely. As Yakub brought about a people (the present white race) who were a completely new people made out of the original of us, another new people must be made to be the ruling voice of tomorrow out of this old world that is now living her last days. They will be completely new people. The Holy Qur'an and the Bible refer to them as being brought about by the power and will of God in Person in the resurrection of the mentally dead, lost-found original people in America. We may not seem to please you or to be pleasing to Allah, but it is written in the Bible that He will give to whom He pleases and chastise whom He pleases.

This is to warn us that we have no choice in the matter. Whatever Allah desires, He will bring into being, whether we like it or not."

-Most Hon. Elijah Muhammad, We Must Teach Our Own

Hadith On The Deviation Of The Orthodox Muslims, Justifies A New Islam Emerging

Volume 3, Book 48, Number 819, Sahih Bukhari Collection:
Narrated Zahdam bin Mudrab: I heard Imran bin Husain saying, "The Prophet said, 'The best people are those living in my generation, then those coming after them, and then those coming after (the second generation)." Imran said "I do not know whether the Prophet mentioned **two or three generations after your present generation. The Prophet added, 'There will be some people after you, who will be dishonest and will not be trustworthy and will give witness (evidences) without being asked to give witness, and will vow but will not fulfill their vows, and fatness will appear among them**."

Volume 5, Book 57, Number 2, Sahih Bukhari Collection:

Narrated Imran bin Husain: "Allah's Apostle said, 'The best of my followers are those living in my generation (i.e. my contemporaries). and then those who will follow the latter" 'Imran added, "I do not remember whether he mentioned two or three generations after his generation, then the Prophet added, **'There will come after you, people who will bear witness without being asked to do so, and will be treacherous and untrustworthy, and they will vow and never fulfill their vows, and fatness will appear among them."**

Volume 8, Book 78, Number 686, Sahih Bukhari Collection:
Narrated Zahdam bin Mudarrab: 'Imran bin Hussain said, "The Prophet said, 'The best of you (people) are my generation, and the second best will be those who will follow them, and then those who will follow the second generation." Imran added, "I do not remember whether he mentioned two or three (generations) after his generation. He added, **'Then will come some people who will make vows but will not fulfill them; and they will be dishonest and will not be trustworthy, and they will give their witness without being asked to give their witness, and fatness will appear among them**.' "

Muhammad (PBUH) prophesied of a New Islam that will come (after the deviation of the ummah). It will appear strange and unorthodox (NOI).
Book 1, Number 0270, Sahih Muslim Collection:
Narrated from Abu Hurairah who said: The Messenger of Allah (peace and blessings of Allah be upon him) said: **"Islam began as something strange and will revert to being strange as it began, so give glad tidings to the strangers."**

Master W. Fard Muhammad's Offer of Forgiveness

"You are alright today if you just will accept your own religion. And no getting on knees to ask for forgiveness for your past. All of that is forgiven. God told me to tell you that He will forgive us all the past; just accept your own, now. Go from here and not think over what happened in the past. You did not know who you were nor the enemy. So that is right and just that you should be forgiven for that which you had no knowledge of. So this what He told me to tell you. And since we don't have to go on our knees for yesterday, be sure that we go on our knees for today. A people that have did everything that the devil did and tried to beat him at some of it, get forgiven for all of that evil."
-Most Hon. Elijah Muhammad, Theology of Time, 8-27-72

So their Lord accepted their prayer, (saying): I will not suffer the work of any worker among you to be lost whether male or female, the one of you being the other. So those who fled and were driven forth from their homes and persecuted in My way and who fought and were slain, **I shall truly remove their evil** and make them enter Gardens wherein flow rivers — a reward from Allah. And with Allah is the best reward.-3:195

And those who believe and do good, and believe in that which has been revealed to Muhammad — and it is the Truth from their Lord — **He will remove their evil from them and improve their condition.**-47:2

O you who believe, turn to Allah with sincere repentance. **It may be your Lord will remove from you your evil** and cause you enter Gardens wherein flow rivers, on the day on which Allah will not abase the Prophet and those who believe with him. Their light will gleam before them and on their right hands — they will say: Our Lord, make perfect for us our light, and grant us protection; surely Thou art Possessor of power over all things.-66:8

That is the command of Allah, which He has revealed to you. And whoever keeps his duty to Allah, **He will remove from him his evils and give him a big reward**.-66:5

Ramadan Day 11-The Believer's Notes

Surah 9:93 – Surah 11:5

Ramadan Day 11-The Believer's Notes

Surah 9:93 – Surah 11:5

Hadith Wisdom For Ramadan Fasting

Narrated by `Abdullah:

The Prophet (ﷺ) fasted for days continuously; the people also did the same but it was difficult for them. So, the Prophet (ﷺ) forbade them (to fast continuously for more than one day). They slid, "But you fast without break (no food was taken in the evening or in the morning)." The Prophet (ﷺ) replied, "I am not like you, for I am provided with food and drink (by Allah).

Day 11	NOI	Regional	Cities	Prayer	Times	2023
City	Fajr	Sunrise	Dhuhr	Asr	Maghrib	Isha
Atlanta	06:15 AM	07:25 AM	01:42 PM	05:15 PM	07:59 PM	09:08 PM
Chicago	05:13 AM	06:31 AM	12:55 PM	04:30 PM	07:17 PM	08:37 PM
Houston	06:04 AM	07:10 AM	01:26 PM	04:58 PM	07:42 PM	08:48 PM
London	04:55 AM	06:27 AM	01:09 PM	04:40 PM	07:42 PM	08:58 PM
Los Angeles	05:30 AM	06:40 AM	12:57 PM	04:31 PM	07:14 PM	08:24 PM
Miami	06:08 AM	07:12 AM	01:25 PM	04:54 PM	07:38 PM	08:42 PM
New York	05:22 AM	06:39 AM	01:00 PM	04:35 PM	07:21 PM	08:38 PM
Philadelphia	05:28 AM	06:44 AM	01:05 PM	04:40 PM	07:25 PM	08:42 PM
Washington DC	05:38 AM	06:53 AM	01:13 PM	04:47 PM	07:32 PM	08:47 PM

The Vindication Of The Most Honorable Elijah Muhammad's Theology Day 12

Hadith: The Light of Islam (Sun) Will Rise In The West (America) in the Last Days

Volume 6, Book 60, Number 159, Sahih Bukhari Collection:
Narrated Abu Huraira: Allah's Apostle said, "The Hour will not be established until the **sun rises from the West**: and when the people see it, then whoever will be living on the surface of the earth will have faith, and that is (the time) when no good will it do to a soul to believe then, if it believed not before." (6.158)

Volume 4, Book 54, Number 421, Sahih Bukhari Collection:
Narrated Abu Dhar: The Prophet asked me at sunset, "Do you know where the sun goes (at the time of sunset)?" I replied, "Allah and His Apostle know better." He said, "It goes (i.e. travels) till it prostrates Itself underneath the Throne and takes the permission to rise again, and it is permitted and then (a time will come when) it will be about to prostrate itself but its prostration will not be accepted, and it will ask permission to go on its course but it will not be permitted, but it will be ordered to return whence it has come and so **it will rise in the west**. And that is the interpretation of the Statement of Allah: "And the sun Runs its fixed course For a term (decreed). that is The Decree of (Allah) The Exalted in Might, The All-Knowing." (36.38)

Volume 6, Book 60, Number 160, Sahih Bukhari Collection:
Narrated Abu Huraira: Allah's Apostle said, "The hour will not be established till **the sun rises from the West; and when it rises (from the West) and the people see it, they all will believe**. And that is (the time) when no good will it do to a soul to believe then." Then he recited the whole Verse (6.158)

Pakistani Islamic Scholar S. Muhammad Tufail Discusses Nation of Islam

"We have been watching the Muslim movement in America with great interest for many years. It is a great movement in this part of the world. It will do a great service not only to their people but to Islam as a whole. There is a tradition of the Prophet that in later times the sun will rise in the West. We interpret this as meaning the sun of Islam will rise in the West.

Q. Do you interpret the fact that a large Muslim movement has come about in America, under the leadership of Mr. Elijah Muhammad, as being a sign of the fulfillment of the Prophet?

A. Yes, this may be. Only the future will decide. In the early times, Islam spread towards the East. But in this instance, it is going to spread and dominate in the Western Hemisphere."

Ramadan Day 12-The Believer's Notes

Surah 11:6 – Surah 12:52

Ramadan Day 12-The Believer's Notes

Surah 11:6 – Surah 12:52

Hadith Wisdom For Ramadan Fasting

Narrated by Abu Huraira:

The Prophet (peace be upon him) said, "If somebody eats or drinks forgetfully then he should complete his fast, for what he has eaten or drunk, has been given to him by Allah."

Day 12	NOI	Regional	Cities	Prayer	Times	2023
City	Fajr	Sunrise	Dhuhr	Asr	Maghrib	Isha
Atlanta	06:14 AM	07:23 AM	01:42 PM	05:15 PM	07:59 PM	09:09 PM
Chicago	05:11 AM	06:30 AM	12:54 PM	04:31 PM	07:19 PM	08:38 PM
Houston	06:02 AM	07:09 AM	01:26 PM	04:58 PM	07:42 PM	08:49 PM
London	04:52 AM	06:24 AM	01:08 PM	04:41 PM	07:44 PM	09:00 PM
Los Angeles	05:29 AM	06:39 AM	12:57 PM	04:31 PM	07:15 PM	08:25 PM
Miami	06:07 AM	07:11 AM	01:25 PM	04:54 PM	07:38 PM	08:43 PM
New York	05:20 AM	06:37 AM	01:00 PM	04:35 PM	07:22 PM	08:40 PM
Philadelphia	05:27 AM	06:43 AM	01:05 PM	04:40 PM	07:26 PM	08:43 PM
Washington DC	05:36 AM	06:51 AM	01:12 PM	04:47 PM	07:33 PM	08:48 PM

The Vindication Of The Most Honorable Elijah Muhammad's Theology Day 13

THE BLACK MAN IS GOD

"The Most Honorable Elijah Muhammad taught that the "the Black man is God."

This idea is certainly not new, despite it being new to most who have labored under the notion that all of the paintings on the ceiling of the Sistine Chapel are accurate portrayals of God as an old white man who lives in the clouds. To the contrary, a close reading of the Bible scriptures describes God as the ancient Black man.

Perhaps Bishop Henry McNeal Turner's bold ministry should be examined to vindicate Muhammad on this critical area of the life-giving teachings. Bishop Turner delivered a sermon where he said, **"God Is A Negro."** He later defended is speech in this letter to a local newspaper:

"We have as much right biblically and otherwise to believe that God is a Negro, as you buckra, or white, people have to believe that God is a fine looking, symmetrical and ornamented white man. For the bulk of you, and all the fool Negroes of the country, believe that God is white- skinned, blue-eyed, straight-haired, projecting-nosed compressed-lipped and finely-robed white gentleman sitting upon a throne somewhere in the heavens.

Every race of people since time began who have attempted to describe their God by words, or by paintings, or by carvings, or by any other form or figure have conveyed the idea that the God who made them and shaped their destinies was symbolized in themselves, and why should not the Negro believe that he resembles God as much as other people? We do not believe that there is any hope for a race of people who do not believe that they look like God.

Demented though we be, whenever we reach the conclusion that God or even that Jesus Christ, while in the flesh, was a white man, we shall hang our gospel trumpet upon the willow and cease to preach.

We had rather be an atheist and believe in no God or a pantheist and believe that all nature is God, than to believe in the personality of a God and not believe that He is Negro. Blackness is much older than whiteness, for black was here before white, if the Hebrew word, coshach, or chasack, has any meaning. We do not believe in the eternity of matter, but we do believe that chaos floated in infinite darkness or blackness, millions, billions, quintillions and eons of years before God said, "Let there be light," and that during that time God had no material light Himself and was shrouded in darkness, so far as human comprehension is able to grasp the situation.

Yet we are no stickler as to God's color, anyway, but if He has any we should prefer to believe that it is nearer symbolized in the blue sky above us and the blue water of the seas and oceans; but we certainly protest against God being a white man or against God being white at all; abstract as this theme must forever remain while we are in the flesh. This is one of the reasons we favor African emigration, or Negro nationalization, wherever we can find a domain, for as long as we remain among whites, the Negro will believe that the devil is black and that he (the Negro) favors the devil, and that God is white and the (the Negro) bears no resemblance to Him, and the effect of such a sentiment is contemptuous and degrading, and one-half of the Negro race will be trying to get white and the other half will spend their days trying to be white men's scullions in order to please the whites; and the time they should be giving to the study of such things will dignify and make our race great will be devoted to studying about how unfortunate they are in not being white.

We conclude these remarks by repeating for the information of the Observer what it adjudged us demented for — God is a Negro."

Bishop Turner's mighty message agrees with the biblical description found in Daniel 7:9

> I kept on watching until the Ancient of Days was seated. His clothes were white, like snow, and the hair on his head was like pure wool. His throne burned with flaming fire, and its wheels burned with fire.

Isaiah 43:13 is similar

> I am God; also from ancient days I am the one. And there is no one who can deliver out of my hand; when I act, who can reverse it?

To be ancient is to be extremely old. And modern archaeologists have been in a continuous pursuit to find the origins of man or the most ancient of man. And they always end up in Africa. The Leakey family is a great family of archaeologists and Louis B. Leakey spoke to the Muhammad Speaks newspaper in 1964 about their findings of human remains in Africa that dated 2,000,000 years old. Referring to him as **homo-habilis**, Leakey discussed his findings and reports that this ancient Black man was advanced in the use of tools and home building.

> The importance of a home-building man at so early a period, at least a million years earlier than our previous findings, lifts man's age millions of years beyond our present thinking. I knew that most wild beasts and even reptiles and birds make homes for themselves. So, I knew that if man with his good brain did not seek to make a home for himself, he was dumber than we thought. Actually, man even millions of years ago was apparently endowed with intelligence.

As Bishop Turner pointed out, the majority of the people around the world have always depicted images of their God or Creator as being in their own image. This is especially true prior to the global expansion of Christianity as the religious arm of European imperialism.

Dr. Wesley Muhammad's brilliant and ground-breaking book **The Book of God: An Encyclopedia of Proof that the Black Man is God** represents a treasure of scholarship from one who is also both believer and scholar of the life-giving teachings. He is a distinguished scholar whose work to vindicate the theology of the Most Honorable Elijah Muhammad earned him a doctorate degree from the University of Michigan. The first section of his encyclopedia ends with the following conclusion based on the facts of his historical research:

> The Creator was a Man-a Black Man. This was acknowledged by all of the ancient spiritual traditions of

> the Original People. This was acknowledged by the original Hebrews (and Jews), the original Christians, and the original Muslim followers of Prophet Muhammad ibn Abdullah (saw). This understanding of God is the hallmark of Traditional Aboriginal Religion and Philosophy as well as the original orthodoxy of the three Hebraic religions. It was the later Greek philosophers who introduced the Spook God to the world.

Dr. Wesley's book is highly recommended to the reader for an exhaustive treatment on this specific content area of the proofs for the life-giving teachings. The non-exhaustive treatment contained in this book is provided to summarize as well as to contextualize our presentation of the Most Honorable Elijah Muhammad as a man who is worthy of great respect, reverence, gratitude and admiration. From Dr. Wesley's work, we learn of the long history of "Black Gods."

> Nearly all of the ancient Gods of the old and new world were black and had wooly hair..." from the texture of the hair I am inclined to assign to the Buddha of India, the Fuhi of China, Xaha of the Japanese the Quetzalcoatl of the Mexicans, the same and indeed an African or rather Nubian origins.

Dr. Wesley's arguments begin with his examining the great and dominant idea of divine embodiment and anthropomorphism within the sacred texts of many of the world's great religious and spiritual systems. From there he provides evidence that not only is there a consensus of a "man-God" being described in scripture, but the "man-God" of scripture is subsequently identified as a **"Black-Man-God."** He quoted Godfrey Higgins who noted:

> **We have found the Black complexion or something relating to it whenever we have approached the origin of nations**. The Alma Mater, the Goddess Multimammia, the founders of the Oracles, the Memnon of first idols, were always Black. Venus, Jupiter, Apollo, Bacchus, Hercules, Asteroth, Adonis, Horus, Apis, Osiris, and Amen: **in short, all the...deities were Black**. They remained as they were first...in very ancient times.

Other scholars are utilized by Dr. Wesley to help drive home the point. Cheikh Anta Diop writes of Ancient Egypt:

> Thus, we can understand why the Egyptians always painted their gods Black as coal, in the image of their race, from the beginning to the end of their history.

A quote from Manley P. Hall's **Man: Grand Symbol of the Mysteries** sheds more light on the Egyptians worship of Black-Man-God.

> Eusebius, on the authority of Porphyry, wrote that the Egyptians acknowledged one intellectual author or creator of the world; that they worshipped him in a ...human form and dark blue complexion(Blue-Black) ...

The Egyptian concept of God is insightful as it is their theological ideas that informed the beliefs and ideas of the Greeks. America's debt to Greek and Roman folkways, ideas and norms is universally acknowledged. Dr. Wesley makes the point that the Greeks bore witness to the "Black-Man-God" by citing the works of Zecharia Sitchin and Godfrey Higgins. From Sitchin:

> The Greeks described their gods as anthropomorphic as physically similar to mortal men and women, and human in character. They could be happy and angry and jealous; they made love, quarreled, fought; and they procreated like humans, bringing forth offspring through sexual intercourse-with each other and humans.

From Higgins:

> The Greek gods were adaptations of the Egyptian ones. Hence, the earliest ones of Greece were Black.

Dr. Wesley's research into the vindication of the Nation of Islam's theology is the strongest academic work on this subject to date. The reader is encouraged to read his writings in tandem with the numerous messages delivered by the Honorable Minister Louis Farrakhan; of particular relevance is the Minister's 1991 Saviours' Day message **"Who Is God?".**

-Demetric Muhammad, Hail Elijah, p. 77-85

Apocryphal Writings Shine Light On Being A “Registered” Muslim

-(p.29 Hail Elijah, The Importance Of Elijah In The Religions of Christianity & Judaism, Apocryphal Psuedo-Titus Epistle)

“Thus Elias, a noble man who still lives in the body...O holy dispensation of God, who has provided for...the coming age! Enoch, the righteous, from among the first people, was commissioned to commit to writing the history of the first man, and the holy Elias (was given the task) of registering the new deeds of this later people.”

Ramadan Day 13-The Believer's Notes

Surah 12:53 – Surah 14:52

Ramadan Day 13-The Believer's Notes

Surah 12:53 – Surah 14:52

Hadith Wisdom For Ramadan Fasting

Narrated by Abu Huraira:

A man came to the Prophet (peace be upon him) and said, "I had sexual intercourse with my wife on Ramadan (while fasting)." The Prophet (peace be upon him) asked him, "Can you afford to manumit a slave?" He replied in the negative. The Prophet (peace be upon him) asked him, "Can you fast for two successive months?" He replied in the negative. He asked him, "Can you afford to feed sixty poor persons?" He replied in the negative. (Abu Huraira added): Then a basket full of dates was brought to the Prophet (peace be upon him) and he said (to that man), "Feed (poor people) with this by way of atonement." He said, "(Should I feed it) to poorer people than we? There is no poorer house than ours between its (Medina's) mountains." The Prophet (peace be upon him) said, "Then feed your family with it."

Day 13	NOI	Regional	Cities	Prayer	Times	2023
City	Fajr	Sunrise	Dhuhr	Asr	Maghrib	Isha
Atlanta	06:12 AM	07:22 AM	01:41 PM	05:15 PM	08:00 PM	09:10 PM
Chicago	05:09 AM	06:28 AM	12:54 PM	04:31 PM	07:20 PM	08:39 PM
Houston	06:01 AM	07:08 AM	01:26 PM	04:58 PM	07:43 PM	08:50 PM
London	04:50 AM	06:22 AM	01:08 PM	04:42 PM	07:45 PM	09:01 PM
Los Angeles	05:27 AM	06:37 AM	12:57 PM	04:31 PM	07:16 PM	08:26 PM
Miami	06:06 AM	07:10 AM	01:25 PM	04:54 PM	07:39 PM	08:43 PM
New York	05:18 AM	06:36 AM	01:00 PM	04:36 PM	07:23 PM	08:41 PM
Philadelphia	05:25 AM	06:41 AM	01:04 PM	04:40 PM	07:27 PM	08:44 PM
Washington DC	05:34 AM	06:50 AM	01:12 PM	04:48 PM	07:34 PM	08:49 PM

The Vindication Of The Most Honorable Elijah Muhammad's Theology Day 14

The Most Honorable Elijah Muhammad explained that the Biblical and Qur'anic prophecies regarding the "coming of God" and the gathering together of His People are being fulfilled among Black People in America. He stated that this major event, predicted within the "end times" prophecies of the world's great religions, began with the coming of Allah (God) in the person of Master W. Fard Muhammad. Some Qur'anic ayats below are witness bearers to Messenger Muhammad's bold teaching.

ALLAH IS GOD 15

We cannot see a spirit; therefore, the teachings of His coming would be false. The spirit of life is and has been with us all of our lives. God is in person among us today. He is a man, He is in His time. God sees, hears, knows, wills, acts and is a person (man). The evil workings of the devil MUST come to an end.

THE COMING OF GOD AND THE GATHERING TOGETHER OF HIS PEOPLE

The prophets have warned us of a time that would come when God would judge the wicked and punish, or rather destroy, the wicked and give the earth over to the rule of a righteous people. So many of us have misunderstood just what we should expect. What will God look like? If we expect the destruction of the devil, what will the devil look like? How will I distinguish him? If the devil should be destroyed, what does that devil look like? In order not to follow him to his destruction I must be able to recognize him so that he won't be able to deceive me. What world's end will come, and what is that world that is going to end? Does that include everything that makes up the solar system? The planet earth? If so, what shall we expect? What kind of solar system will we have after the destruction of the present one? Think over these things. We must get down to the facts so that we can recognize them when they are presented to us. But you never questioned the first teacher. Shouldn't we be fair about this? Let us go after the thing right!

If we want to give each teacher justice, we should start with the first one. When Moses began to preach to the Hebrews to make themselves ready to go out to another country that God had promised their fathers on the condition that they believe and obey, here was the reply: "Who made you a judge over us?"

2:210-They wait for naught but that **Allah should come to them** in the shadows of the clouds with angels, and the matter has (already) been decided. And to Allah are (all) matters returned.

89:22-And **thy Lord comes with the angels**, ranks on ranks

59:2-He it is Who caused those who disbelieved of the People of the Book to go forth from their homes at the first banishment. You deemed not that they would go forth, while they thought that their fortresses would defend them against Allah. **But Allah came to them from place they expected not** and cast terror into their hearts — they demolished their houses with their own hands and the hands of the believers. So take a lesson, O you who have eyes!

16:33-Await they aught but that **the angels should come to them or that thy Lord's command should come to pass**. Thus did those before them. And Allah wronged them not, but they wronged themselves.

Ramadan Day 14-The Believer's Notes

Surah 15:1 – Surah 16:128

Ramadan Day 14-The Believer's Notes

Surah 15:1 – Surah 16:128

Hadith Wisdom For Ramadan Fasting

Narrated by Jabir bin `Abdullah:

Allah's Messenger (peace be upon him) was on a journey and saw a crowd of people, and a man was being shaded (by them). He asked, "What is the matter?" They said, "He (the man) is fasting." The Prophet (peace be upon him) said, "It is not righteousness that you fast on a journey."

Day 14	NOI	Regional	Cities	Prayer	Times	2023
City	Fajr	Sunrise	Dhuhr	Asr	Maghrib	Isha
Atlanta	06:11 AM	07:21 AM	01:41 PM	05:16 PM	08:01 PM	09:11 PM
Chicago	05:07 AM	06:26 AM	12:54 PM	04:32 PM	07:21 PM	08:41 PM
Houston	06:00 AM	07:06 AM	01:25 PM	04:58 PM	07:43 PM	08:51 PM
London	04:48 AM	06:20 AM	01:08 PM	04:43 PM	07:47 PM	09:03 PM
Los Angeles	05:26 AM	06:36 AM	12:56 PM	04:31 PM	07:17 PM	08:27 PM
Miami	06:05 AM	07:09 AM	01:24 PM	04:54 PM	07:39 PM	08:44 PM
New York	05:16 AM	06:34 AM	12:59 PM	04:36 PM	07:24 PM	08:42 PM
Philadelphia	05:23 AM	06:40 AM	01:04 PM	04:41 PM	07:28 PM	08:45 PM
Washington DC	05:33 AM	06:48 AM	01:12 PM	04:48 PM	07:35 PM	08:51 PM

Hadith al-Ruya

Dr. Wesley Muhammad

"Of all the "ahadith al-sura", or "form traditions," those that are most menacing to the transcendentalists (those who advocate a mystery God) describe a theophany in which God appeared to the Prophet in a particular form. Ibn Hanbal reported in his Musnad:

> "One morning, the Messenger of God went out to them [his companions] in a joyous mood and [with] a radiant face. We said [to him]: "Oh Messenger of God, here you are in a joyous mood, with a glowing face!" "How could I not be?" he answered. "My Lord came to me last night under the most beautiful form (fi ahsan sura), and He said [to me]: 'Oh Muhammad!' - 'Here I am, Lord, at Your order!' He said [to me]: 'Over what disputes the Sublime Council?' - 'I do not know, Lord.' He posed [to me] two or three times the same question. Then He put His palm between my shoulder blades, to the point where I felt its coolness between my nipples, and from that moment appeared to me [all] that is in the heavens and on the earth."

Not only is God's "most beautiful form" of interest; the physical contact between Lord and Prophet described here establishes divine corporeality in a manner unrivaled by other traditions. For Ignaz Goldziher, this report is "flagrant anthropomorphism." Yet the imam's actual narration of this hadith, reported on the authority of 'Abd al-Rahman ibn 'A'ish, has not gone unquestioned. Ibn Hajar al-'Asqalani reports from Abu Zur'a (d. 878) that the latter asked Ibn Hanbal about this report, and he replied: "This is of no consequence *(hadha laysa bi-shay')*." Ibn al-Jawzi (d. 1200) reports a similar position from Ahmad in his *Daf' shubah al-tashbih bi-aka.ff al-tanzih.*

He quotes the imam as stating, "The origins of this hadith and its sources are incongruous (mudtarib)." Yet Ibn al-Jawzi reports this very narration from Ibn Hanbal in his *al-'Ilal al-mutanahiya fl al-aJ:iadrth al-wahiya.* 'Abd Allah ibn Ahmad (d.903), the imam's son, likewise narrates the hadith from his father in the latter's Kitab al-Sunna. According to Nur al-Din 'Ali ibn Abi Bakr al-Haythami (d. 1405), when Ibn Hanbal was asked about the report, he declared it to be correct or right (sawab).

Whatever qualms Ibn Hanbal may have had about this particular isnad (chain of narration), as that was allegedly the object of his criticism, he had no issues with the matn (text). He reported it three other times with different chains of narration and explicitly declared *sahih* a similar hadith from Mu'adh ibn Jabal. The question, then, is how did the revered imam understand this report? Did he understand God truly to possess a "beautiful form"? The answer varies according to whose testimony one consults. Ibn al-Jawzi reports from Abu

Ya'la's (d. 1066) *Kitab al-Kifaya* that Ahmad stated, **"'I saw my Lord in the most beautiful form,' i.e., in the best position (mawdi')."** Interpreting "most beautiful form" as "best position" effectively eliminates the anthropomorphism of the text. But there are problems with this report. First, it is at variance with Abu Ya'la's own exegesis of this narration, as found in his *Kitab al-mu'tamad fi usul al-din.*

According to what we read, God truly has a most beautiful form in the same manner He has a soul and an essence: If it is said, "He is a person (shakhs) or form (:fura)," it (should be) said: the report from different routes on the night of the Mi'raj mentioned, "I saw my Lord in the most beautiful form." And then He said, "Over what does the Sublime Council dispute?" And the application of that is not to be refused. Just as "soul" (nafs) not like souls and essence (dhat) not like essences weren't denied Him. Likewise form unlike forms, for the Shari'a (uses it in this manner).

Second, 'Abd Allah ibn Ahmad, the person most responsible for the publication of Ibn Hanbal's dogmatic works, quotes from his father a different exegesis of this hadith, which is startling in its frank anthropomorphist suggestions:

My father reported to me ... from 'Abd al-Rahman ibn al-'A'ish from some of the companions of the Prophet: "He came out to them one morning while in a joyous mood and [with] a radiant face. We said [to him]: 'Oh Messenger of God, here you are in a joyous mood, with a glowing face!' -'How could I not be?' he answered. **'My Lord came to me last night under the most beautiful form,** and He said [to me]: "'O Muhammad!' ... " And my father [Ibn Hanbal] reported to us, 'Abd al-Razzaq from Ma'mar from Qatada [from the Prophet], **"Allah created Adam according to His form."** My father reported to us, 'Abd al-Razzaq from Ma'mar from Qatada, "'in the best stature (fi ahsan taqwim)' meaning 'in the most beautiful form (fi ahsan sura)' ." Ibrahim ibn al-Hajjaj reported to us, Hammad (ibn Salama) reported to us ... that the Prophet said, "Allah is beautiful (jamil) and He loves beauty."

The implication of this collection of traditions is unmistakable. **The "most beautiful form" is first identified with that form of God according to which Adam was created. This identification is further supported by the imam's interpretation of sura 95:4: "Surely We created man in the best stature (fi ahsan taqwim)."**

Ibn Hanbal accepts the tafsir or exegesis of Qatada identifying man's "best stature" with God's "most beautiful form." Because Adam was created according to God's own form, this identification is logical. **It is then affirmed that God is beautiful in the physical sense.** Such an exegesis demonstrates a capacity for hermeneutical exercise, against the minimalist fideism popularly imputed to Ibn Hanbal. If he was anthropomorphist in his thought, this was not due to irrationalism or blind adherence to the "letter" of scripture. The report quoted here betrays the employment of the rational faculties, albeit in a traditionalist context."

Master W. Fard Muhammad's Love

"I have treasured all my life love for the lost-found nation of Islam..."

September 7, 1933

Ramadan Day 15-The Believer's Notes

Surah 17:1 – Surah 18:74

Ramadan Day 15-The Believer's Notes

Surah 17:1 – Surah 18:74

Hadith Wisdom For Ramadan Fasting

Narrated by Anas bin Malik:

We used to travel with the Prophet (peace be upon him) and neither did the fasting persons criticize those who were not fasting, nor did those who were not fasting criticize the fasting ones.

Narrated by Tawus:

Ibn `Abbas said, "Allah's Messenger (peace be upon him) set out from Medina to Mecca and he fasted till he reached 'Usfan, where he asked for water and raised his hand to let the people see him, and then broke the fast, and did not fast after that till he reached Mecca, and that happened in Ramadan." Ibn `Abbas used to say, "Allah's Messenger (peace be upon him) (sometimes) fasted and (sometimes) did not fast during the journeys so whoever wished to fast could fast, and whoever wished not to fast, could do so."

Day 15	NOI	Regional	Cities	Prayer	Times	2023
City	Fajr	Sunrise	Dhuhr	Asr	Maghrib	Isha
Atlanta	06:09 AM	07:19 AM	01:41 PM	05:16 PM	08:02 PM	09:12 PM
Chicago	05:05 AM	06:25 AM	12:53 PM	04:32 PM	07:22 PM	08:42 PM
Houston	05:59 AM	07:05 AM	01:25 PM	04:58 PM	07:44 PM	08:51 PM
London	04:46 AM	06:18 AM	01:08 PM	04:44 PM	07:49 PM	09:05 PM
Los Angeles	05:24 AM	06:35 AM	12:56 PM	04:31 PM	07:17 PM	08:28 PM
Miami	06:04 AM	07:08 AM	01:24 PM	04:53 PM	07:40 PM	08:44 PM
New York	05:14 AM	06:33 AM	12:59 PM	04:37 PM	07:25 PM	08:43 PM
Philadelphia	05:21 AM	06:38 AM	01:04 PM	04:41 PM	07:29 PM	08:46 PM
Washington DC	05:31 AM	06:46 AM	01:11 PM	04:48 PM	07:36 PM	08:52 PM

Master W. Fard Muhammad:

"The Proof of The Message Is The Proof Of The Man"

Demetric Muhammad

"Allah has promised to those of you who believe and do good that He will surely make them rulers in the earth as He made those before them rulers, and that He will surely establish for them their religion, which He has chosen for them, and that He will surely give them security in exchange after their fear. They will serve Me, not associated aught with Me. And whoever is ungrateful after this, they are the transgressors."

Holy Qur'an-24:55

Divine Secrets Revealed To A Black Man From America

I must admit that when I think about Saviours' Day and the reason for Saviours' Day, my eyes begin to fill with tears. These are tears of joy and gratitude when I think about the goodness of God. I am so happy to be a Muslim. I am so happy to be a believer in the life-giving teachings of the Most Honorable Elijah Muhammad. I am overjoyed and my heart if filled with profound gratitude. Saviours' Day reminds me, more so than any other time during the year of the profoundness of what we believe and what we bear witness has occurred among us, the Black people of America.

We believe and emphatically exclaim that it is Allah (God), who appeared to us in the person of Master Wallace Fard Muhammad. We believe that it is He that is, and has been, the teacher of the Most Honorable Elijah Muhammad, and the protector and maker of the Honorable Minister Louis Farrakhan.

There are many in the world of religion, who disagree with us. There are many in the Muslim world that consider our theological beliefs to be "outside the pale" of permissible Islamic beliefs. And despite this, the Most Honorable Elijah Muhammad and the Honorable Minister Louis Farrakhan have proven unafraid to stand on this belief, in spite of this world's religious and spiritual leader's rejection of it.

I reflect upon this Saviours' Day, the 146th birth anniversary of Master W. Fard Muhammad, and how the 92 years of the presence of the Nation of Islam in America is now at a point where there is an overwhelming abundance of facts and evidence to prove the veracity and truth of what Master W. Fard Muhammad revealed to His servant, the Most Honorable Elijah Muhammad.

There are 2 companion passages of scripture, one from the Bible and the other found within the Holy Qur'an that have direct bearing on the controversial belief and teaching of the Nation of Islam. From the Bible we read:

Surely the Lord GOD does nothing, Unless He reveals His secret to His servants the prophets.-Amos 3:7

And From the Holy Qur'an we read:

The Knower of the unseen, so He makes His secrets known to none; Except a messenger whom He chooses. For surely He makes a guard to go before him and after him, That He may know that they have truly delivered the messages of their Lord; and He encompasses what is with them, and He keeps account of all things.-72:26-28

These important passages of scripture contextualize the controversial nature of when Allah (God) blesses a people with the gift of the divine revelation of previously hidden truths. The scriptures refer to this process as Allah (God) divulging His "secrets." Controversy is inherent in the very nature of what is held as "secret" information. But we are assured that in Allah's own good time that He will vindicate His Messengers who courageously teach to their people the divine wisdom of Allah's divinely revealed "secrets."

Farrakhan: "Minister of The Confirmation"

What brings me so much joy, in a time like this is that for so long the teachings of the Most Honorable Elijah Muhammad, revealed to Him by Master W. Fard Muhammad, were mocked and ridiculed. At best, Messenger Muhammad was paid a "back-handed" compliment, when it was said of him that he was a social reformer who could rehabilitate criminals. His message was portrayed in the media and by various critics as being filled with the kind of ideas that could never attract serious thinkers. The critics have painted Muhammad's message as crude, unsophisticated, void of nuance, bereft of complexity, without beauty and only consumable on a very pedestrian level.

Modern times however do violence to the old critics of Messenger Muhammad! The events and happenings of today are conspiring to vindicate the message of Muhammad. Moreover, the vindication of the Message is the vindication of the Messenger. For the scripture points out that the "proof of the Message is the proof of the Messenger."(See Deuteronomy 18:20-22)

This current season, where close observers are noticing that Master W. Fard Muhammad's revelations to the Most Honorable Elijah Muhammad are being proven true, compares perfectly to the period of time mentioned in the Holy Qur'an when Moses prayed to Allah to give him his brother Aaron (Haroon) as a helper **to "confirm"** what Allah had revealed to Moses (Musa). Consider this powerful passage:

> "And my brother, Aaron, he is more eloquent in speech than I, **so send him with me as a helper to confirm me**. Surely I fear that they would reject me. He said: We will strengthen thine arm with thy brother, and We will give you both an authority, so that they shall not reach you. With Our signs, you two and those who follow you, will triumph."-28:34-35

When something is "confirmed" it is strengthened (firmed up) via the agency of proofs, facts, evidence, empirical, scientific, mathematical, quantitative and qualitative sources. What has, no doubt, spawned the season of vindication for Master W. Fard Muhammad and what He revealed, is the ministry of the Honorable Minister Louis Farrakhan. Farrakhan is the Minister of "The Confirmation of The Revelation." Minister Farrakhan has strengthened the message in its believability among a mass of "non-believers", many of whom who have been compelled into becoming believers through the sheer force of Minister Farrakhan's unimpeachable arguments.

Not only has Minister Farrakhan bowled us over with the majesty of His unique God-given representation of Muhammad's message, but His spiritual depth and anointing has produced a budding community of scholarship devoted to the protection, preservation and widespread proliferation of what Master W. Fard Muhammad revealed to the Most Honorable Elijah Muhammad.

The Confirmation Of The Revelation

The Confirmation of the Revelation of Master W. Fard Muhammad to His Servant, the Most Honorable Elijah Muhammad, fortifies the believers. I personally see it as Allah working through many and varied men, women and circumstances to do what He promised in the Holy Qur'an wherein it reads and "He will surely establish for them their religion, which He has chosen for them.."

Space will not permit us to include all that we know of the proofs and evidences that confirm what the Nation of Islam exclusively possesses of the most recent of Allah's divine revelations to the human family of our planet. But we conclude and pause to reflect on just a few sources from modern scientific discovery that serve as reminders, witness bearers and confirmations, that despite what our critics have attempted to destroy us, the truth as revealed by Master W. Fard Muhammad keeps marching on!

The Making of The White Race

> "Incredibly, Dr. Jonathan Pritchard estimates that the point in time when the genes of the Asian and European populations were altered was 6,600 years ago, the exact date that the Honorable Elijah Muhammad taught that Mr. Yacub began his Patmos Island grafting process.
> These scientists Cooper, Eiberg, Cheng and Pritchard have scientifically zeroed in on a date in time that corresponds exactly to the Teachings of the Honorable Elijah Muhammad; but the scientists are yet unable to account for the reason for this dramatic, genetic convulsion in the human family."-Hon. Min. Louis Farrakhan, The Time & What Must Be Done part 39

The Original People Are The Black People of The Planet Earth

> Every modern ancestor's origins can be traced back to Africa...All humans share a common direct maternal ancestor known as Mitochondrial Eve. She is believed to be a part of a small group of humans who lived in Africa...Mitochondrial DNA found in our cells is the genetic signature that has been passed from mother to child. Mitochondrial Eve was a woman who lived 200,000 years ago who had enough daughters in a continuous chain that her Mitochondrial DNA survived.
> - Mitochondrial Eve and Homo Sapiens in Africa's Great Rift Valley | Africa's Great Civilizations (pbslearningmedia.org)

UFOs are Real

> The U.S. government officials said there is no doubt that identified UAPs were physical objects, tamping down speculation that sightings could be optical illusions caused by atmospheric conditions or sensor malfunctions. "From a safety of flight issue, we absolutely do believe that what we are seeing are not simply sensor artifacts. These are things that physically exist," a senior government official said. "They

are physical objects."- Pentagon task force's UFO report released — many cases remain unexplained (cbsnews.com)

American Under Divine Judgment

North America — and the USA in particular — has the world's wildest weather extremes: No other part of the planet can boast its ferocious weather stew of hurricanes, tornadoes, droughts, floods, wildfires, blizzards, heat waves and cold snaps. "You'd be hard-pressed to find another patch of land on Earth the size of the USA that boasts such a variety of such intensely extreme weather inside its borders," says meteorologist and author Robert Henson of Boulder, Colo. "We get more high-impact weather than any other country on the planet," agrees Sean Potter, a meteorologist and weather historian in New York City. - USA has the world's most extreme weather (usatoday.com)

One Meal A Day For A Long Life

A recent study based on depriving mice of food for a certain length of time reveals that longer intervals between meals may, in fact, improve health, lengthen life and prevent disease. The research was reported in the recent Proceedings of the National Academy of Sciences.

Dr. Mark P. Mattson, chief of the laboratory of neurosciences at the National Institute on Aging, which is part of The National Institutes of Health, said, "I would be very confident in saying that healthy adults don't need three full meals a day and would be better off skipping one or two. When you go without food, there are benefits. Your cells become more efficient. "- FCN Editorial - Muhammad already said it: Our diets are killing us! (finalcall.com)

There Is Life On Mars

"And while NASA hasn't found any evidence of life now, we've found lots of evidence that Mars could have supported life in the past," Graham explained. "There are lots of pieces of evidence that say there was once a huge ocean on Mars and an atmosphere that could have supported life."- Is there life on Mars? A NASA scientist explains in new video (space.com)

Master W. Fard Muhammad's Love

"HE GREATLY rejoiced over us and was real happy that He had found us. He said that He would made a new people out of us who submit to Him by causing us to grow into a new growth, not an entirely new body but a reversal of the old decayed body into a new growth, which He said would make us all as we were at the age of 16."
-Most Hon. Elijah Muhammad
June 9, 1956

Ramadan Day 16-The Believer's Notes

Surah 18:75 – Surah 20:135

Ramadan Day 16-The Believer's Notes

Surah 18:75 – Surah 20:135

Hadith Wisdom For Ramadan Fasting

Narrated `by Abdullah bin Abi `Aufa:

We were traveling with Allah's Messenger (peace be upon him) and he was fasting, and when the sun set, he said to (someone), "Get down and mix Sawiq with water for us." He replied, "O Allah's Messenger (peace be upon him)! (Will you wait) till it is evening?" The Prophet (peace be upon him) again said, "Get down and mix Sawiq with water for us." He replied, "O Allah's Messenger (peace be upon him)! It is still daytime." The Prophet (peace be upon him) said again, "Get down and mix Sawiq with water for us." So, he got down and carried out that order. The Prophet (peace be upon him) then said, "When you see night falling from this side, the fasting person should break his fast," and he beckoned with his finger towards the east.

Day 16	NOI	Regional	Cities	Prayer	Times	2023
City	Fajr	Sunrise	Dhuhr	Asr	Maghrib	Isha
Atlanta	06:08 AM	07:18 AM	01:40 PM	05:16 PM	08:02 PM	09:13 PM
Chicago	05:03 AM	06:23 AM	12:53 PM	04:32 PM	07:23 PM	08:43 PM
Houston	05:57 AM	07:04 AM	01:25 PM	04:58 PM	07:45 PM	08:52 PM
London	04:43 AM	06:15 AM	01:07 PM	04:44 PM	07:50 PM	09:05 PM
Los Angeles	05:23 AM	06:33 AM	12:56 PM	04:31 PM	07:18 PM	08:29 PM
Miami	06:03 AM	07:07 AM	01:24 PM	04:53 PM	07:40 PM	08:45 PM
New York	05:13 AM	06:31 AM	12:59 PM	04:37 PM	07:26 PM	08:45 PM
Philadelphia	05:19 AM	06:37 AM	01:04 PM	04:42 PM	07:30 PM	08:48 PM
Washington DC	05:29 AM	06:45 AM	01:11 PM	04:49 PM	07:37 PM	08:53 PM

The Vindication Of
The Most Honorable Elijah Muhammad's Theology
Day 17

GOD'S JUDGEMENT OF AMERICA

Another major content area of the life-giving teachings of the Most Honorable Elijah Muhammad involves his bold and controversial prophesy that America was doomed by Allah(God) to fall and ruin, if she refused to do justice by God's chosen people-the Black man and woman of America.

That America is to receive a divinely ordained punishment is a belief that many Christian writers have advanced. I discussed this in an article written for the March 30, 2016 online edition of the FinalCall.com[1]. In that article, we cite the following writers and theologians:

Edward Tracy: "**On what comfortable and convenient grounds can the U.S.A. claim immunity from divine judgement? The nation that forgets God goes backward—backward to defeat, backward to destruction.** That we (U.S.A.) are going backward cannot be denied? We are regressing spiritually, morally, legally, financially, governmentally, and at an alarming acceleration."[2]

Herbert W. Armstrong: "Just as God has bestowed on us such material blessings as never before came to any nations, now to correct us so we may enjoy such blessings, **He is going to bring upon our peoples such national disaster as has never before struck any nation! Many prophecies describe this**!"[3]

Ruth Graham (wife of famous evangelist Billy Graham): "**If God doesn't punish America, He'll have to apologize to Sodom and Gomorrah.**"[4]

---

[1] Demetric Muhammad, "Is America In the Crosshairs of God's Wrath? Christian scholars, biblical scripture, Jewish historians and natural disasters support Farrakhan's divine warnings", The Final Call Newspaper Online Edition, http://www.finalcall.com/artman/publish/Perspectives_1/article_102992.shtml
[2] Edward Tracy, The United States in Prophecy, Convale Publishing, ©1969
[3] Herbert Armstrong, The United States and Britain in Prophecy, Worldwide Church of God, ©1967
[4] Ruth Graham, as quoted by Billy Graham in "My Heart Aches for America", July 19, 2012, https://billygraham.org/story/billy-graham-my-heart-aches-for-america/

Dr. Martin Luther King Jr: "This integration movement is beginning to unfold things that I had never quite envisioned and **I wonder if we are not in fact integrating into a burning house**." And he then began to, it was the first time that I had heard him utter anything that suggested that there was another dimension to this whole theory. We were going, going, we were all going to have to go someplace else.[5]

Christian author and student of prophecy S. Franklin Logsdon has also studied Biblical prophecy. His writings agree with the Most Honorable Elijah Muhammad the America fits the description of the prophetic "mystery Babylon" that is identified in the Bible's book of Revelations. Logsdon writes boldly and clearly:

> We proceed logically and reasonable to extract from divine revelation the descriptions of an unnamed nation. Then, deductively, giving careful attention to relationships, endeavors, accomplishments and character, we press toward a crystallization for identification.
>
> Applying basic truths relative to God's dealing with nations, we observe the tendencies and trends of national behavior on the part of one nation Biblically described. We note how, though singularly blessed, this prophesied nation incurs the displeasure and eventual indignation of the Most High God, and how she places herself in line for His severe judgment.
>
> We notice how she diminishes in world influence and deteriorates internally. Boasting of superb power and mighty defenses, but living lustfully and godlessly, she finally is plunged into desolation. **Because the details of this whole scriptural portrayal of an end time nation bears such a striking and convincing resemblance to the U.S.A., one more courageous than the author would forthrightly declare, "She's the one."**[6]

Of particular power and importance is the candid and visceral commentary written by one of America's founding fathers, **Thomas Jefferson**. Jefferson, a deist and slave owner appears to arrive at a moment of clarity to discuss the dastardly deeds of he and his fellow slave owners, pondering their fate in the eyes of the God of justice.:

There must doubtless be an unhappy influence on the manners of our people produced by the existence of slavery among us. The whole commerce between master and slave is a perpetual exercise of the most boisterous passions, the most unremitting despotism on the one part, and degrading submissions on the other. Our children see this, and learn to imitate it; for man is an imitative animal. This quality is the germ of all education in him. From his cradle to his grave he is learning to do what he sees others do. If a parent could find no motive either in his philanthropy or his self-love, for restraining the intemperance of passion towards his slave, it should always be a sufficient one that his child is present. But generally, it is not sufficient. The parent storms, the child looks on, catches the lineaments of wrath, puts on the same airs in the circle of smaller slaves, gives a loose to his worst of passions, and thus nursed, educated, and daily exercised in tyranny, cannot but be stamped by it with odious peculiarities.... For if a slave can have a country in this world, it must be any other in preference to that in which he is born to live and labor for another: in which he must lock up the faculties of his nature, contribute as far as depends on his individual endeavors to the evanishment of the human race, or entail his own miserable condition on the endless generations proceeding from him. With the morals of the people, their industry also is destroyed. For in a warm climate, no man will labor for himself who can make another labor for him. This is so true, that of the proprietors of slaves a very small

---

[5] Dr. Martin Luther King Jr., as quoted by Harry Belafonte in Interview by Blackside, Inc. on May 15, 1989, for Washington University Libraries, Film and Media Archive, Henry Hampton Collection.

[6] S. Franklin Logsdon, Is the U.S.A. in Prophecy, Zondervan Publishing, ©1968, p.3-4.

proportion indeed are ever seen to labor. And can the liberties of a nation be thought secure when we have removed their only firm basis, a conviction in the minds of the people that these liberties are of the gift of God? That they are not to be violated but with his wrath? ***Indeed, I tremble for my country when I reflect that God is just: that his justice cannot sleep for ever: that considering numbers, nature and natural means only, a revolution of the wheel of fortune, an exchange of situation, is among possible events: that it may become probable by supernatural interference! The Almighty has no attribute which can take side with us in such a contest.***[7]

[7] Thomas Jefferson, Notes on the State of Virginia, Query XVIII: Manners, ©1781, http://teachingamericanhistory.org/library/document/notes-on-the-state-of-virginia-query-xviii-manners/

Ramadan Day 17-The Believer's Notes

Surah 21:1 – Surah 22:78

Ramadan Day 17-The Believer's Notes

Surah 21:1 – Surah 22:78

Hadith Wisdom For Ramadan Fasting

Narrated by Abu Juhaifa:

The Prophet (peace be upon him) made a bond of brotherhood between Salman and Abu Ad-Darda.' Salman paid a visit to Abu Ad-Darda' and found Um Ad-Darda' dressed in shabby clothes and asked her why she was in that state. She replied, "Your brother Abu Ad-Darda' is not interested in (the luxuries of) this world." In the meantime Abu Ad-Darda' came and prepared a meal for Salman. Salman requested Abu Ad- Darda' to eat (with him), but Abu Ad-Darda' said, "I am fasting." Salman said, "I am not going to eat unless you eat." So, Abu Ad-Darda' ate (with Salman). When it was night and (a part of the night passed), Abu Ad-Darda' got up (to offer the night prayer), but Salman told him to sleep and Abu Ad- Darda' slept. After sometime Abu Ad-Darda' again got up but Salman told him to sleep. When it was the last hours of the night, Salman told him to get up then, and both of them offered the prayer. Salman told Abu Ad-Darda', "Your Lord has a right on you, your soul has a right on you, and your family has a right on you; so you should give the rights of all those who has a right on you." Abu Ad- Darda' came to the Prophet (peace be upon him) and narrated the whole story. The Prophet (peace be upon him) said, "Salman has spoken the truth."

Day 17	NOI	Regional	Cities	Prayer	Times	2023
City	Fajr	Sunrise	Dhuhr	Asr	Maghrib	Isha
Atlanta	06:06 AM	07:17 AM	01:40 PM	05:16 PM	08:03 PM	09:14 PM
Chicago	05:01 AM	06:21 AM	12:53 PM	04:33 PM	07:24 PM	08:45 PM
Houston	05:56 AM	07:03 AM	01:24 PM	04:58 PM	07:45 PM	08:53 PM
London	04:41 AM	06:13 AM	01:07 PM	04:45 PM	07:52 PM	09:07 PM
Los Angeles	05:21 AM	06:32 AM	12:56 PM	04:32 PM	07:19 PM	08:30 PM
Miami	06:02 AM	07:06 AM	01:23 PM	04:53 PM	07:41 PM	08:45 PM
New York	05:11 AM	06:29 AM	12:58 PM	04:37 PM	07:27 PM	08:46 PM
Philadelphia	05:18 AM	06:35 AM	01:03 PM	04:42 PM	07:31 PM	08:49 PM
Washington DC	05:28 AM	06:43 AM	01:11 PM	04:49 PM	07:38 PM	08:54 PM

The Vindication Of
The Most Honorable Elijah Muhammad's Theology
Day 18

THE TRUE REALITY OF SATAN

Imam Michael Saahir in his excellent book **The Man Behind the Men: The Most Honorable Elijah Muhammad**[8] shares with his readers that the idea that the evil treatment of Black people by their white slave masters is demonic is not a new idea. He quotes from famous Black activists and thinkers. From Fredrick Douglass we read, "**Those ministers who defended slavery from the Bible, were of their father the devil**; and those churches which fellowshipped slaveholders as Christians, were synagogues of Satan, and our nation was a nation of liars."[9]

In addition to Douglass's use of the term devil, we find also legendary abolitionist and writer David Walker who wrote:

> The whites have always been an unjust, jealous, unmerciful, avaricious and blood-thirsty set of beings, always seeking after power and authority. --We view them all over the confederacy of Greece, where they were first known to be anything, (in consequence of education) we see them there, cutting each other's throats--trying to subject each other to wretchedness and misery--to effect which, they used all kinds of deceitful, unfair, and unmerciful means. We view them next in Rome, where the spirit of tyranny and deceit raged still higher. We view them in Gaul, Spain, and in Britain. --In fine, we view them all over Europe, together with what were scattered about in Asia and Africa, as heathens, and **we see them acting more like devils than accountable men.**[10]

Imam Saahir includes a quote from Henry Highland Garnet: "Remember the stripes your fathers bore. Think of the torture and disgrace of your noble mothers. Think of your wretched sisters, loving virtue and purity as they are driven into concubinage, and are **exposed to the unbridled lust of incarnate devils**.... Yes, tyrants would meet with plagues more terrible than those of Pharaoh. But you are a patient

[8] Imam Michael Saahir, The Man Behind the Men: The Honorable Elijah Muhammad, ©2011, p.98.
[9] Fredrick Douglass, My Bondage My Freedom, Miller, Orton & Mulligan, New York, © 1855.
[10] David Walker, Walker's Appeal in Four Articles together with a Preamble to the Colored Citizens of the World But in particular and very expressly to those of the United States of America, Boston, MA, September 28, 1829.

people. **You act as though you were made for special use of these devils.**"[11]

In addition to what Black historical figures identified as the collective white man's devilish behavior we find similar expressions from Whites. The dictionary defines devil as:

> The Devil (from Greek: diábolos = slanderer or accuser)[1] is believed in many religions, myths and cultures to be a supernatural entity that is **the personification of evil and the enemy of God and humankind**; the chief spirit of evil and enemy of God, often represented as the ruler of hell and **often depicted as a human figure** with horns, cloven hoofs, and tail; one of the subordinate evil spirits of traditional Jewish and Christian belief; **a person or animal regarded as cruel, wicked, or ill-natured; a person or animal regarded as unfortunate or wretched; a person or animal regarded as clever, daring, mischievous, or energetic**; the opposite of truth; an error, lie, or false belief in sin, sickness, and death.[12]

The Maulana Muhammad Ali English translation of the Holy Qur'an points out that the devil (shaitan) is regularly conceived of as human in form and expression. The footnote to Surah 22 Ayat 3 reads:

> 22:3. And among men is he who disputes about Allah without knowledge, and follows every rebellious devil. Footnote 3a: The devil here is, as very frequently in the Holy Qur'an, the devil in human form.

The index of this English translation of the Holy Qur'an includes the various places throughout the Quranic text where a human devil is portrayed.

> **Devil**, the, in human form, 2:102, footnote 102a; 3:175, footnote 175a; 8:48, footnote 48a; 14:22, footnote 22a; 22:3, footnote 3a; as signifying leaders in unbelief, 2:14, footnote 14a; standing for wicked opponents, 23:97, footnote 97a, footnote 99a; evil-doers are forces of,17:64, footnote 64b; as applied to foreign tribes,38:37–38, footnote 38a; signifying divers,21:82, footnote 82a; applied to soothsayers,15:16 –18, footnote 18a; 37:7, footnote 7a; 67:5, footnote 5a

These definitions and scriptural markers, when used to describe the collective behavior of Caucasian world dominance, provides justification for the use of the term devil. White thinkers and writers have also used this term to describe the conduct of "white offenses in the aggregate." In 1968 Colorado College associate professor Frank Tucker wrote a book entitled **The White Conscience: An analysis of the white man's mind and conduct**. In his section entitle "white offenses in the aggregate" he includes several indictments of the collective devilishment of white world dominance.

From Tucker, we read of U.S. Senator J.J. Ingalls who said on the floor of the U.S. Senate:

Mr. President, **the race to which we belong is the most arrogant and rapacious**, the most exclusive and indomitable in history. It is the conquering and the unconquerable race, through which alone man has taken possession of the physical and moral world.... **All other races have been its enemies or its victims.**"

Tucker also quotes author Gerald W. Johnson who wrote: "Of all the creatures to appear on this earth, **the white man is the fiercest by far.**"[13]

British economist John A. Hobson said that "wherever Europeans had found less highly organized peoples with promising mineral or agricultural lands, they had if possible taken over

---

[11] Henry Highland Garnet, A Memorial Discourse (Philadelphia: J. M. Wilson, 1865), p. 44-51.
[12] Collins Dictionary of the English Language, Online Version, Found at: https://www.collinsdictionary.com/dictionary/english/devil
[13] Frank Tucker, The White Conscience, Frederick Ungar Publishing Co., New York, ©1968, p.3.

these lands compelling the inhabitants to work for the Europeans benefit. If the natives could not be reduced to useful forms of servitude, they were expelled or exterminated."[14]

And British poet Wilfred S. Blunt exclaimed "**The whole white race is reveling openly in violence**, as though it had never pretended to be Christian. God's equal curse be on them all!"[15]

All of this history and documentation serves to vindicate the Honorable Elijah Muhammad's use of that term. And in the early 1970s he asked his National Representative Minister Louis Farrakhan to stop using that term "devil". He instructed his top minister that the evil of Caucasian people could be best described at that time under titles such as "the slave master's children", "the enemy" or "Satan". Each of these terms, one historical, the other political and the last one spiritual would best cover the more modern "white offenses in the aggregate."

As a final thought on this particular area of the "life-giving teachings" science also vindicates Muhammad's controversial teaching. In his most popular and beloved book Message to the Blackman in America, the Honorable Elijah Muhammad discusses the origin of Caucasian people being no more than 6,000 years in length. And recent genetic research has come forward to support Muhammad's once ridiculed teaching.

Consider the following excerpt from his top minister, National Representative and best helper and defender, the Honorable Minister Louis Farrakhan. In part 39 of Minister Farrakhan's historic year long webcast series The Time and What Must Be Done, the Minister takes time to showcase the scientific research that bears witness to this area of the life-giving teachings. From the Minister's words, we cite the following:

Guess what? The scientists are now agreeing with the Honorable Elijah Muhammad about the time of the White race's appearance on our planet, and their nature! ***Oh, so many have mocked and ridiculed Mr. Muhammad's Teachings about "Yakub"; that he said, "Allah taught him" that the White man first appeared 6,000 years ago on an island in the Aegean Sea called Pelan, or "Patmos"—but White scientists are now confirming the reality of this event in their history, and this revelation from Allah to the Honorable Elijah Muhammad!***

According to the National Geographic Society, scientists studying DNA have now confirmed, "Europeans as a people are younger than we thought"—this is in an article published April 23, 2013 in National Geographic's Daily News titled "Modern Europe's History Starts in Stone Age" written by Ker Than. ***Professor Alan Cooper, director of the Australian Centre for Ancient DNA at the University of Adelaide, analyzed DNA from ancient skeletons and found that the genetic makeup of modern Europe was established just 6,500 years ago****. According to the National Geographic Daily News article, Professor Cooper said: "The genetics show that something around that point caused the genetic signatures of previous populations to disappear. However, we don't know what happened or why ..."*

Other scientists have come to the same conclusions: ***Dr. Keith Cheng, a geneticist at the Pennsylvania State University College of Medicine, led a study that shows the evolution of a gene for skin color; and suggests that Europeans "lightened up quite recently, perhaps only 6,000 to 12,000 years ago."*** *[Reference: An April 20, 2007 article in Science*

---

[14] John A. Hobson, Imperialism: A Study, James & Co., New York, 1902, p.262, 271-272.
[15] Wilfrid S. Blunt, My Diaries: Being a Personal Narrative of Events, 1888-1914, Martin Secker, London, ©1919 p.464.

magazine titled "European Skin Turned Pale Only Recently, Gene Suggests" (Vol. 316, No. 5823, pg. 364).] ***Dr. Hans Eiberg of the University of Copenhagen confirmed that all blue-eyed humans have a "genetic mutation" that he says occurred "six-10,000 years ago."*** *His team found a specific gene, known as the "OCA2 gene," which, if altered, would result in human beings without melanin in their hair, eyes, or skin color, a condition known as "albinism." [Reference: A January 30, 2008 article in The Telegraph (U.K.) titled* ***"Blue eyes result of ancient 'genetic mutation': Blue eye color originated near The Black Sea" by Roger Highfield, Science Editor.] Thus, this OCA2 gene seems to have been targeted and manipulated by some force or event around 6,000-plus years ago.***

You know, that makes us, as Muslims, feel real good, because the Honorable Elijah Muhammad taught us this—and we have brought it before scholars and scientists, and they mocked us and laughed at us.

Also, Dr. Jonathan Pritchard, with other researchers at The University of Chicago, had found "where genes appear to have been reshaped by natural selection ... within the last 5,000 to 15,000 years." *[Reference: March 7, 2006 in The New York Times "Science" section titled "Still Evolving, Human Genes Tell New Story" by Nicholas Wade.] Refer to pages 110 and 125-126 of Message to The Blackman:* ***Incredibly, Dr. Pritchard estimates that the point in time when the genes of the Asian and European populations were altered was "6,600 years ago"—the exact date that the Honorable Elijah Muhammad taught that Mr. Yakub began his Patmos Island grafting process!***

These scientists, Cooper, Eiberg, Cheng and Pritchard, have scientifically "zeroed in" on a date in time that corresponds exactly to The Teachings of the Honorable Elijah Muhammad; but the scientists are yet unable to account for the reason for this dramatic genetic convulsion in the human family. According to the National Geographic Daily News article, Professor Cooper said: ***"This population moves in around 4,000 to 5,000 [B.C.]"—that's about 6,500 years ago— "but where it came from remains a mystery,"—of course, it's not a "mystery" today! — "as we can't see anything like it in the areas surrounding Europe."***[16]

[16] Honorable Minister Louis Farrakhan, The Time and What Must Be Done Webcast Series, The Final Call Incorporated, ©2013.

Legendary Black Educator & Historian Carter G. Woodson On The Need For A New Theology Among Black People in America

"In schools of theology Negroes are taught the interpretation of the Bible worked out by those who have justified segregation and winked at the economic debasement of the Negro sometimes almost to the point of starvation...
In theology, literature, social science, and education, however, radical reconstruction is necessary. **The old worn-out theories as to man's relation to God and his fellowman, the system of thought which has permitted one man to exploit, oppress, and exterminate another and still be regarded as righteous must be discarded** for the new thought of men as brethren and the idea of God as the lover of all mankind...."

Ramadan Day 18-The Believer's Notes

Surah 23:1 – Surah 25:20

Ramadan Day 18-The Believer's Notes

Surah 23:1 – Surah 25:20

Hadith Wisdom For Ramadan Fasting

Narrated by Al-Bara:

It was the custom among the companions of Muhammad that if any of them was fasting and the food was presented (for breaking his fast), but he slept before eating, he would not eat that night and the following day till sunset. Qais bin Sirma-al-Ansari was fasting and came to his wife at the time of Iftar (breaking one's fast) and asked her whether she had anything to eat. She replied, "No, but I would go and bring some for you." He used to do hard work during the day, so he was overwhelmed by sleep and slept. When his wife came and saw him, she said, "Disappointment for you." When it was midday on the following day, he fainted and the Prophet (peace be upon him) was informed about the whole matter and the following verses were revealed: "You are permitted To go to your wives (for sexual relation) At the night of fasting." So, they were overjoyed by it. And then Allah also revealed: "And eat and drink Until the white thread Of dawn appears to you Distinct from the black thread (of the night)."

Day 18	NOI	Regional	Cities	Prayer	Times	2023
City	Fajr	Sunrise	Dhuhr	Asr	Maghrib	Isha
Atlanta	06:05 AM	07:15 AM	01:40 PM	05:16 PM	08:04 PM	09:15 PM
Chicago	04:59 AM	06:20 AM	12:53 PM	04:33 PM	07:25 PM	08:46 PM
Houston	05:55 AM	07:02 AM	01:24 PM	04:58 PM	07:46 PM	08:53 PM
London	04:39 AM	06:11 AM	01:07 PM	04:46 PM	07:54 PM	09:09 PM
Los Angeles	05:20 AM	06:31 AM	12:55 PM	04:32 PM	07:20 PM	08:31 PM
Miami	06:00 AM	07:04 AM	01:23 PM	04:53 PM	07:41 PM	08:46 PM
New York	05:09 AM	06:28 AM	12:58 PM	04:38 PM	07:28 PM	08:47 PM
Philadelphia	05:16 AM	06:33 AM	01:03 PM	04:42 PM	07:32 PM	08:50 PM
Washington DC	05:26 AM	06:42 AM	01:10 PM	04:49 PM	07:39 PM	08:55 PM

The Vindication Of
The Most Honorable Elijah Muhammad's Theology
Day 19

"This Book, there is no doubt in it, is a guide to those who keep their duty, Who believe in the Unseen and keep up prayer and spend out of what We have given them, And who believe in that which has been revealed to thee and that which was revealed before thee, and of the Hereafter they are sure."

-Holy Qur'an 2:2-4

The Holy Qur'an states in the above that Muslims believe in that which has been revealed to Prophet Muhammad (peace be upon him) and that which has been revealed before Muhammad. This is because the same God revealed the Holy Qur'an and the scriptures revealed to the prophets and messengers that came before him. To be clear the God of Prophet Muhammad is the same God that Jesus worshipped, is also the same God Moses worshipped and the same God Abraham worshipped.

Consider the following passages from that which was revealed before the Holy Qur'an, namely the Torah and Gospel.

Adam's God was a man

"And they heard the [c]sound of the Lord God walking in the garden in the [d]cool of the day, and Adam and his wife hid themselves from the presence of the Lord God among the trees of the garden."

-Genesis 3:8

Abraham's God was a man

"Then the Lord appeared to him by [a]the terebinth trees of Mamre, as he was sitting in the tent door in the heat of the day. So he lifted his eyes and looked, and behold, three men were standing by him; and when he saw them, he ran from the tent door to meet them, and bowed himself to the ground, and said, "My Lord, if I have now found favor in Your sight, do not pass on by Your servant. Please let a little water be brought, and wash your feet, and rest yourselves under the tree. And I will bring a morsel of bread, that you may refresh your hearts. After that you may pass by, inasmuch as you have come to your servant."

-Genesis 18:1-5

Moses God was a man

"Suddenly the Lord said to Moses, Aaron, and Miriam, "Come out, you three, to the tabernacle of meeting!" So the three came out. Then the Lord came down in the pillar of cloud and stood in the door of the tabernacle, and called Aaron and Miriam. And they both went forward. Then He said, "Hear now My words: If there is a prophet among you, I, the Lord, make Myself known to him in a vision; I speak to him in a dream. Not so with My servant Moses; He is faithful in all My house. I speak with him face to face, Even plainly,[c] and not in [d]dark sayings; And he sees the form of the Lord. Why then were you not afraid To speak against My servant Moses?"

-Numbers 12:4-8

Jesus God was a man

"The Pharisees therefore said to Him, "You bear witness of Yourself; Your witness is not [l]true." Jesus answered and said to them, "Even if I bear witness of Myself, My witness is true, for I know where I came from and where I am going; but you do not know where I come from and where I am going. You judge according to the flesh; I judge no one. And yet if I do judge, My judgment is true; for I am not alone, but I am with the Father who sent Me. It is also written in your law that the testimony of two men is true. I am One who bears witness of Myself, and the Father who sent Me bears witness of Me."

-John 8:13-18

Muhammad's God is a man

"Say: O disbelievers, I serve not that which you serve, Nor do you serve Him Whom I serve, Nor shall I serve that which ye serve, Nor do you serve Him Whom I serve. For you is your recompense and for me my recompense."

-Surah 109:1-6

These passages vindicate the teaching of the Most Honorable Elijah Muhammad that His God also is a man.

"God is a man and we just cannot make Him other than man, lest we make him an inferior one; for man's intelligence has no equal in other than man. His wisdom is infinite; capable of accomplishing anything that his brain can conceive. A spirit is subjected to us and not we to the spirit. Habakkuk uses the pronoun "He" in reference to God. This pronoun "He" is only used in the case when we refer to a man or boy or something of the male sex."

-Most Hon. Elijah Muhammad, Is God A Man or Spirit

Despite Spike Lee's use of creative license in his epic film about Malcolm X, the truth of Malcolm's prison house "road to Damascus"-type spiritual epiphany was not a vision of his teacher the Most Honorable Elijah Muhammad. It was instead a vision that Malcolm concluded was of his teacher's teacher, Allah (God) in the person of Master W. Fard Muhammad

The Greatness of Master W. Fard Muhammad

"I prayed for some kind of relief from my confusion. It was the next night, as I lay on my bed, I suddenly, with a start, became aware of a man sitting beside me in my chair. He had on a dark suit. I remember. I could see him as plainly as I see anyone I look at. He wasn't black, and he wasn't white. He was light-brown-skinned, an Asiatic cast of countenance, and he had oily black hair. I looked right into his face. I didn't get frightened. I knew I wasn't dreaming. I couldn't move, I didn't speak, and he didn't. I couldn't place him racially-other than that I knew he was a non- European. I had no idea whatsoever who he was. He just sat there. Then, suddenly as he had come, he was gone. ...I would later come to believe that my pre-vision was of Master W. D. Fard,... the Messiah; the one whom Elijah Muhammad said had appointed him-Elijah Muhammad-as His Last Messenger..."-Malcolm X

Ramadan Day 19-The Believer's Notes

Surah 25:21 – Surah 27:55

Ramadan Day 19-The Believer's Notes

Surah 25:21 – Surah 27:55

Hadith Wisdom For Ramadan Fasting

Narrated by `Aisha:

Allah's Messenger (peace be upon him) used to fast till one would say that he would never stop fasting, and he would abandon fasting till one would say that he would never fast. I never saw Allah's Messenger (peace be upon him) fasting for a whole month except the month of Ramadan, and did not see him fasting in any month more than in the month of Sha'ban.

Day 19	NOI	Regional	Cities	Prayer	Times	2023
City	Fajr	Sunrise	Dhuhr	Asr	Maghrib	Isha
Atlanta	06:04 AM	07:14 AM	01:40 PM	05:16 PM	08:05 PM	09:15 PM
Chicago	04:57 AM	06:18 AM	12:52 PM	04:34 PM	07:26 PM	08:47 PM
Houston	05:54 AM	07:01 AM	01:24 PM	04:58 PM	07:46 PM	08:54 PM
London	04:37 AM	06:09 AM	01:06 PM	04:47 PM	07:55 PM	09:10 PM
Los Angeles	05:18 AM	06:29 AM	12:55 PM	04:32 PM	07:20 PM	08:32 PM
Miami	05:59 AM	07:03 AM	01:23 PM	04:53 PM	07:42 PM	08:46 PM
New York	05:07 AM	06:26 AM	12:58 PM	04:38 PM	07:29 PM	08:49 PM
Philadelphia	05:14 AM	06:32 AM	01:03 PM	04:43 PM	07:33 PM	08:51 PM
Washington DC	05:24 AM	06:40 AM	01:10 PM	04:50 PM	07:40 PM	08:56 PM

The Vindication Of
The Most Honorable Elijah Muhammad's Theology
Day 20

Theologians have a specialized word to describe the instances when God appears to human beings. A visible manifestation of God within the Old Testament is called a theophany. The word theophany derives from two Greek words, the word for God (theos) and the word for appearing(phainō, which in the passive means appear). That is, a theophany is an appearance of God....The theme of theophany—the theme of God appearing—is important for several reasons. First, as we just observed, the theme has at its center the person of Christ, who is the permanent theophany anticipated by the temporary theophanies in the Old Testament. Second, the theme finds its culmination in the final vision of God described in the book of Revelation: "They [the saints] will see his face, and his name will be on their foreheads"...

"The appearances in human form have part of their basis in the fact that God created man "in the image of God" (Gen. 1:27). On the level of the Creator, God acts in a way analogous to human action, and his nature is fittingly represented in human form, rather than the form of an animal or a plant. He speaks, he thinks, he knows, he hears, and he acts in power. Human beings through their bodily actions imitate his actions. Their imitation is fitting, because God's action is the archetype or original pattern for human action. In addition, human appearances of God have a special weight. Even though in the Old Testament such appearances are temporary, they anticipate the permanent coming of God in permanent human form."

Ramadan Day 20-The Believer's Notes

Surah 27:56 – Surah 29:45

Ramadan Day 20-The Believer's Notes

Surah 27:56 – Surah 29:45

Hadith Wisdom For Ramadan Fasting

Narrated `by Abdullah bin `Amr bin Al-`As:

The Prophet (peace be upon him) said to me, "You fast daily all the year and pray every night all the night?" I replied in the affirmative. The Prophet (ﷺ) said, "If you keep on doing this, your eyes will become weak and your body will get tired. He who fasts all the year is as he who did not fast at all. The fasting of three days (a month) will be equal to the fasting of the whole year." I replied, "I have the power for more than this." The Prophet (ﷺ) said, "Then fast like the fasting of David who used to fast on alternate days and would never flee from the battle field, on meeting the enemy."

Day 20	NOI	Regional	Cities	Prayer	Times	2023
City	Fajr	Sunrise	Dhuhr	Asr	Maghrib	Isha
Atlanta	06:02 AM	07:13 AM	01:39 PM	05:16 PM	08:05 PM	09:16 PM
Chicago	04:56 AM	06:16 AM	12:52 PM	04:34 PM	07:27 PM	08:49 PM
Houston	05:52 AM	07:00 AM	01:24 PM	04:58 PM	07:47 PM	08:55 PM
London	04:35 AM	06:07 AM	01:06 PM	04:48 PM	07:57 PM	09:12 PM
Los Angeles	05:17 AM	06:28 AM	12:55 PM	04:32 PM	07:21 PM	08:32 PM
Miami	05:58 AM	07:02 AM	01:23 PM	04:53 PM	07:42 PM	08:47 PM
New York	05:05 AM	06:24 AM	12:58 PM	04:38 PM	07:30 PM	08:50 PM
Philadelphia	05:12 AM	06:30 AM	01:02 PM	04:43 PM	07:34 PM	08:52 PM
Washington DC	05:22 AM	06:39 AM	01:10 PM	04:50 PM	07:41 PM	08:58 PM

The Vindication Of
The Most Honorable Elijah Muhammad's Theology
Day 21

How To Eat To Live Confirmed

The Most Honorable Elijah Muhammad and the Nation of Islam are known for being some of the first in the Black community to promote healthy lifestyles through diet and nutrition. The hallmark of all of the life-giving teachings is the 2-book series entitled How to Eat to Live. In the these two powerful volumes of ancient and divinely prescribed dietary wisdom, Muhammad drives home the major key to long life and good health: eat 1 meal a day!

Over time many health researchers and medical scientists have conducted research that supports Muhammad's teaching of eating one meal every 24 hours.

Keiara Butler writes in a 2015 Mother Jones article entitled **Why You Should Stop Eating Breakfast, Lunch, and Dinner**:

> The one thing that might actually improve your metabolism is periodic fasting—that's right, the very same eating pattern that the early European settlers deemed uncivilized. Mark Mattson, a neuroscientist at the National Institute on Aging, has observed in a series of mice experiments over the past two decades that **mice who skip feedings are leaner and live longer than their nonskipping counterparts. The fasting mice also have more robust brain cells than those who consume regular meals.** Mattson, who skips breakfast and lunch most days, theorizes that **caloric deprivation acts as a mild stress that helps cells build up their defenses—warding off damage from aging, environmental toxins, and other threats.** Other research has shown that periodic fasting may also prevent heart disease.[17]

The diet of the Most Honorable Elijah Muhammad –one meal a day-has inspired scientific research and even the marketing and promotion of this diet under other and various names and labels.

A 2007 study titled Impact of Reduced Meal Frequency Without Caloric Restriction on Glucose Regulation in Healthy, Normal Weight Middle-Aged Men and Women concluded:

> Collectively, the available data therefore suggest that meal skipping or intermittent CR diets can result in health benefits including improved glucose regulation, but only if there is an overall reduction in energy intake.[18]

The proofs we have provided only serve as a brief summation of the major components of the life-giving teachings. Much more can be provided to vindicate and support Muhammad and

[17] Kiera Butler, Mother Jones.com, Mar. 4, 2015, http://www.motherjones.com/environment/2015/03/against-meals-breakfast-lunch-dinner/

[18] Carlson, Olga et al., Impact of reduced meal frequency without caloric restriction on glucose regulation in healthy, normal-weight middle-aged men and women, Metabolism - Clinical and Experimental, Volume 56, Issue 12, 1729 - 1734

these powerful teachings. Suffice it to say that what was given to him by his teacher is revelation which modern research is daily proving to be true and proper; right and exact.

Eat once every few days and fast once a month (Unity Fast):

Volume 3, Book 31, Number 196, Sahih Bukhari Collection:
Narrated 'Abdullah bin 'Amr bin Al-'As: Allah's Apostle said to me, "O 'Abdullah! Have I not been informed that you fast during the day and offer prayers all the night." 'Abdullah replied, "Yes, O Allah's Apostle!" The Prophet said, "Don't do that; **fast for few days and then give it up for few days, offer prayers and also sleep at night,** as your body has a right on you, and your wife has a right on you, and your guest has a right on you. **And it is sufficient for you to fast three days in a month, as the reward of a good deed is multiplied ten times, so it will be like fasting throughout the year.**" I insisted (on fasting) and so I was given a hard instruction. I said, "O Allah's Apostle! I have power." The Prophet said, "**Fast like the fasting of the Prophet David and do not fast more than that.**" I said, "How was the fasting of the Prophet of Allah, David?" He said, "Half of the year," ***(i.e. he used to fast on every alternate day).***
Afterwards when 'Abdullah became old, he used to say, "It would have been better for me if I had accepted the permission of the Prophet (which he gave me i.e. to fast only three days a month)."

Fasting three days a month is consistent with the Nation of Islam's Unity Fast, which is done for three days (the first weekend of each month).

Volume 3, Book 31, Number 201, Sahih Bukhari Collection:
Narrated 'Abdullah bin 'Amr: Allah's Apostle was informed about my fasts, and he came to me and I spread for him a leather cushion stuffed with palm fires, but he sat on the ground and the cushion remained between me and him, and then he said, **"Isn't it sufficient for you to fast three days a month?"** I replied, "O Allah's Apostle! (I can fast more)." He said, "Five?" I replied, "O Allah's Apostle! (I can fast more)." He said, "Seven?" I replied, "O Allah's Apostle! (I can fast more)." He said, "Nine (days per month)?" I replied, "O Allah's Apostle! (I can fast more)" He said, "Eleven (days per month)?" And then the Prophet said, **"There is no fast superior to that of the Prophet David it was for half of the year. So, fast on alternate days."**

Volume 8, Book 74, Number 294, Sahih Bukhari Collection:
Narrated Abdullah bin 'Amr: The news of my fasting was mentioned to the Prophet . So he entered upon me and I put for him a leather cushion stuffed with palm-fibers. The Prophet sat on the floor and the cushion was between me and him. He said to me, "Isn't it sufficient for you (that you fast) three days a month?" I said, "O Allah's Apostle! (I can fast more than this)." He said, "You may fast) five days a month." I said, "O Allah's Apostle! (I can fast more than this)." He said, "(You may fast) seven days." I said, "O Allah's Apostle!" He said, "Nine." I said, "O Allah's Apostle!" He said, "Eleven." I said, "O Allah's Apostle!" He said, **"No fasting is superior to the fasting of (the Prophet David) which was one half of a year, and he used, to fast on alternate days**. (See Hadith No. 300, Vol 3)

Volume 3, Book 31, Number 202, Sahih Bukhari Collection:
Narrated Abu Huraira: My friend (the Prophet) advised me to observe three things:
(1) **to fast three days a month**;
(2) to pray two Rakat of Dzuhr prayer (fore-noon prayer); and
(3) to pray Witr before sleeping.

The Most Honorable Elijah Muhammad

A Target of World Leaders ??

August 1964 Esquire Magazine prints political cartoon of French President Charles DeGaulle speaking among world leaders as he identifies the cartoonist's image of the Hon. Elijah Muhammad as the man producing trouble for him and his fellow "crooks" among the global political and cultural leaders.

Ramadan Day 21-The Believer's Notes

Surah 29:46 – Surah 33:30

Ramadan Day 21-The Believer's Notes

Surah 29:46 – Surah 33:30

Hadith Wisdom For Ramadan Fasting

Narrated by Abu Sa`id:

The Prophet (peace be upon him) forbade the fasting of `Id-ul-Fitr and `Id-ul-Adha (two feast days) and also the wearing of As-Samma' (a single garment covering the whole body), and sitting with one's leg drawn up while being wrapped in one garment. He also forbade the prayers after the Fajr (morning) and the `Asr (afternoon) prayers.

Day 21	NOI	Regional	Cities	Prayer	Times	2023
City	Fajr	Sunrise	Dhuhr	Asr	Maghrib	Isha
Atlanta	06:01 AM	07:12 AM	01:39 PM	05:16 PM	08:06 PM	09:17 PM
Chicago	04:54 AM	06:15 AM	12:52 PM	04:34 PM	07:29 PM	08:50 PM
Houston	05:51 AM	06:58 AM	01:23 PM	04:57 PM	07:48 PM	08:56 PM
London	04:32 AM	06:04 AM	01:06 PM	04:48 PM	07:59 PM	09:14 PM
Los Angeles	05:16 AM	06:27 AM	12:54 PM	04:32 PM	07:22 PM	08:33 PM
Miami	05:57 AM	07:01 AM	01:22 PM	04:52 PM	07:43 PM	08:48 PM
New York	05:04 AM	06:23 AM	12:57 PM	04:39 PM	07:31 PM	08:51 PM
Philadelphia	05:11 AM	06:29 AM	01:02 PM	04:43 PM	07:35 PM	08:54 PM
Washington DC	05:21 AM	06:37 AM	01:10 PM	04:50 PM	07:42 PM	08:59 PM

The Vindication Of

The Most Honorable Elijah Muhammad's Theology

Day 22

Master W. Fard Muhammad

& 25,000 Holy Names

"The slaves had been stripped of their status, their names, their families and friends, and their customs and culture. They were surrounded by fear, distrust, and sometimes hatred. No wonder it was commonplace for newly arrived slaves to try to run away or sink into a deep, sometimes suicidal depression. They stood naked to misery, not knowing what would happen to them."(Slavery In America by Dorothy and Carl Schneider p. 78)

THE NAMES WHICH THE HOLY PROPHET CHANGED

123. 'Ayishah (peace be on her), narrates, that the Holy Prophet (peace and blessings of God be upon him) used to change ugly names (of persons). (Tirmzi.)

124. Abu Horairah (peace be on him), narrates, that the original name of Zainab, the daughter of Abi Salmah was Barrah (purification), hence people used to say (to her) " Dost thou purify thy ownself "? So the Holy Prophet (peace and blessings of God be upon him) changed her name to Zainab. (Shaikhain.)

125. Ibn-i-'Abbās (peace be on him), narrates, that the original name of Juvairiah, the daughter of Hariṭh was Barrah (purification), the Holy Prophet (peace and blessings of God be upon him) changed it to Juvairiah He (the Holy Prophet) detested (that it should be said) Barrah (purification) had gone out of him (or passed from him). (Muslim)

126. Shoraih, son of Háni (peace be on him), narrates, through his father, that it came to the notice of the Holy Prophet (peace and blessings of God be upon him) that his (Hāni's) people (called him by the) surname of Abul Hakam (meaning the doer of Justice). The Holy Prophet (peace and blessings of God be upon him) sent for him and said : "Only Allah, the Almighty, is "Hakam" (the Judge), and to Him only becomes the justice, so why hast thou surnamed

When Master W. Fard Muhammad came to Detroit he ultimately impacted 25,000 Black people with His powerful teachings. According to the Supreme Wisdom Lessons:

"Now, the Messenger and his Laborers worked day and night for the last three and one-half years, and their accomplishments are approximately twenty-five thousand."

The practice of changing the names of His followers and students is both a part of the Islamic tradition practiced by Prophet Muhammad and also a fulfillment of certain prophecies that predicted that one day at the end of this present world of sin, Allah (God) would come and give to His people His names.

Some scriptural references on the changing of names by God is found below:

And ye shall leave your name for a curse unto my chosen: for the Lord GOD shall slay thee, and call his servants by another name — Isaiah 65:15

The LORD will establish you as His holy people, just as He has sworn to you, if you keep the commandments of the LORD your God and walk in His ways. So all the peoples of the earth will see that you are called by the name of the Lord, and they will be afraid of you.
-Deuteronomy 28:9-10

Insist on Arabian Names

City Clerk Richard W. Reading said that for four years his clerks have struggled with Negroes who insisted upon being registered by weird Arabian names. They became so incensed upon the refusal of authorities to do so, that he brought the matter to the attention of James R. Walsh, assistant corporation counsel. Mr. Walsh wrote a notice forbidding the clerks to countenance signatures such as Mohammed, or Ali, or Bey, and had it posted on the wall of the Election Commission's offices. It is still there.

Welfare workers, too, have suffered from the cult's fanatic zeal. Negro Welfare workers have for some time reported that they had been insulted as "devils," and in many cases threatened with bodily harm.

City officials in Detroit were angry over the powerful impact of Master W. Fard Muhammad and what He produced of a strong desire among Black people to give up their old slave masters names

"All who believe in the Devil must be called by his name and that is the one you carry now. So when you become a servant of another master, that master compels you to go in his name if you are his servant. So it is with Allah (God). The difference is other master's names is that Allah's Names live forever while others vanish from the earth. There is no people on the Earth that will survive in the Hereafter without the Name of Allah (God)."

-Most Hon. Elijah Muhammad, Names of Allah

[1] This shows that the Holy Prophet wanted his followers to adopt good names along with their good beliefs and good actions. This was an encouragement for the Muslims to adopt good names. But there was no idea that some

Master W. Fard Muhammad's Perfect Love Casts Out Fear

The Detroit "Islam" cult seems to inspire the fighting spirit much as the genuine religion did in its earliest days.

"**In so far as he is Islamized, the Negro's warlike propensities will be inflamed**, and he will be used as the tool of Arab Pan-Islamism seeking to drive the white man from Africa and make the continent its very own.... With very few exceptions the colored races of Africa are preeminently fighters....**To them the fierce, warlike spirit inherent in Mohammedanism is infinitely more attractive**... Islam has thus two avenues of approach to the African negro **his natural preference for a militant faith** and his resentment at white tutelage."

-T. Lothrop Stoddard, The Rising Tide of Color Against White World Supremacy

Ramadan Day 22-The Believer's Notes

Surah 33:31 - Surah 36:27

Ramadan Day 22-The Believer's Notes

Surah 33:31 - Surah 36:27

Hadith Wisdom For Ramadan Fasting

Narrated by Ahmad:

Abdullah ibn `Amr (may Allah be pleased with him and his father) narrated that the Messenger of Allah (peace be upon him) said: "Fasting and the Qur'an will intercede for a person on the Day of Resurrection. Fasting will say, 'O Lord, I deprived him of his food and his desires at day, so let me intercede for him.' And the Qur'an will say: 'I deprived him of his sleep at night so let me intercede for him.' Then they will intercede."

Day 22	NOI	Regional	Cities	Prayer	Times	2023
City	Fajr	Sunrise	Dhuhr	Asr	Maghrib	Isha
Atlanta	05:59 AM	07:10 AM	01:39 PM	05:16 PM	08:07 PM	09:18 PM
Chicago	04:52 AM	06:13 AM	12:52 PM	04:35 PM	07:30 PM	08:51 PM
Houston	05:50 AM	06:57 AM	01:23 PM	04:57 PM	07:48 PM	08:56 PM
London	04:30 AM	06:02 AM	01:06 PM	04:49 PM	08:00 PM	09:15 PM
Los Angeles	05:14 AM	06:25 AM	12:54 PM	04:32 PM	07:23 PM	08:34 PM
Miami	05:56 AM	07:00 AM	01:22 PM	04:52 PM	07:43 PM	08:48 PM
New York	05:02 AM	06:21 AM	12:57 PM	04:39 PM	07:32 PM	08:52 PM
Philadelphia	05:09 AM	06:27 AM	01:02 PM	04:43 PM	07:36 PM	08:55 PM
Washington DC	05:19 AM	06:36 AM	01:09 PM	04:50 PM	07:43 PM	09:00 PM

The Vindication Of
The Most Honorable Elijah Muhammad's Theology
Day 23

ALLAH'S THRONE OF POWER SHOWN TO ELIJAH MUHAMMAD

Ilia Rashad Muhammad

"The Knower of the unseen, so He makes His secrets known to none Except a messenger whom He chooses. For surely He makes a guard to go before him and after him."

Surah 72:26-27

The concept of God revealing his secrets to his designated messenger clearly distinguishes and authenticates the divinity of this recipient from others. Elijah Muhammad proved that he was granted the divine secrets of the all-wise true and living God and he brought tangible proof of the divine secrets revealed to him. This included the foremost, firsthand knowledge about the Mother Plane and its host of 1500 smaller wheel-shaped planes that the world now refer to as unidentified flying objects (UFOs). If these planes exist as the Honorable Elijah Muhammad first illustrated, then it would be grossly negligent not to consult the man who presented this truth to the world. As remarkable as Mr. Muhammad's authentication about these planes have proven to become, his evidence about these crafts cannot be isolated from the source that disclosed these objects to him because all of his teachings are predicated upon him meeting and being taught by Allah (God) who came in the Person of Master Fard Muhammad. It is this central reality that scholars, UFO researchers, leaders, and even critics have negligently omitted from public discourse.

Since so much has been said, hypothesized, postulated, accused, and believed about UFOs from outside sources, it would be fitting to focus research around the most credible firsthand data. Since the Honorable Elijah Muhammad is the foremost authority on this subject matter, then his data, claims, and hypothesis should most deservingly be examined and tested. Moreover, his publicly anointed National Representative—the Honorable Minister Louis Farrakhan cannot be overlooked, ignored, or unacknowledged because he has been supremely designated as the official representative of that same power.

In his famous book titled, Fall of America, the Honorable Elijah Muhammad was forthrightly clear on the power behind this phenomena stating, "The Mother Plane and her work is a display of the power of the mightiest God, Master Fard Muhammad, to Whom praises are due forever."

Before the evidence of these planes became readily accessible, many Muslims in the mainstream Islamic world severely criticized the Nation of Islam's teachings concerning the

Mother Wheel and its smaller flying wheels (UFOs) as heretical and inherently un-Islamic. While the NOI is clearly distinguished as the first to offer such explicit teachings, the Muslims who attempt to challenge the NOI on this point do so from a strictly traditional perspective. Like some Christian evangelists, those Muslim clerics who charge the NOI with shirk have not offered any proof to substantiate their charges. Interestingly, most of those who have criticized the NOI followers for their belief in the Mother Wheel don't acknowledge the Holy Qur'an's many references to Allah's Throne of Power that is stationed in the heavens, nor do they mention the myriad Hadith references that Prophet Muhammad (PBUH) made about Allah's dwelling place. Like the Bible, the Holy Qur'an too depicts God in a tangibly celestial position along with his host of angels. Even more perplexing is that traditional Islamic worldviews include the belief that the Prophet Muhammad (PBUH) was taken on a Night Journey from Mecca to Jerusalem on a legendary winged creature called Al-Buraq. Apparently, the traditional Muslims' charge against the Nation of Islam's position on the evidential wheel-shaped planes (so-called UFOs) is based solely on an argument that would easily invalidate their own traditional beliefs.

Now that the reality of these so-called UFOs exist just as the Honorable Elijah Muhammad and the Honorable Minister Farrakhan represent, it would be extremely hypocritical for Muslims, scholars, or thinking people to ignore the vast body of evidence that prove the Nation of Islam was right and exact all along.

The Hon. Elijah Muhammad teaches that the most popular English slaver John Hawkins began bringing Africans as slaves to the Americas also in the year 1555. To date we are 468 years in bondage. "The transatlantic slave trade was, in many ways, still in its infancy during the 16th century, but thousands of captive Africans were already being loaded onto European ships and transported across the sea to Spanish America and Brazil every, year, especially after 1560. In this vein, an expedition under the command of John Lok reportedly returned to England with "certayne blacke slaves" in 1555." (Slaves and Englishmen: Human Bondage in the Early Modern Atlantic World by Michael Guasco p. 67)

Children of Israel in Bondage for 400 years (Acts 7:6-7; Genesis 15:13-15)

"an expedition under the command of John Lok reportedly returned to England with "certayne blacke slaves" in 1555."

Ramadan Day 23-The Believer's Notes

Surah 36:28 - Surah 39:31

Ramadan Day 23-The Believer's Notes

Surah 36:28 - Surah 39:31

Hadith Wisdom For Ramadan Fasting

Narrated by An-Nasa'i:

It was narrated that Abu Umamah said: "I said: 'O Messenger of Allah, tell me of an act (that I should do).' He (peace be upon him) said: 'Take to fasting, for there is nothing equal to it."

Day 23	NOI	Regional	Cities	Prayer	Times	2023
City	Fajr	Sunrise	Dhuhr	Asr	Maghrib	Isha
Atlanta	05:58 AM	07:09 AM	01:38 PM	05:16 PM	08:08 PM	09:19 PM
Chicago	04:50 AM	06:12 AM	12:51 PM	04:35 PM	07:31 PM	08:53 PM
Houston	05:48 AM	06:56 AM	01:23 PM	04:57 PM	07:49 PM	08:57 PM
London	04:28 AM	06:00 AM	01:05 PM	04:50 PM	08:02 PM	09:17 PM
Los Angeles	05:13 AM	06:24 AM	12:54 PM	04:32 PM	07:23 PM	08:35 PM
Miami	05:55 AM	07:00 AM	01:22 PM	04:52 PM	07:44 PM	08:49 PM
New York	05:00 AM	06:20 AM	12:57 PM	04:39 PM	07:34 PM	08:54 PM
Philadelphia	05:07 AM	06:26 AM	01:02 PM	04:44 PM	07:37 PM	08:56 PM
Washington DC	05:17 AM	06:34 AM	01:09 PM	04:51 PM	07:44 PM	09:01 PM

The Vindication Of
The Most Honorable Elijah Muhammad's Theology
Day 24

The Reality of God

Student Minister Willie Muhammad

"Of all the knowledge that one may have or obtain, the knowledge of God is the greatest and the most necessary of all knowledge. I would say that 98% of the people of earth are without knowledge of the God, the Supreme Being."
Most Hon. Elijah Muhammad, Our Savior Has Arrived

It's not by accident that the Most Honorable Elijah Muhammad in the opening chapters of one of the most read books composed of articles written by him, "Message to the Black Man in America," that the first ten chapters are aimed at exposing the lies that have been taught about God. All throughout these chapters the Most Honorable Elijah Muhammad focuses in on teaching the reader the reality of God and revealing the dangerous teaching about the "Mystery God."

In my many years of discussions and/or debates about the identity of Master Fard Muhammad, I have noticed that the disagreement of many was rooted in their incorrect understanding about the Reality of God. From the perspective of the Teachings of the Most Honorable Elijah Muhammad, when the subject of the Reality of God is discussed, we are talking about the understanding that God, the Supreme Being exists in the form of a human being. We are saying that to have a Reality of God one must understand that God is not a spirit, spook or ghost that cannot be seen, heard or touched. Yes, God has a spirit, but that Spirit has and always will be housed in a human body. Thus, to possess a view of God outside of this truth, is to possess a view that is not based upon the Reality of God as expressed in BOTH the Bible and the Holy Qur'an.

Since we are in the month of Ramadan, we want to use scriptures taken from the Holy Quran to accomplish two goals. One, to lay a foundation that will help those who desire to understand the concept of Allah in the Person of Master Fard Muhammad. Two, to show that what the Most Honorable Elijah Muhammad taught about the Reality of God is in accord and supported by scriptures, science and common sense.

Let's look at a few versus from just ONE chapter in the Holy Qur'an. While reading these verses I would like for you to underline all of the pronouns that refer to Allah (God) such as His, Him and He.

> "This it is of which Allah gives the good news to **His** servants, who believe and do good. Say: I ask of you naught in return for it but love for relatives. And whoever earns good, We give him more of good therein. Surely Allah is Forgiving, Grateful. "Or say they: **He** has forged a lie against Allah? So, if Allah please, **He** would seal thy heart (against them). And Allah blots out the falsehood and confirms the Truth with **His**

> words. Surely **He** is Knower of what is in the breasts. And **He** it is Who accepts repentance from **His** servants and pardons evil deeds, and **He** knows what you do; And **He** answers those who believe and do good deeds, and gives them more out of **His** grace. And for the disbelievers is a severe chastisement. And if Allah were to amplify the provision for **His** servants, they would rebel in the earth; but **He** sends (it) down by measure, as **He** pleases. Surely **He** is Aware, Seer of **His** servants. And **He** it is Who sends down the rain after they have despaired, and **He** unfolds **His** mercy. And **He** is the Friend, the Praised One. And of **His** signs is the creation of the heavens and the earth and what **He** has spread forth in both of them of living beings. And **He** is All-powerful to gather them together, when **He** will."
> Surah 42: 23-29

When I read the verses, I counted 21 times Allah (God) refers to Himself and instructs the Prophet to use very specific terms regarding Him. This is just ONE chapter and only SIX verses! This same occurrence happens throughout the entire Holy Qur'an. Now I asked you to do that exercise in preparation for the next example I want to use.

Imagine you are approached by a man on the street in a frantic but non-threatening manner. His left eye is blackened; the right side of his face is swollen. His top lip is swollen and busted. He says, "I need your help? He who blackened my eye, he caused my face to be swollen. He busted my lip! Can you take out your cellphone and take a picture of him so I can show it to the police?" You decide to help the man. When you take out your cellphone and prepare to take a picture, are you looking to take a picture of a man/human or a spirit/ghost? If I were a betting man, I would say that 100% of you all who are reading this would say you would be planning to take a picture of a man! A human being!

Why would you be expecting such? You would be expecting to take a picture of a man because the brother who came asking for your help used pronouns such as he and him. Now here is my question, how could you look for a man in that situation but then read verses of the Holy Qur'an like the ones above which refer to Allah with the same pronouns and allow someone to cause you to cast aside the same logic you used in the above example? Shouldn't you be thinking about a man/human being as well when you read the Holy Qur'an? The deception of Satan has also touched the Islamic world causing them to bring the belief of the Mystery God into Islam where they try to say that Allah is immaterial, has no gender and that believing such is shirk! They say this despite the Arabic word for God, which is Allah being masculine in grammar. One of the dangers of not knowing the truth about the Reality of God is that it causes one to cast aside common sense. Thus, void of common sense one can read the numerous scriptures that bear witness to the Reality of God and not realize such. Below is yet another example of the many supporting verses that are present in the Holy Qur'an.

Allah is said to have human characteristics and attributes in the Holy Qur'an. Allah is said to possess **a face** (wajh, 55:26) with **eyes** (20:39; 11:37); **two hands** (yadayya, 38:75; 5:64), **a leg** (saq, 68:42), **side** (janb, 39:56) **a soul** (nafs, 3:28, 5:116) and **a spirit** (ruh, 66:12); **He** is in the heavens (67:16) established (istawa) on **His throne** (7:54). From there **He** will "come" to earth (2:210). He also has human behaviors: He gets angry (1:7, 2:61, 3:112 and 162, 4:93, etc.); **He** is a wise planner (3:54, 8:30, 10:21, 13:42, etc.); **He** pokes fun (2:15).

I would highly encourage you to get the scholarly writings of Brother Dr. Wesley Muhammad. In your efforts to learn more about the Reality of God. I would encourage you to begin with these titles – The Truth of God, The Book of God: An Encyclopedia of Proof that the Black Man is God. In the book 'the Truth of God,' Dr. Wesley deconstructs the incorrect interpretation of several verses that those who oppose our belief attempt to use in their rebuttals.

For the sake of brevity, I will highlight one such example and provide Dr.Wesley's scholarly rebuttal of their incorrect interpretation. The objectors use Surah 42:11 which states:

> "Nothing is like Him; and He is the Hearing, the Seeing."

They say that this verse dispels what Mr. Muhammad teaches. I totally disagree and assert that it proves what the Most Honorable Elijah Muhammad teaches. As a male I am a him, I am a he. As a human being, we hear and see. If the above verse is meant to say that 'nothing is like him,' then how could we explain the points I just made about me being a he and a him? That I and you hear and see?

This is a simple example that proves their interpretation as being wrong. Brother Dr. Wesley goes further by analyzing and explaining what the actual Arabic says. Dr. Wesley states:

> "Laysa kamithlihi shay" (There is none like Him) and they try to use this to negate all anthropomorphism(descriptions of Allah as a man). This is a wrong translation. The correct translation is: "There is none like (ka) His likeness (mithlihi)". Mithlihi is actually mithl = like or likeness, joined to the possessive pronoun His. This doesn't mean that God is formless, but he possesses a likeness or form that is incomparable."
> Source: Transcendent Anthropomorphism - Dr. Wesley Muhammad

Let's go further in Surah 57:4, Allah is said to be mounted on a throne nearly exactly as what is stated in the Book of Revelation 5:

> "He it is who created the heavens and the earth in six days; then He mounted the throne."

In Dr. Wesley's books, he explains how the Arabic word for throne is the same word for throne that is used when describing the physical and literal thrones kings sit on. In other verses in the Holy Qur'an, it speaks about angels sitting around the throne and even carrying it.

More irrefutable truth bearing witness to the Reality of God

Here are additional Qur'anic verses. The first is speaking about a Muhammad who saw Allah. The verse that follows reaffirms what this Muhammad saw because there were those who doubted and attempted to refute what he saw.

> "By the Star when it goes down,- Your Companion is neither astray nor being misled. Nor does he say (aught) of (his own) Desire. It is no less than inspiration sent down to him: He was taught by one Mighty in Power, Endued with Wisdom: **FOR HE APPEARED (in stately form)**; While he was in the highest part of the horizon: **THEN HE APPROACHED HIM AND CAME CLOSER**, And was at a distance of but two bow-lengths or (even) nearer; **SO DID HE (Allah) CONVEY THE INSPIRATION TO HIS SERVANT**(conveyed) what He (meant) to convey."
> Surah 53:1-10 (emphasis mine)

Some Islamic scholars have tried to say that the one seen by this Muhammad was the Angel Gabriel. How could this be? Is the Angel Gabriel worthy to wear the title, "one Mighty in Power, Endued with Wisdom?" Allah in the Qur'an reveals the following to Prophet Muhammad in support of what this Muhammad would see.

> "Verily this is the word of a most honourable Messenger, Endued with Power, with rank before THE LORD OF THE THRONE, With authority there, (and) faithful to his trust. And (O people!) your companion is not one possessed; And without doubt HE SAW HIM IN THE CLEAR HORIZON. Neither doth he withhold grudgingly a knowledge of the Unseen. Nor is it the word of an evil spirit accursed."
> Surah 81:1-25 Yusef Ali

These are scriptures from the Holy Qur'an. There are also Hadiths or sayings of the Prophet that affirm what the Most Honorable Elijah Muhammad teaches about the Reality of God. Here is one found in Hadith Tirmidhi 245 where Prophet Muhammad is said to be taken in the presence of Allah and sees Allah and is touched by Allah.

> "I got up in the night and performed ablution and observed the prayer as had been ordained for me. I dozed in my prayer till I was overcome by (sleep) and lo, I found myself in the presence of my Lord, the Blessed and the Glorious, in the best FORM. He said: Muhammad! I said: At Thy service, my Lord. He said: What these highest angels contend about? I said: I do not know. He repeated it thrice.
> He said: Then I SAW Him put HIS PALMS between my shoulder blades till I felt the coldness of HIS FINGERS between the two sides of my chest. Then everything was illuminated for me and I could recognize everything..."

Of course, there are attempts to rebut what we have shown from Qur'anic scriptures and the Hadith. The existence of rebuttals does not take away from the truth.

We close this chapter with a simple but effective explanation given by the Honorable Minister Louis Farrakhan, where he uses science to prove the Reality of God. The Minister states:

> "Anything that exists, exists in one of three stages: liquid, solid or gas. We do not see God as liquid and we do not see Him as gas. Some of the old writers called Him, "The Rock of Ages". You can stand on Him, depend upon Him. He is solid. If He is solid, He must be animate or inanimate. We do not look at God as an inanimate object. We see Him full of life and spirit: A Life-Giver. We have to say He is animate. "Animate" means He is either animal, plant or human. We do not speak of God as a plant, even though some describe Him as the "Rose of Sharon" and the "Lilly of the valley". We do not speak of God as vegetable, but we do speak of Him in terms of the animal kingdom. In the animal kingdom, we have the lowest form and the highest manifestation. The highest manifestation in the animal kingdom is man or woman, male and female."
> -The Knowledge of God

The Most Honorable Elijah Muhammad's words written in Message to the Black Man in America still stands undefeated:

> "God is a man, and we just cannot make Him other than a man, lest we make Him an inferior one."

Master W. Fard Muhammad As Mahdi

Allah, to whom be praised, came in the person of Master W. F. Mu-hammad, the Great Mahdi expected by the Muslims and the anti-Christs (the devils) under the names: Jesus Christ, Messiah, God, Lord, Jehovah, the last (Jehovah) and the Christ. These meanings are good and befitting as titles, but the meaning of His name "Mahdi," as mentioned in the Holy Qur-an Sharieff 22:54, is better. All of these names refer to Him. His name, FARD MUHAMMAD, is beautiful in its meaning. He must bring an end to war, and the only way to end war between man and man is to destroy the war-maker (the trouble-maker).

-Most Hon. Elijah Muhammad, 12-14-57

Ramadan Day 24-The Believer's Notes

Surah 39:32 – Surah 41:46

Ramadan Day 24-The Believer's Notes

Surah 39:32 – Surah 41:46

Hadith Wisdom For Ramadan Fasting

Narrated by Abu Hurairah:

The Messenger of Allah (peace be upon him) said: 'There has come to you Ramadan, a blessed month, which Allah, the Mighty and Sublime, has enjoined you to fast. In it the gates of Heaven are opened and the gates of Hell are closed, and every devil is chained up. In it Allah has a night which is better than a thousand months; whoever is deprived of its goodness is indeed deprived."'

Day 24	NOI	Regional	Cities	Prayer	Times	2023
City	Fajr	Sunrise	Dhuhr	Asr	Maghrib	Isha
Atlanta	05:56 AM	07:08 AM	01:38 PM	05:17 PM	08:08 PM	09:20 PM
Chicago	04:48 AM	06:10 AM	12:51 PM	04:36 PM	07:32 PM	08:54 PM
Houston	05:47 AM	06:55 AM	01:23 PM	04:57 PM	07:49 PM	08:58 PM
London	04:26 AM	05:58 AM	01:05 PM	04:51 PM	08:04 PM	09:18 PM
Los Angeles	05:11 AM	06:23 AM	12:54 PM	04:32 PM	07:24 PM	08:36 PM
Miami	05:54 AM	06:59 AM	01:22 PM	04:52 PM	07:44 PM	08:49 PM
New York	04:58 AM	06:18 AM	12:57 PM	04:40 PM	07:35 PM	08:55 PM
Philadelphia	05:05 AM	06:24 AM	01:01 PM	04:44 PM	07:38 PM	08:57 PM
Washington DC	05:16 AM	06:33 AM	01:09 PM	04:51 PM	07:45 PM	09:02 PM

The Vindication Of

The Most Honorable Elijah Muhammad's Theology

Day 25

Black God Black Messiah

وَإِذْ قَالَ رَبُّكَ لِلْمَلَٰٓئِكَةِ إِنِّى خَٰلِقٌۢ بَشَرًا مِّن صَلْصَٰلٍ مِّنْ حَمَإٍ مَّسْنُونٍ

And when thy Lord said to the angels: I am going to create a mortal of sounding clay, of **black mud** fashioned into shape.

Holy Qur'an 15:28

Hama' حمأ

حمأ: يحمأ

To clean out mud (from a well). *Hama'un* حَمَاءٌ: Black feted mud, slime (a combination of earth and water, earth having the source of body and water of the soul or life; Mud transmuted or moulded into shape; Slack mud. *Hami'atun* حَمَأَةٌ: *f.* of *Hami'un.*

Hama'in حَمإٍ (*n.*): Clay (15:26; 28:33). ***Hami'atin*** حَمِئَةٍ (*n.*): Black mud (18:86). (L; T; R; LL; Râzî)

The Holy Qur'an States Adam Is Created From Black Mud

MUHAMMAD SPEAKS

ARE WE THE BLACK MUSLIMS?

By Elijah Muhammad
Messenger of Allah

SURE, WE ARE BLACK MUSLIMS! As white people call themselves white Christians, we are Black Muslims!

OF COURSE IT STARTED at first from the press. But we do not get indignant about being called Black for that is what we are.

WE WERE BLACK IN THE VERY BEGINNING of the Creation of the Father, who was Black. Black is what we prefer to be called. There is no white scholar or scientist of history and religion that will dare say otherwise.

WHY SHOULD YOU FEEL OFFENDED when you are called a Black Muslim? The white people are not offended if you call them white Christians.

IT IS DUE TO THE FACT that the so-called American Negro has been mocked by the white slave-master, after the white slave-master, attracted them with the power of unalike. He attracted the slave so much so, that he desired to be white instead of his own nature color, Black, in which he was created. White is a made color and not a created color.

THE WHITE PEOPLE WHO ENSLAVED our fathers had an unrestrained hand and power over the Black slave. They could beat and force the slave to believe, answer to and obey anything they taught the Black slave without hindrance for we had no teachers among our slave-parents. The poor slave had no help here or there for centuries. I should say until today, on The Coming of Our God and Saviour, in the Person of Master Fard Muhammad, To Whom Praises are Due forever.

BUT I SAY, BROTHERS AND SISTERS, be happy that you are Black. It is the first color, original of man, in the sun. It is honorable, durable and lasting. It is not easy to be changed even under climatic conditions.

ALLAH (GOD) is the Father of the Creation of the Heavens and the Earth. His Color is Black. It is the best and purest of all the colors. It is Unchangeable as His Wisdom, which is Superior over All.

IT IS TRUE WE ARE BLACK MUSLIMS. Our very Nation is Black People. Our Creator was a Black God.

SO DO NOT BE ASHAMED TO ACCEPT YOUR OWN BLACK SELF. It is an honorable color. IT IS THE FIRST AND THE LAST.

"Why should you feel offended when you are called a Black Muslim? The White people are not offended if you call them white Christians. It is due to the fact that the so-called American Negro has been mocked by the white slave-master, after the white slave-master attracted them with the power of unalike. He attracted the slave so much so, that he desires to be white instead of his own nature of Black , in which he was created. White is a made color and not a created one....

But I say brothers and sisters, **be happy that you are Black**. It is the first color, original of man, in the sun. It is honorable, durable and lasting. It is not easy to be changed even under climatic conditions.

Allah (God) is the Father of the Creation of the Heavens and the Earth. His color is Black. It is the best and purest of all the colors. It is unchangeable as His Wisdom, which is superior over ALL."

-Most Hon. Elijah Muhammad, Are We The Black Muslims?

"NEARLY all religious history is prophetic of the coming of Saviors, Messiahs, Redeemers, and virgin-born Gods. Most religious countries, and more than a score of religious systems, had a standing prophecy that a divine deliverer would descend from heaven and relieve them from their depressed state, and ameliorate their condition. And in most cases that prophecy was believed to have been fulfilled by the birth of a being, who, as he approached the goal of moral and intellectual manhood exhibited such remarkable proof of superiority of mind as to be readily accepted as the promised Messiah.... "Here we will note it as a curious circumstance, that Several of the above-named Saviors are represented as being black, Jesus Christ included with this number. There is as much evidence that the Christian Savior was a black man, or at least a dark man, as there is of his being the son of the Virgin Mary, or that he once lived and moved upon the earth. And that evidence is the testimony of his disciples, who had nearly as good an opportunity of knowing what his complexion was as the evangelists, who omit to say anything about it. In the pictures and portraits of Christ by the early Christians, he is uniformly represented as being black. And to make this the more certain, the red tinge is given to the lips; and the only text in the Christian bible quoted by orthodox Christians, as describing his complexion, represents it as being black.

Solomon's declaration, "I am black, but comely, O ye daughters of Jerusalem" (Sol. i. 5), is often cited as referring to Christ. According to the bible itself, then, Jesus Christ was a black man." -Kersey Graves, The World's 16 Crucified Saviours

Ramadan Day 25-The Believer's Notes

Surah 41:47 – Surah 45:37

Ramadan Day 25-The Believer's Notes

Surah 41:47 – Surah 45:37

Hadith Wisdom For Ramadan Fasting

Narrated by Zaid bin Khalid Al-Juhani:

“The Prophet (peace be upon him) said, "He who provides a fasting person with something to break his fast, will earn the same reward as the one who was observing the fast, without diminishing in any way the reward of the latter."

Day 25	NOI	Regional	Cities	Prayer	Times	2023
City	Fajr	Sunrise	Dhuhr	Asr	Maghrib	Isha
Atlanta	05:55 AM	07:06 AM	01:38 PM	05:17 PM	08:09 PM	09:21 PM
Chicago	04:46 AM	06:08 AM	12:51 PM	04:36 PM	07:33 PM	08:56 PM
Houston	05:46 AM	06:54 AM	01:22 PM	04:57 PM	07:50 PM	08:59 PM
London	04:23 AM	05:56 AM	01:05 PM	04:52 PM	08:05 PM	09:19 PM
Los Angeles	05:10 AM	06:22 AM	12:53 PM	04:32 PM	07:25 PM	08:37 PM
Miami	05:53 AM	06:58 AM	01:21 PM	04:51 PM	07:44 PM	08:50 PM
New York	04:56 AM	06:17 AM	12:56 PM	04:40 PM	07:36 PM	08:56 PM
Philadelphia	05:04 AM	06:23 AM	01:01 PM	04:44 PM	07:39 PM	08:59 PM
Washington DC	05:14 AM	06:31 AM	01:09 PM	04:51 PM	07:46 PM	09:03 PM

The Vindication Of The Most Honorable Elijah Muhammad's Theology

Day 26

"More Than A Vision"

"By the star when it sets! Your companion errs not, nor does he deviate. Nor does he speak out of desire. It is naught but revelation that is revealed —One Mighty in Power has taught him, The Lord of Strength. So he attained to perfection, And he is in the highest part of the horizon. Then he drew near, drew nearer yet, So he was the measure of two bows or closer still. So He revealed to His servant what He revealed. The heart was not untrue in seeing what he saw. Do you then dispute with him as to what he saw? And certainly he saw Him in another descent, At the farthest lote-tree. Near it is the Garden of Abode. When that which covers covered the lote-tree; The eye turned not aside, nor did it exceed the limit. Certainly he saw of the greatest signs of his Lord."-Surah 53:1-19

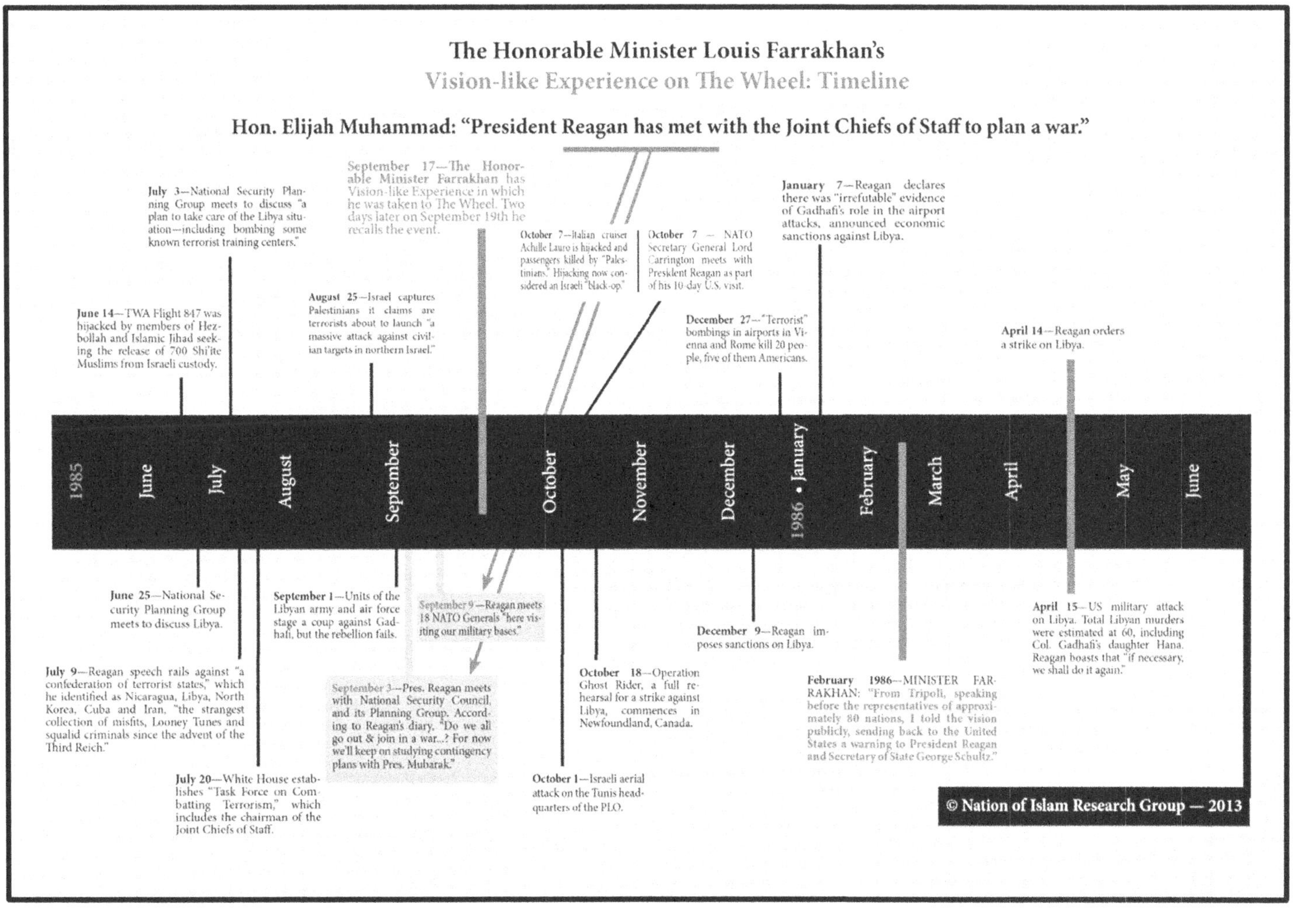

Ramadan Day 26-The Believer's Notes

Surah 46:1 – Surah 51:30

Ramadan Day 26-The Believer's Notes

Surah 46:1 – Surah 51:30

Hadith Wisdom For Ramadan Fasting

Narrated by Anas:

"The Messenger of Allah (peace be upon him) used to break his fasting before performing Maghrib (Sunset) prayer with three fresh date-fruits; if there were no fresh date- fruits, he would eat three dry dates; and if there were no dry date- fruits; he would take three draughts of water."

Day 26	NOI	Regional	Cities	Prayer	Times	2023
City	Fajr	Sunrise	Dhuhr	Asr	Maghrib	Isha
Atlanta	05:54 AM	07:05 AM	01:38 PM	05:17 PM	08:10 PM	09:22 PM
Chicago	04:44 AM	06:07 AM	12:51 PM	04:36 PM	07:34 PM	08:57 PM
Houston	05:45 AM	06:53 AM	01:22 PM	04:57 PM	07:51 PM	08:59 PM
London	04:21 AM	05:54 AM	01:05 PM	04:52 PM	08:07 PM	09:21 PM
Los Angeles	05:10 AM	06:22 AM	12:53 PM	04:32 PM	07:25 PM	08:37 PM
Miami	05:52 AM	06:57 AM	01:21 PM	04:51 PM	07:45 PM	08:51 PM
New York	04:54 AM	06:15 AM	12:56 PM	04:40 PM	07:37 PM	08:58 PM
Philadelphia	05:02 AM	06:21 AM	01:01 PM	04:45 PM	07:40 PM	09:00 PM
Washington DC	05:12 AM	06:30 AM	01:08 PM	04:52 PM	07:47 PM	09:05 PM

The Vindication Of
The Most Honorable Elijah Muhammad's Theology
Day 27

The Greek Philosophic Origins of Divine Incorporeality

Wesley Muhammad

Hebrew as well as NT Greek spirituality, even divine spirituality, was therefore corporeal*; that is to say it was characterized by a luminous, subtle materiality. It is in Greek philosophic tradition that such ideas as divine *in*corporeality* begin: in fact, it is to this tradition that we owe the very concept of "immateriality." As R. Renehan notes in his important study, "On the Greek Origins of the Concepts Incorporeality and Immateriality"[19]:

> Few concepts have been more influential, for better or worse, in the history of Western philosophy and theology than those of incorporeal beings and immaterial essences. Their importance for the particular directions which European thought long took pondering such problems as the nature of deity, soul, intellect, in short, of ultimate reality, is not easily exaggerated...Such concepts are the creation of Greek philosophy. Prior to that even 'spirit' was material, in Egypt, Greece, and elsewhere.[20]

Plato
"The Father of Immaterialism"

A number of Presocratics (i.e. Greek philosophers before the time of Socrates) laid 'stepping stones' leading to a fully explicit notion of incorporeality/immateriality. The Ionian philosopher of Colophon Xenophanes (570-475 BC), in rejecting the anthropomorphic gods of the Greeks and the surrounding Near East, posited an abstract and non-anthropomorphic deity* that would be highly influential to the development of the Christian doctrine of divine transcendence* with its characteristic notion of divine incorporeality/immateriality.[21] But for all its abstraction Xenophanes' deity was still corporeal in a sense.[22] "When all is said and done, it must be recognized that one man was responsible

[19] Renehan, "On the Greek Origins."
[20] Renehan, "On the Greek Origins," 105.
[21] On Xenophanes' deity v. Werner Jaeger, ***The Theology of the Early Greek Philosophers. The Gifford Lectures, 1936*** (Oxford: The Clarendon Press, 1947) 43ff. On Xenophanes' influence on Christian thought v. Eric Osborn, "Iranaeus on God-Argument and Parody," ***StPtr*** 36 (2001): 270-281; William R. Schoedel, "Enclosing, Not Enclosed: The Early Christian Doctrine of God," in W.R. Schoedel and R.L. Wilcken (edd.), ***Early Christian Literature and the Classical Tradition. In Honerem R.M. Grant*** (Théologie historique 54; Paris: Éditions Beauchesne, 1979) 75-86.
[22] See discussion in Vernant, "Dim Body, Dazzling Body," 21; Jaeger, ***Theology of the Early Greek***, 43.

for the creation of an ontology which culminates in incorporeal Being as the truest and highest reality. That man was Plato."[23] Renehan suggests that it was Plato (Figure 4) who coined the term ασωματος, *asomatos* (incorporeal).[24] Plato's incorporeal Form (ειδος/ιδεα) of the Good, however, was not God.[25] It seems to have been his student Aristotle (384-322 BC) who, understanding the full implications of the term ασωματος *asomatos*, first used it of the deity, his Unmoved Mover (*Cael.* 279a17ff, *Metaph.* 1073a5ff).[26] This novel Platonic/Aristotelian notion of divine incorporeality/immateriality will be taken up and elaborated in Hellenistic Judaism, Patristic Christianity, and heterodox Islam.[27]

---

[23] Renehan, "On the Greek Origins," 138.
[24] Renehan, "On the Greek Origins," 127-130.
[25] J.B. Skemp, "Plato's Concept of Deity," in *Zetesis. Album amicorum door vrienden en* **collega's** *aangeboden aan Prof. Dr. E. de Strycker ter gelegenheid van zijn 65e verjaardag* (Antwerpen, De Nederlandsche Boekhandel, 1973) 115-121.

[26] Renehan, "On the Greek Origins,"134-5.
[27] Schoedel, "Enclosing, Not Enclosed," notes:

> the antithesis, 'enclosing, not enclosed', first gains currency in Philo as a description of God and seems to owe its striking formulation to an impulse to go beyond the Greek tradition in emphasizing the divine transcendence.
> To say that God encloses all things and is not enclosed means for Philo (a) that God is immaterial and not in a place, (b) that he is unknowable in his essence, and (c) that he is creator of all things (*Migr. Abr.* 183; cf. *Leg.. alleg.* 3:51...) Such themes presuppose a God who transcends the cosmos and is not simply (as in Greek philosophy) a factor in the totality of things. *To be sure, the emphasis on God's immateriality reflects, as an isolate them, Plato more than the Bible* (emph. mine-WW). But it points here in a new direction. For ultimately, it was to provide a context within which the infinite 'could be detached from the concept of the corporeal, with which it had been essentially united in Greek thought'. An indication of the novelty of Philo's thought in this connection is the emphasis, perhaps for the first time, on the idea that the essence of God is unknowable.

See also John M. Dillon, "The Transcendence of God in Philo: Some Possible Sources," ***Protocol of the Colloquy of the Center for Hermeneutical Studies in Hellenism and Modern Culture*** 16 (1975): 1-22; Harry A. Wolfson, "Maimonides of the Unity and Incorporeality of God," ***JQR*** 56 (1965): 112-136. On Patristic Christianity see Wiles, ***Christian Fathers*** 13, 17, and above. See also Schoedel, "Enclosing, Not Enclosed"; Robert P. Casey, "Clement of Alexandria and the Beginnings of Christian Platonism," ***HTR*** 18 (1925): 39-101; Gedaliahu Stroumsa, "The Incorporeality of God: Context and Implication of Origen's Position," ***Rel*** 13 (1983): 345-358; Frances M. Young, "The God of the Greeks and the Nature of Religious Language," in William R. Schoedel and Robert L. Wilekn (eds.), ***Early Christian literature and the classical intellectual tradition. In Honorem Robert M. Grant*** (Theologie historique 53; Paris: Editions Beauchesne, 1979) 45-74; G. Jantzen, ***God's World, God's Body*** (Philadelphia: Westminster Press, 1984), 23-35. On Islam see above and below.

"Dig your heels deep into the faith that God is a Man, who came in the Person of Master W. Fard Muhammad and He came with a work to do."

-Hon. Min. Louis Farrakhan

February 23, 2023

Ramadan Day 27-The Believer's Notes

Surah 51:31 – Surah 57:29

Ramadan Day 27-The Believer's Notes

Surah 51:31 – Surah 57:29

Hadith Wisdom For Ramadan Fasting

Narrated `by Aishah:

“The Messenger of Allah (peace be upon him) used to kiss and embrace while he was fasting, but he was the one of you who had most control over his desire.”

Day 27	NOI	Regional	Cities	Prayer	Times	2023
City	Fajr	Sunrise	Dhuhr	Asr	Maghrib	Isha
Atlanta	05:52 AM	07:04 AM	01:38 PM	05:17 PM	08:11 PM	09:23 PM
Chicago	04:42 AM	06:05 AM	12:50 PM	04:37 PM	07:35 PM	08:58 PM
Houston	05:44 AM	06:52 AM	01:22 PM	04:57 PM	07:51 PM	09:00 PM
London	04:19 AM	05:52 AM	01:05 PM	04:53 PM	08:09 PM	09:23 PM
Los Angeles	05:07 AM	06:19 AM	12:53 PM	04:32 PM	07:26 PM	08:39 PM
Miami	05:51 AM	06:56 AM	01:21 PM	04:51 PM	07:45 PM	08:51 PM
New York	4:53 AM	06:14 AM	12:56 PM	04:41 PM	07:38 PM	08:59 PM
Philadelphia	05:00 AM	06:20 AM	01:01 PM	04:45 PM	07:41 PM	09:01 PM
Washington DC	05:11 AM	06:29 AM	01:08 PM	04:52 PM	07:48 PM	09:06 PM

The Vindication Of
The Most Honorable Elijah Muhammad's Theology
Day 28

Muqatil b. Sulayman, the Hon. Elijah Muhammad, and Point Number 12

Wesley Muhammad

A wonderful opportunity to examine the place of the Honorable Elijah Muhammad's doctrines in the history of Islamic theology is found in an analysis of the doctrine of an early qur'anic exegete, Muqatil b. Sulayman (d. 150/767) from Balkh. Herbert Berg has already suggested a similarity between the two.[28] Muqatil, like Elijah Muhammad, is known for an explicit and unabashed anthropomorphic theology. Al-Ash'ari, in his ***Maqal§t al-IslamÊyin***, described Muqatil's views as follows:

> God is a body; He has hair, He has the form of a man; He has flesh, blood, hair and bone; He has limbs and organs, such as hand, foot, head, eyes. It is [a] dense (*mußmat*) [body]. And in spite of this, He resembles nothing and nothing resembles Him.[29]

This bold description of God has negatively colored Muqatil's image with posterity and in the academic literature.[30] There has recently been some debate, however, over the accuracy of this charge. The publication of his exegetical works did little to bring clarity to Muqatil's doctrines in this regard. Claude Gilliot's lengthy study of the question yielded no conclusive answer.[31] Binyamin Abrahamov concluded that a survey of Muqatil's exegesis shows that he was not a *mushabbiha* (anthropomorphist).[32] Josef van Ess,[33] on the other hand, as well as Claud Gilliot, have demonstrated that, while figurative interpretations to qur''anic anthropomorphisms can certainly be found in the various recensions of Muqatil's ***Tafsir***, literal interpretations to these anthropomorphisms are not at all lacking. There exists in the material itself ample justification for believing the reports of Muqatil's anthropomorphist theology. Not only does he explain the "hand" (*yad*) of God anthropomorphically, he applies the same exegetical method to the "leg" (*saq*), the "descent" (*nazul*), the "vision" (*ru'ya*) and the "establishment on the Throne." (*'istawa ala l-arsh*).[34] That Muqatil was a *mujassima* or corporealist who attributed a body to God is clearly attested in his exegesis of Surat *al-Ikhl§ß*. He understands *as-ßamad* (112:2) as dense, not hollow and as "he who has no [hollow

[28] *Art. cited,* 345.
[29] *Op. cited.*
[30] Cf. M. Plessner's article, "al-Mukatil B. Sulaiman," ***EI2***, 711-12.
[31] Gilliot, *art. cited,* 83.
[32] Binyamin Abrahamov, ***Al-Kasim B. Ibrahim on the Proof of God's Existence: Kitab al-Dalil al-Kabir*** (Leiden: E. J. Brill, 1990) 5.
[33] Van Ess, **TG II**, pp. 529f.; Gilliot, *art. cited,* 54ff.
[34] Cf. Gilliot, *art. cited,* 54ff.

stomach] similar to the hollow (stomach) of creatures."[35] God is thus massive in his body and differs from creatures in that he lacks a stomach cavity.

The most revealing passage is found in the extensive extract of Muqatil's ***At-tafsir fi mutashabih al-Qur'an*** preserved in Malati's (d. 377/987) ***Kitab at-tanbih wa ar-radd.***[36] We read there the incredible statement: "Everywhere it is said in the Qur'an, 'and He sat Himself (*wa-stawa*') is meant: He is 32 years old, and settles, istaqarra."[37] Muqatil's description of God as 32 years old means that God appears to the people in the ideal shape of a man of that age.[38] This is obviously based on the hadith of the "youthful God." Instead of using the designation *sh§bb* as found in most versions of the hadith Muqatil uses *kahl* which indicates a man who has reached his maturity but has not yet begun to gray.[39] That this is the ideal age according to Muqatil is shown by the fact that he gave the "virgins of Paradise" of Sura 56:37 this same age.[40]

The "charge" of anthropomorphism is thus substantiated. It seems appropriate here to cite the parallels between the doctrines of Muqatil and the Honorable Elijah Muhammad. For the latter, God is also a man of flesh and blood. In a famous speech in Atlanta, the Hon. Elijah Muhammad stated:

> God is a man, a flesh and blood being, but He is a Divine Being. Why do we call God a Divine Being? Because He is a Being like we are but His wisdom, power and other capacities and attributes are Supreme, making Him the Highest Power...He has the Divine Power to will whatever He wishes and to bring it into existence with His Divine Will.[41]

The Hon. Elijah Muhammad's description of the difference between God as a flesh and blood man, a Divine Being, and regular humans is paralleled in Muqatil's exegesis of Sura 42 and the so-called 'anti-anthropomorphic injunction,' "There is none like Him." As we saw above, Muqatil concludes his description of God as a man of flesh and blood with the words: "*And in spite of this, He resembles nothing and nothing resembles Him.*" This is no doubt to conform to the Qur'anic mandate to acknowledge a difference between God and His creation. But wherein lies the difference? In his exegesis of this passage as found in his ***Tafsir***, Muqatil comments: "in power" (*bi-l-qudra*).[42] God differs from man "in power."

Muqatil and the Hon. Elijah Muhammad likewise agree in their physical description of God. Muqatil's God is in the image of the youths of Paradise, beardless (*amrad*).[43] He has rich, black hair,[44] not curly (*ja'd*) as the traditions of the "youthful God" going back to Ibn Abbas maintain. Muqatil describes the hair as *muwaffar*:[45] it goes to the earlobe or even farther.[46] God's black hair, as we saw above, was contrasted with His white

[35] Ibid., 55. Gilliot correctly observes that, as density and "mass" are characteristic of bodies, this interpretation betrays a corporealist orientation. Nevertheless, he is incorrect in suggesting that Muqatil's refusal to attribute a *jawf* or stomach to God "rules out" an anthropomorphist interpretation (55). As we have shown above (37ff.), the absence of the stomach cavity was a part of the anthropomorphist doctrine. Dawud al-Jawaribi, a generation later, propagated an even cruder anthropomorphist doctrine which likewise denied God a stomach cavity; van Ess, **TG II**: 432ff.
[36] Ed. by Sven Dedering ("Bibliotheca Islamica" IX [Istanbul, 1936]).
[37] ***Tanbih*** 60, 12/75.
[38] Van Ess, **TG II**:530.
[39] Ibid.; idem., "Youthful God", 11.
[40] ***Tanbih*** 60, 7f./75, 5f.
[41] As quoted in Louis Lomax, ***When the Word is Given*** (Cleveland: World Publishing Company, 1962) 127f.
[42] Muqatil b. Sulayman, ***Tafsir***, III:465; cf. also Gilliot, *art. cited*, 56.
[43] Cf. Gimaret, ***Diea a l'image***, 157 n. 2.
[44] Al-Ash'ari, ***Maqalat***,153, 1.
[45] Van Ess **TG** IV:381.
[46] Gimaret, ***Diea a l'image***, 157 n. 2.

skin.[47] Muqatil's God was a young man, around 32-33 years old, with white skin and black hair that goes to his earlobes or beyond. He is beardless. If one were to glance at a picture of Fard Muhammad, God Himself according to the Honorable Elijah Muhammad, one would instantly recognize the similarity. Fard is a young man, 33 years old when He first arrived in America in 1910. His rich black hair that reaches to His earlobes outlines His white skin. (Figure 6). His beardless face is a conspicuous departure from the wearing of beards that has become characteristic of Muslims since the Prophet's time. It is as if Muqatil's God has appeared in America.

Descriptions of God paralleling those articulated by the Honorable Elijah Muhammad are thus found articulated in the early period of Islam. With Muqatil, we are talking about the end of the Umayyad period[48] and the beginning of the era of theological discourse in Islam. The question that remains is whether this anthropomorphist theology was as anathema* to Muqatil's contemporaries as it will be to later theologians. To answer this question, we must take a look at the theological milieu of the time.

[47] See above. Cf. van Ess **TG** I:342ff.
[48] The Umayyad period was c. 661-749 AD.

Ramadan Day 28-The Believer's Notes

Surah 58:1 – Surah 66:12

Ramadan Day 28-The Believer's Notes

Surah 58:1 – Surah 66:12

Hadith Wisdom For Ramadan Fasting

Narrated by Abu Hurairah:

“The Messenger of Allah (peace be upon him) said, "When any one of you is observing fasting on a day, he should neither indulge in obscene language nor should he raise the voice; and if anyone reviles him or tries to quarrel with him he should say: 'I am observing the fast."'

Day 28	NOI	Regional	Cities	Prayer	Times	2023
City	Fajr	Sunrise	Dhuhr	Asr	Maghrib	Isha
Atlanta	05:51 AM	07:03 AM	01:37 PM	05:17 PM	08:11 PM	09:24 PM
Chicago	04:41 AM	06:04 AM	12:50 PM	04:37 PM	07:36 PM	09:00 PM
Houston	05:42 AM	06:51 AM	01:22 PM	04:57 PM	07:52 PM	09:01 PM
London	04:16 AM	05:50 AM	01:04 PM	04:54 PM	08:10 PM	09:24 PM
Los Angeles	05:06 AM	06:18 AM	12:53 PM	04:33 PM	07:27 PM	08:40 PM
Miami	05:49 AM	06:55 AM	01:21 PM	04:51 PM	07:46 PM	08:52 PM
New York	04:51 AM	06:12 AM	12:56 PM	04:41 PM	07:39 PM	09:00 PM
Philadelphia	04:58 AM	06:18 AM	01:00 PM	04:45 PM	07:42 PM	09:03 PM
Washington DC	05:09 AM	06:27 AM	01:08 PM	04:52 PM	07:48 PM	09:07 PM

The Vindication Of
The Most Honorable Elijah Muhammad's Theology
Day 29

"Why does he fear, now, since he is a big man? Because the Devil taught him to eat the wrong food."

Fascinating Scientific Research Points To Truth of Master W. Fard Muhammad's English Lesson C1

Science News *from research organizations*

Bacteria are connected to how babies experience fear

New research shows that an infant's gut microbiome could contain clues to help monitor and support healthy neurological development

Date: June 4, 2021

Source: Michigan State University

Summary: Why do some babies react to perceived danger more than others? According to new research, part of the answer may be found in a surprising place: an infant's digestive system.

Why do some babies react to perceived danger more than others? According to new research from Michigan State University and the University of North Carolina, Chapel Hill, part of the answer may be found in a surprising place: an infant's digestive system.

The human digestive system is home to a vast community of microorganisms known as the gut microbiome. The MSU-UNC research team discovered that the gut microbiome was different in infants with strong fear responses and infants with milder reactions.

These fear responses -- how someone reacts to a scary situation -- in early life can be indicators of future mental health. And there is growing evidence tying neurological well-being to the microbiome in the gut.

The new findings suggest that the gut microbiome could one day provide researchers and physicians with a new tool to monitor and support healthy neurological development.

"This early developmental period is a time of tremendous opportunity for promoting healthy brain development," said MSU's Rebecca Knickmeyer, leader of the new study published June 2 in the journal Nature Communications. "The microbiome is an exciting new target that can be potentially used for that."

Studies of this connection and its role in fear response in animals led Knickmeyer, an associate professor in the College of Human Medicine's Department of Pediatrics and Human Development, and her team to look for something similar in humans. And studying how humans, especially young children, handle fear is important because it can help forecast mental health in some cases.

"Fear reactions are a normal part of child development. Children should be aware of threats in their environment and be ready to respond to them" said Knickmeyer, who also works in MSU's Institute for Quantitative Health Science and Engineering, or IQ. "But if they can't dampen that response when they're safe, they may be at heightened risk to develop anxiety and depression later on in life."

6. He likes the Devil because the Devil gives him nothing.
7. Why does he like the Devil?
8. Because the Devil put fear in him when he was a little boy.
9. Why does he fear, now, since he is a big man?
10. Because the Devil taught him to eat the wrong food.
11. Does that have anything to do with the above question, No. 10?
12. Yes, sir! That makes him other than his own self.
13. What is his own self?
14. His own self is a righteous Muslim.

On the other end of the response spectrum, children with exceptionally muted fear responses may go on to develop callous, unemotional traits associated with antisocial behavior, Knickmeyer said.

To determine whether the gut microbiome was connected to fear response in humans, Knickmeyer and her co-workers designed a pilot study with about 30 infants. The researchers selected the cohort carefully to keep as many factors impacting the gut microbiome as consistent as possible. For example, all of the children were breastfed and none was on antibiotics.

The researchers then characterized the children's microbiome by analyzing stool samples and assessed a child's fear response using a simple test: observing how a child reacted to someone entering the room while wearing a Halloween mask.

"We really wanted the experience to be enjoyable for both the kids and their parents. The parents were there the whole time and they could jump in whenever they wanted," Knickmeyer said. "These are really the kinds of experiences infants would have in their everyday lives."

Compiling all the data, the researchers saw significant associations between specific features of the gut microbiome and the strength of infant fear responses.

For example, children with uneven microbiomes at 1 month of age were more fearful at 1 year of age. Uneven microbiomes are dominated by a small set of bacteria, whereas even microbiomes are more balanced.

The researchers also discovered that the content of the microbial community at 1 year of age related to fear responses. Compared with less fearful children, infants with heightened responses had more of some types of bacteria and less of others.

The team, however, did not observe a connection between the children's gut microbiome and how the children reacted to strangers who weren't wearing masks. Knickmeyer said this is likely due to the different parts of the brain involved with processing potentially frightening situations.

"With strangers, there is a social element. So children may have a social wariness, but they don't see strangers as immediate threats," Knickmeyer said. "When children see a mask, they don't see it as social. It goes into that quick-and-dirty assessment part of the brain."

As part of the study, the team also imaged the children's brains using MRI technology. They found that the content of the microbial community at 1 year was associated with the size of the amygdala, which is part of the brain involved in making quick decisions about potential threats.

Connecting the dots suggests that the microbiome may influence how the amygdala develops and operates. That's one of many interesting possibilities uncovered by this new study, which the team is currently working to replicate. Knickmeyer is also preparing to start up new lines of inquiry with new collaborations at IQ, asking new questions that she's excited to answer.

"We have a great opportunity to support neurological health early on," she said. "Our long-term goal is that we'll learn what we can do to foster healthy growth and development."

SOURCE: https://www.sciencedaily.com/releases/2021/06/210604135433.htm

https://www.nature.com/articles/s41467-021-23281-y?utm_medium=affiliate&utm_source=commission_junction&utm_campaign=CONR_PF018_ECOM_GL_PHSS_AALWY_DEEPLINK&utm_content=textlink&utm_term=PID100090912&CJEVENT=42bfe194bfb611ed83b2a4630a88b824

Ramadan Day 29-The Believer's Notes

Surah 67:1 – Surah 77:50

Ramadan Day 29-The Believer's Notes

Surah 67:1 – Surah 77:50

Hadith Wisdom For Ramadan Fasting

Narrated by Abu Hurairah:

“The Prophet (peace be upon him) said, "If one does not eschew lies and false conduct, Allah has no need that he should abstain from his food and his drink."

Narrated by Abu Hurairah:

“The Prophet (peace be upon him) said, "Whosoever performs Qiyam (Night Prayer) during Lailat-ul-Qadr (Night of Power), with Faith and being hopeful of Allah's reward, will have his former sins forgiven."

Day 29	NOI	Regional	Cities	Prayer	Times	2023
City	Fajr	Sunrise	Dhuhr	Asr	Maghrib	Isha
Atlanta	05:49 AM	07:02 AM	01:37 PM	05:17 PM	08:12 PM	09:25 PM
Chicago	04:39 AM	06:02 AM	12:50 PM	04:37 PM	07:37 PM	09:01 PM
Houston	05:41 AM	06:50 AM	01:21 PM	04:57 PM	07:53 PM	09:02 PM
London	04:14 AM	05:48 AM	01:04 PM	04:54 PM	08:12 PM	09:26 PM
Los Angeles	05:04 AM	06:17 AM	12:53 PM	04:33 PM	07:28 PM	08:41 PM
Miami	05:48 AM	06:54 AM	01:20 PM	04:51 PM	07:46 PM	08:52 PM
New York	04:49 AM	06:11 AM	12:55 PM	04:41 PM	07:40 PM	09:02 PM
Philadelphia	04:57 AM	06:17 AM	01:00 PM	04:46 PM	07:43 PM	09:04 PM
Washington DC	05:07 AM	06:26 AM	01:08 PM	04:52 PM	07:49 PM	09:08 PM

Allah's 99 Beautiful Names

The idea of this section book emerges out of the belief that it is the study of God that reveals the blueprint for the complete and proper development of human potential. In the religion of Islam, in order to help the believer to have a deeper and more comprehensive knowledge of Allah(God), 99 principle characteristics or attributes of Allah(God) have been identified and defined. They are referred to in the Arabic as **"Al Asma Ul Husna"** and are referred to in several places throughout the Holy Qur'an.

These 99 names provide for men and women characteristics that we should strive to embody in our own lives. These 99 characteristics comprise the noblest of human virtues and locate them within the Originator and Creator of the heavens and the earth. They outline and provide a basic overview to answer the question "what is God like?" Islam is frequently and sometimes colloquially defined as submission to the will of Allah(God). However in practical application (i.e. the real world) we have a need to repair, restore and rebuild our lives after having suffered underneath the evil sinful conditions that serve as component parts of the Black experience in America. Rebuilding involves both removal and addition. In spiritual terms, as it relates to the subject of rebuilding our lives, we must not only submit to the Will of Allah (God); we must also adopt the Characteristics of Allah (God) as our own.

This section is an introduction to the 99 Attributes of Allah (God) that includes brief commentary cited from various sources including: Sufi Scholar H. Inayat Khan, The Dictionary of the Holy Qur'an by A.M. Omar, Maqsad al-Asna by Imam Ghazalli and The English Translation of the Holy Qur'an by M.Muhammad Ali.

Al-Rahman

The Most Lovingly Beneficent, The Most Kind and Giving, The Most Gracious, The Infinitely Good

AR-RAHMAN
The All-Compassionate

The One who continually showers all of creation with blessings and prosperity without any disparity. The One who is most kind, loving and merciful. The One whose endless, loving mercy is perfect and inclusive. The One who is overflowing with the quality of loving mercy and is continually pouring it upon all of creation.

The One whose perfect mercy and loving beneficence endlessly embrace all of creation. The One who loves and cherishes all of creation. The One who is most loving, gentle and merciful.

From the root r-h-m which has the following classical Arabic connotations: to have tenderness, gentleness, kindness; to love; to have mercy, to have pity; to show favor and goodness; to have all that is required for beneficence;

This name is used in the Qur'ān. For example, see 1:1

The root r-h-m also indicates womb; meaning that which provides protection and nourishment, and that from which all of creation is brought into being.

Rahmān conveys the idea of fullness and extensiveness, indicating the great quality of love and mercy which engulfs all of creation without any effort or request on our part, while Rahīm conveys the idea of constant renewal and giving liberal reward to those who are deserving.

Al-Rahmān is the Beneficent One whose endless outpouring of love and mercy are continually showered upon all of creation, while al-Rahīm is the Merciful One whose love and mercy are manifested as that which is received as the consequence of one's deeds.

According to Ibn Qayyum (1350 AD), Rahmān describes the quality of abounding Grace which is inherent in and inseparable from the Almighty.

In Muhammad Ali's translation of the Qur'ān, he refers to classical sources (as indicated by the initials in parenthesis) who said:

Rahmān and Rahīm are both derived from the root rahmat, signifying tenderness requiring the exercise of beneficence [kindness] (R), and thus comprising the ideas of love and mercy.

Al-Rahmān and al-Rahīm are both active participle nouns of different measures denoting intensiveness of significance, the former being of the measure of fa'lān and indicating the greatest preponderance of the quality of mercy, and the later being of the measure of fa'īl and being expressive of a constant repetition and manifestation of the attribute (AH).

The Prophet is reported to have said: "Al-Rahmān is the beneficent One whose love and mercy are manifested in the creation of the world, and al-Rahīm is the merciful One whose love and mercy are manifested in the state that comes after" (AH), i.e as a consequence of the deeds of men. Thus the former is expressive of the utmost degree of love and generosity, the latter of unbounded and constant favor and mercy.

Lexicologists agree in holding that the former includes both the believer and the unbeliever for its objects, while the latter relates specifically to the believer (LL).

In the Dictionary of the Holy Qur'ān, Abdul Omar quotes from classical resources:

Rahmān is an active participle noun of the measure fa'lān which conveys the idea of fullness and extensiveness and indicates the greatest preponderance of the quality of love and mercy which comprehends the entire universe without regard to our effort or asking, even before we are born. The creation of the sun, the moon, air and water, etc are all there because of this attribute.... the term Rahmān circumscribes the quality of abounding Grace inherent in and inseparable from the Almighty.

Al Rahim

The Most Merciful, The Most Compassionate

The One who grants even more grace and greater rewards in response to our good actions and high thoughts. The One who greatly rewards those who use the Divine bounties and beneficence in a good way. The One who has mercy on the merciful.

From the root r-h-m which has the following classical Arabic connotations: to have tenderness,

AR-RAHEEM
The All Mercifull

gentleness, kindness; to love; to have mercy; to have pity; to show favor and goodness; to have all that is required for beneficence

This name is used in the Qur'ān. For example, see 1:1

The root r-h-m also indicates womb; meaning that which provides protection and nourishment, and that from which all of creation is brought into being.

According to Ibn Qayyum (1350 AD), Rahīm expresses the continuous manifestation of the Grace in our lives and its effect upon us as a result of our own activities.

In Muhammad Ali's translation of the Qur'ān, he refers to classical sources (as indicated by the initials in parenthesis) who said:

Rahmān and Rahīm are both derived from the root rahmat, signifying tenderness requiring the exercise of beneficence [kindness] (R), and thus comprising the ideas of love and mercy.

Rahīm is in the measure of fa'īl and denotes the idea of constant repetition and giving of a liberal reward to those who deserve it and seek it. The Manifestation of this attribute is in response to and is a result of the action of the human being. That is, Rahīm indicates that which is extremely and continuously loving and merciful, and who is the dispenser of grace and love as a result of our deeds and supplications, and the One in whom the attribute is constantly and [endlessly] repeated.

Al-Malik

The King, The Ruler

The One who is king of all beings. The One who is the owner and ruler of this world. The One who has supreme authority, and who is relied upon by everyone. The One who has all ruling power over all beings, and is ruled by none.

AL-MALIK
The Absolute Ruler

From the root m-l-k which has the following classical Arabic connotations: to possess, to own exclusively ; to exercise authority to command; to have power over, command, reign; to have dominion over, to have ruling power; to have kingship

This name is used in the Qur'ān. For example, see 59:23

The name Malik signifies king, while the name the name Mālik, by virtue of the ā which intensifies the meaning, signifies something that is in some way greater than a king, and is often translated as master or lord. However, the exact differences between these names are not universally agreed upon.

By some traditions, al-Malik is considered to be the owner and king of this world, or of the beings of this world, while Mālik al-Mulk is considered to be the supreme lord and master of all worlds, the known and the unknown, the manifest and the un-manifest.

Al-Quddus

The Most Holy, The Most Pure, The All-Perfect

The One who is pure, spotless, without blemish or fault. The One who is far from, and untouched by, worldly imperfections or faults. The One whose essence and attributes are of unimaginable purity and perfection. The One who is beyond all human understanding of purity, perfection and holiness.

AL-QUDDUS

The Pure One

From the root q-d-s which has the following classical Arabic connotations: to be pure, clean, spotless; to be far removed from impurity or imperfection; to be holy, sacred, hallowed

This name is used in the Qur'ān. For example, see 59:23

The ancient roots of the Arabic word Quddūs, as well as the Hebrew word Kadosh, point toward that which is set apart, different, that which is 'other'. Thus, al-Quddūs is known as the One who is set apart, distinctly different and separate from all worldly imperfections, sins and faults, the One whose perfection and righteousness are so 'other' that they cannot be grasped by mankind, the truly Blessed One.

The name al-Quddūs describes the unique, unimaginable purity and perfection that is Allāh, the One whose goodness and righteousness are beyond our understanding.

According to al-Qurturbi, the name al-Quddūs also describes the One who is glorified and revered by the angels.

The Merriam-Webster dictionary defines the word holy as: Holy -- Exalted or worthy of complete devotion as one perfect in goodness and righteousness.

As-Salaam

The Source of Peace, The Flawless, The Source of Wholeness and Well-Being

The One who is perfect, whole, prosperous and content.

AS SALAM

The One who is the source of all peace, wholeness and safety. The One who has rendered all of creation to be perfect, whole, prosperous and content. The One whose creation is free of imperfections, free of faults and free of error.

From the root s-l-m which has the following classical Arabic connotations: to be peaceful, quiet, tranquil, content, friendly, reconciled; to be free from imperfections, free from faults, complete, whole, sound; to be safe, secure, well, healthy, prosperous

This name is used in the Qur'ān. For example, see 59:23

This ancient Semitic root of s-l-m implies every manner of wholeness, completeness and prosperity.

Many seek peace by struggling, battling and trying to impose their will on others, yet external peace will only prevail as a reflection of inner peace. The only path to outer peace is awareness of the tranquil depths of inner peace, and the only source of such inner peace is the One known as as-Salām.

According to Rāghib, the word Islam, which arises form this same s-l-m root, means to enter into salm... which means to enter into peace, or to enter into wholeness. That is, the word Islam means to be at peace with or reconciled with the ways and decrees of Allāh, and is often described as self-resignation, surrender or submission to the will of Allāh.

Al-Mumin

The Remover of Fear, The Giver of Tranquility, The Source of Faith

Al-Mu`min
The Inspirer of Faith

The One who faithfully bestows the gifts of peace, safety and security. The One who grants freedom from fear. The One who illuminates the heart with faith. The One who is most trustworthy.

From the root ā-m-n which has the following classical Arabic connotations: to be secure, safe, free from fear; to be quiet, tranquil; to grant protection, safeguard; to be trusted, trustworthy; to believe in

This name is used in the Qur'ān. For example, see 59:23

The word īmān, often simply translated simply as faith or belief, comes from this same ā-m-n root, and could well be translated as has been granted peace and security.

The word āmīn, often translated simply as amen, also comes from this same ā-m-n root, and could be translated as in this we trust or in this we are free from fear.

The root ā-m-n root is also the original source of the name al-Muhaymin (the protector).

Related names: **Raqīb** refers to the One who has the attribute of watchfulness. **Wakīl** refers to the One who is the trusted administrator. **Hafīz** refers to the One who protects and preserves. **Māni'** is the One who protects and defends against harmful situations. **Muhaymin** refers to the One who is the ever-watchful guardian and protector. **Mu'min** is The One who grants security and freedom from fear.

Al-Muhaymin

The Protector, The Bestower of Security, The Guardian, The Safeguarder

The One who ensures well-being. The One who extends wings of Love to cover and protect creation. The One who is ever watchful. The One who protects and guards. The One who offers peace and security. The One who proclaims the Truth.

AL-MUHAYMIN
The Guardian

From the root h-y-m-n which has the following classical Arabic connotations: to watch over, oversee, protect, guard ;to be a witness to; to offer security and peace; to determine what is true; to extend a wing (like a hen protecting her chicks)

This name is used in the Qur'ān. For example, see 59:23

According to E.W. Lane, the root of Muhaymin was originally ā-m-n, the same root as al-Mu'min (remover of fear).

Al-Aziz

The Mighty, The Strong, Dignified and Powerful, The Eminent

AL AZIZ

The One who is the most Powerful and most Cherished. The victorious One whose strength, glory and power are overwhelming and cannot be overcome or resisted.

The One whose dignity, majesty and power are unique, precious and unattainable by mankind. The One whose respectability and nobility are above all others. The One who is the ultimate in honor and nobility.

The One who has complete mastery over all of creation. The One who overcomes everything. The One who is incomparable and unparalleled. The One who is the cherished source of all strength, power and potency.

From the root '-z-z which has the following classical Arabic connotations: to be mighty, potent, strong, powerful to be high, elevated, noble, exalted; to be honorable, noble, glorious, illustrious; to be indomitable, invincible; to be respected, cherished, dear; to be scarce, rare, precious, unattainable

This name is used in the Qur'ān. For example, see 59:23

Al-Jabbar

The Restorer, The Repairer, The All-Compelling, The Irresistible

The One who irresistibly restores all of creation to soundness and sufficiency. The One who repairs, reforms and completes. The One who irresistibly compels things to be set aright. The One who compels each and every thing according to divine will, yet is never compelled. The

One who is high, above all creation and utterly irresistible.

AL-JABBAR
The Compeller

From the root j-b-r which has the following classical Arabic connotations: to restore something to sound, right or good state; to bring back to normal, reform; to benefit, to confer a benefit; to be supreme, high, above all of creation; to be compelling, irresistible

This name is used in the Qur'ān. For example, see 59:23

The essence of the root j-b-r is the irresistible restoration of something, and the name al-Jabbār describes the nature of the One who is the ultimate restorer of the soundness, wholeness and righteousness of all things. For a human being, any claim to such irresistible power would be false pride and arrogance, but for Allāh it is simply the truth.

Al-Mutakabbir

The Supremely Great, The Possessor of all Rights, The Perfection of Greatness

Al-Mutakabbir
The Greatest

The One who is supremely great. The One who is greater than all of creation. The One who manifests greatness in all things and in all ways. The One who has rights, privileges and attributes which others have not.

From the root k-b-r which has the following classical Arabic connotations: to be great in size, rank or dignity; to be great in size, to be vast, formidable; to be great in age, oldest; to be great in dignity, noble, majestic; to be great in learning, most knowing to have rights above all others

This name is used in the Qur'ān. For example, see 59:23

Mutakabbir is an empathic form of the root k-b-r which denotes actively using rights, privileges and attributes that are above and beyond the rights of everyone else. In mankind, this would be called pride or arrogance, but for the One this is simply the truth.

Al-Qurtubi reported that this name was understood to mean Grand, Great One.

Related names: **Jalīl** is considered to be greatness in attributes.

Kabīr denotes the One whose essence is greatness. **Azīm** is greatness in both attributes and self. **Mutakabbir** is an empathic form which denotes actively using rights, privileges, rank and attributes that are above and beyond the rights of everyone else.

Al-Khaliq

The Creator, The Planner

The One who determines and creates according to the proper measure and proportion of each thing. The One who plans and determines how, when and where to create.

The One whose works are perfectly suited, appropriate, fitting and proper. The One who creates something from nothing. The One who creates both the inner and the outer in just proportions. The One who brings things into existence from a state of non-existence. The One who has the power to change things back and forth between the states of existing and non-existing.

Al-Khaliq
The Creator

From the root kh-l-q which has the following classical Arabic connotations: to measure accurately; to determine the proper measure or proportion for something; to proportion one thing according to another; to create something based on a pattern or model which one has devised; to bring a thing into existence from non-existence

This name is used in the Qur'ān. For example, see 59:24

Related names: **Bāri'** denotes the way the One works with substances, often creating from existing matter, making and evolving that which is free and clear of any other thing, free and clear of imperfections. **Badī'** denotes the One who creates in wonderful, amazingly original ways that have no precedent whatsoever, ways that are awesome innovation. **Khāliq** denotes the One who continues to plan, measure out and create, and who has the power to change things from non-existing to existing. **Musawwir** denotes the One who arranges forms and colors, and who is the shaper of beauty. **Mubdi'** denotes the One who starts or begins all things, or that which has precedence given to it.

Also expressed as al-Khallāq (great creator).

Al-Bari

The Maker, The Producer, The Evolver, The Maker from Nothing

The One who creates form out of nothing. The One who creates with no model or similarity. The One who evolves and re-creates that which exists, both physically and spiritually. The One who sends new forms into existence. The One who manifests that which is in perfect harmony and proportion, without blemish or fault.

From the root b-r-' which has the following classical Arabic connotations: to create, to form

out of nothing, to manifest; to create using pre-existing matter, evolve; to be individual, free and clear of another thing; to be free and clear of fault or blemish

This name is used in the Qur'ān. For example, see 59:24

The Qur'ān commentary of al-Baydāwi says that the primary meaning of the root b-r-' is to denote a thing's becoming free and clear of another thing, either by being released or by being created.

The ancient Semitic roots point toward a manifestation or emanation which is the fruition of a great power, and which contains the potentiality of that which brought it into being.

Al-Musawwir

The Fashioner, The Bestower of Forms, The Shaper

The One who is the fashioner and former of each and every thing in all of creation. The One who has given everything in creation a special inclination or desire. The One who has given everything a special form and a special manner whereby it is distinguished.

From the root s-w-r which has the following classical Arabic connotations: to make something incline, lean or bend towards; to form, fashion, sculpt, imagine or picture something; to have an inclination or desire towards something

This name is used in the Qur'ān. For example, see 59:24

Al-Ghaffar

The All-Forgiving, The Absolver, The Veiler of Sins and Faults, The Most Protecting One

The One who accepts repentance and veils or forgives our faults and sins, time and time again. The One who sets us free from the guilt and shame of our own sins and faults, such that we may discover inner harmony and peace.

The One who protects us from the effects of our faults and sins, both in the present world and the future. The One who accepts repentance and sets aright our faults and sins.

The One who veils, forgives or transforms our faults and sins in such a manner that we may go on without guilt or shame. The One who can set aright, or transform, wrong deeds and change them into what become good deeds.

From the root gh-f-r which has the following classical Arabic connotations: to cover, veil, conceal, hide; to pardon, to forgive, to set aright; to cover a thing to protect it from dirt

This name is used in the Qur'ān. For example, see 40:3

Abū Hāmid al-Ghazālī said: Every creature is bound to have perfection and imperfection, or ugliness and beauty, so whoever overlooks the ugly and mentions only the beautiful is one who shares in this attribute.

Note that the root gh-f-r has given rise to three Beautiful Names that are all used in the Qur'ān: Ghaffār, Ghafūr and Ghāfir. However, only Ghaffār and Ghafūr were included in the list of 99 Names narrated by Tirmidhi.

In Qastalānī's commentary on Bukhārī, it is said that the root gh-f-r means a covering or protection which is either between man and the commission of sin [protecting, or watching over], or between sin and the effects of that sin [forgiving, veiling or concealing].

In al-Nihāyah (a dictionary of hadīth), it is said that Ghāfir refers to the One who protects us from the commission of sins, and that Ghafūr refers to the One who forgives our sins and faults.

Sheikh Tosun Bayrak portrays the differences as:

al-Ghāfir, the veiler of our faults from the eyes of other men; al-Ghafūr, who keeps the knowledge of our faults even from the angels; and al-Ghaffār who relieves us from the suffering of continual remembrance of our faults.

The Arabic word astaghfirullāh (sometimes written as astghfrallāh or estaferallah) is from this same gh-f-r root, and is an invocation of Divine Protection having a range of possible connotations that include Allāh please forgive me, Allāh please hide away my faults, Allāh please watch over me and protect me from faults.

The Arabic lexicon and commentary Tāj al-'Arūs reminds us that truly asking for forgiveness must be by both word and deed, not by the tongue alone.

The names Ghafūr, Ghaffār and Ghāfir denote forgiving or protecting, while 'Afūw indicates complete removal or obliteration of the condition.

Al-Qahhar

The Ever-Dominating, The Conqueror, The Prevailer

The One who prevails over all of creation. The One who overcomes all obstacles. The One who is victorious over any opposition. The One whose will is irresistible. The One who is dominant. The Ever-Dominating One.

AL-QAHHAR
The Subduer

The One who is master of all. The One to whom all submit.

From the root q-h-r which has the following classical Arabic connotations: to overcome, conquer; to overpower, master; to dominate over, prevail; to subdue, subjugate,to compel against one's wishes

This name is used in the Qur'ān. For example, see 39:4

The names Qahhār (ever-dominating, overpowering) and Latīf (subtle, refined) are sometimes used together to honor and appreciate the opposing, yet complementary, ways of the One.

Related names: **Qawī** - Strong - the One who is all-mighty and possesses inexhaustible strength. **Matīn** - Firm - the One whose nature it is to be firm, determined and steadfast. **Qahhār** - Dominator - the One who dominates, conquers, overpowers. **Muqtadir** - Determiner - the One who uses supreme power to enforce whatever Divine wisdom decrees or decides.

Al-Wahhab

The Most Liberal Bestower, The Great Giver, The Giver of Gifts

AL-WAHAB

The Giver Of All

The One who continually bestows gifts, favors and blessings upon all of creation. The One who is the most generous and liberal giver. The One who gives freely and endlessly, without expectation of any return.

From the root w-h-b which has the following classical Arabic connotations: to give for no compensation, to give as a gift; to donate, to offer as a present, bestow; to give liberally and freely to grant, endow to cause something to be

This name is used in the Qur'ān. For example, see 3:8

With regard to mankind's role in giving, Abū Hāmid al-Ghazālī notes that: Whoever bestows gifts with an eye to some interest to be realized by it sooner or later, be it appreciation, affection or release from blame, or or acquiring distinction of mention - he is neither a giver nor generous, but rather engaged in transaction and recompense. But the one who sacrifices all he owns, even his life, for the sake of God alone - such a one is worthy of being named giver and generous.

Ar-Razzaq

The Provider, The Providence, The Supplier, The Bestower of Sustenance

The One who creates all means of nourishment and subsistence. The One who is the giver of all things beneficial, both physical and spiritual. The One who provides everything that is needed.

The One who causes the means of subsistence to come. The One who bestows all means of support and growth, for the body, the mind and the spiritual life.

AR-RAZZAQ
The Sustainer

From the root r-z-q which has the following classical Arabic connotations: to receive something beneficial, especially as a gift; to be provided with the necessities of life; to receive a portion, share or lot; to be supplied with a means of subsistence

This name is used in the Qur'ān. For example, see 51:58

The root r-z-q points to the idea of the receiving of anything beneficial, particularly a gift, whereby something is nourished, sustained, or helped to grow physically, mentally or spiritually.

Al-Fattah

The Opener, The Revealer, The Granter of Success

AL FATTAAH

The One who is the judge and revealer. The One who opens what is closed. The One who is the judge of what shall be opened. The One by whose guidance that which was closed is opened and the unclear is made clear. The One who lifts veils and who opens the heart. The One who unties the knots, and softens that which was hardened. The One who continually offers goodness and mercy.

The One who gives victory. The One who opens the door to success. The One who holds the keys to victory and success. The One who reveals the solution to all problems.

From the root f-t-h which has the following classical Arabic connotations:to open, unlock, unfold; to make victorious; to reveal, inform, explain, make clear; to judge, decide; to grant, permit

This name is used in the Qur'ān. For example, see 34:26

The name of first chapter of the Qur'ān, al-Fātiha, is based on this same root, and is generally translated as The Opener, or The Opening.

The Arabic word miftāhī, translated as key, meaning that which opens or unlocks, is also based on this same root.

Al-Alim

The All-Knowing, The Omniscient, The Certain-Knowing

The One who comprehends everything. The One who is intuitively aware of all things, even before they happen. The One who knows with certainty. The One whose knowledge of past, present and future is deeply rooted and complete in all respects.

AL-ALIM
The Knower Of All

One from whom no knowledge is concealed. The One who is aware of the complete details of all matters. The Omniscient One.

From the root 'a-l-m which has the following classical Arabic connotations: to have knowledge, be cognizant, be certain; to be aware, thoroughly informed; to be find out, gather information; to have intuitive knowledge; to have firmly rooted knowledge of the minute particulars; to act according to knowledge

This name is used in the Qur'ān. For example, see 2:32

Related names: **'Alīm** denotes knowing with certainty, especially intuitive knowing, omniscience. **Khabīr** denotes an understanding of the inner qualities, secrets and true reality.

Al-Qabid

The Withholder, The Restrainer, The Constrictor

AL QAABID

The One whose wisdom causes withholding, either physically or spiritually. The One whose wisdom decides when to withhold something, or make something scarce. The One whose wisdom may elect to withhold joy and expansion of the heart.

The One in whose hand all hearts are held. The One whose hand collects all souls at the time of death.

From the root q-b-d which has the following classical Arabic connotations: to take in the hand, clutch, lay hold of; to grasp, grip, seize, hold firmly; to have absolute ownership of something (hold in the hand); to give and take (hand over and take in hand), barter; to contract, shrink, draw together, collect together; to draw in (as a bird contracting a wing); to withhold, make scanty, make scarce; to contract the heart, i.e. distress, depression, lack of joy

The name Qābid is not specifically used as a Beautiful Name in the Qur'ān.

The underlying roots of Qābid give a sense of give and take, a movement back and forth, an underlying rhythm of ebb and flow, like the rhythmical folding and unfolding of a bird's wings in flight, or the rising and setting of the sun, or the endless cycles of life and death.

Qābid (constrictor) and Bāsit (expander) are opposites.

The Arabic lexicon and commentary Tāj al-'Arūs, as interpreted by E.W. Lane, says: **Qabd** [Qābid] and **Bast** [Bāsit] are terms applied by the investigators of truth among the Sūfis to the two contrary states of the heart, from both of which it is seldom or never free: the former being an affection of the heart withholding it from dilation and joy; whether the cause thereof be known, as the remembrance of a sin or an offense, or of an omission, or be not known..

Al-Basit

The Unfolder, The Expander, The Releaser

AL-BASIT
The Reliever

The One who makes ample and plentiful all that is needed. The One who expands and amplifies all abundance. The One who makes the way wide and open. The One who stretches out a helping hand to mankind. The One whose open hand releases joy, comfort and abundance.

The One who infuses the soul into body. The One who has filled the heart with spiritual abundance. The One whose glory and abundance fill and expand the heart.

From the root b-s-t which has the following classical Arabic connotations: to expand, enlarge, extend; to grant abundance, to provide amply; to spread, widen, to make spacious; to extend a hand

The term Bāsit is not specifically used as a Beautiful Name in the Qur'ān.

The term Bāsit includes a powerful and majestic sense of infusing into something a gift which will grow and flourish in great abundance.

Al-Khafid

The Humbler, The One who Softens, The Lowerer

AL KHAAFIDH

The One who chooses the ones to be humbled, softened, made gentle. The One who decides which ones to weaken or diminish. The One who humbles the proud, haughty or insolent, to awaken them from their sleep.

From the root kh-f-d which has the following classical Arabic connotations: to lower, weaken, depress; to make humble, abase; to relax, diminish, subdue; to make gentle, tranquil, easy to deal with; to soften, make easy, facilitate

The name Khāfid is not specifically used as a Beautiful Name in the Qur'ān.

Rāfi' (uplifter) is the opposite of **Khāfid** (humbler).

The names Khāfid and Rāfi' are often used together to acknowledge the way that balance and harmony are established and maintained though the interplay of cause and effect.

Mudhill (dishonorer) is similar to, but much more intensive and unpleasant than, **Khāfid** (humbler). The phrase al Khāfid ur Rāfi' is often used to honor these complimentary attributes.

Ar-Rafi

The Uplifter, The Exalter

AR-RAFE
The Exalter

The One whose wisdom chooses the ones to be uplifted. The One who uplifts and elevates mankind above petty desires and selfishness. The One who makes it possible to rise above the differences and distinctions that divide mankind.

From the root r-f-' which has the following classical Arabic connotations: to raise or elevate something; to uplift, to take it up; to make high, lofty; to exalt, make honorable, make eminent; to bring a thing near

The name Rāfi' is not specifically used as a Beautiful Name in the Qur'ān.

Al-Mu'iz

The Honorer, The Strengthener, The Glorifier

AL MU'IZZ

The One who gives invincible strength and honor. The One who grants honor and power. The One who strengthens and glorifies. The One who makes it possible for someone or something to be respected, cherished and mighty.

From the root '-z-z which has the following classical Arabic connotations: to be mighty, potent, strong, powerful; to be high, elevated, noble, exalted; to be honorable, noble, glorious, illustrious; to be indomitable, invincible; to be respected, cherished, dearto be scarce, rare, precious, unattainable

The name Mu'izz is not specifically used as a Beautiful Name in the Qur'ān. The name al-'Azīz (mighty) is also from this same '-z-z root. **Mu'izz** (honorer) is the opposite of **Mudhill** (dishonorer).

Mu'izz (honorer) is similar to, but much more more intensive and glorious than, Rāfi' (uplifter).

Al-Mudhill

The Dishonorer, The Disgracer, The Degrader, The Humiliator

The One whose wisdom creates situations that are low and despicable. The One who creates the appearance of dishonor or degradation. The One whose wisdom produces circumstances of humiliation and disgrace.

From the root dh-l-l which has the following classical Arabic connotations:to be low, base, abject, paltry; to be vile, contemptible, despicable; to be inglorious, abased, humble; to be lowly, submissive, weak; to be tractable, easy, manageable

AL-MUZILL
The Humiliator

The name Mudhill is not specifically used as a Beautiful Name in the Qur'ān.

According to Classical Arabic definitions, Mudhill is an intensive epithet which denotes exceeding lowness or baseness.

Mudhill (dishonorer) is the opposite of Mu'izz (honorer).

Mudhill (dishonorer) is similar to, but much more intensive and unpleasant than, Khāfid (humbler).

As-Sami

The All-Hearing, The Ever-Listening

AS-SAMI
The Hearer Of All

The One whose hearing and attention comprehends everything. The One who pays attention to every supplication and invocation.

The One who listens to every voice. The One who hears and accepts every word, thought and secret. The One who listens to everything, perfectly, eternally, without limitations.

From the root s-m-' which has the following classical Arabic connotations:to hear, to listen; to accept, to receive, to be told; to pay attention to, pay regard to; to understand the meaning

This name is used in the Qur'ān. For example, see 17:1

The word samā' (often written sema in Turkish), which literally means hearing or paying attention to, is commonly used to describe the musical gatherings of the Sufis, especially the great whirling dance of the dervishes.

Al-Basir

The All-Seeing, The All-Perceiving, The All-Comprehending

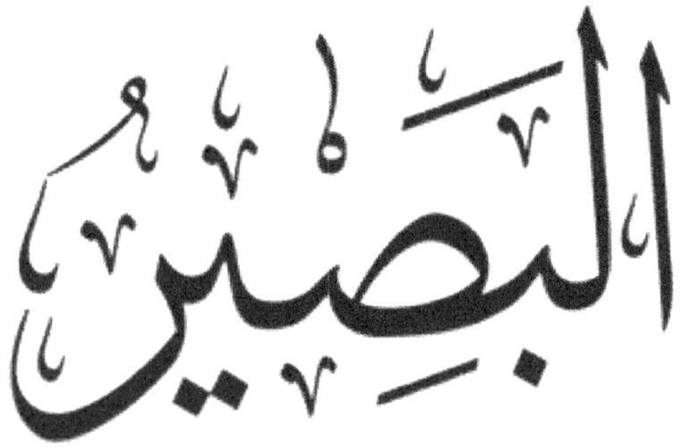

AL BASEER

The One whose insight sees all things clearly, both the apparent and the hidden. The One who sees and understands all that has been, and all that will be. The One who has insight into all things. The One who perceives every detail. The One who understands all things, both outer and inner. The One who has given to mankind the outer eye of the body, and the inner eye of the heart.

From the root b-s-r which has the following classical Arabic connotations: to see, behold, notice; to understand, to know; to perceive, to have insightto be acutely aware

This name is used in the Qur'ān. For example, see 17:1

Al-Hakam

The Judge, The Giver of Justice, The Arbitrator

The One who is the supreme arbitrating magistrate. The One who is the only true judge. The One who always delivers justice in every situation. The One whose judgments and decrees are never over-turned or thwarted. The One who makes the final decision of the nature of all matters. The One who arbitrates all disputes.

AL HAKAM

From the root h-k-m which has the following classical Arabic connotations: to be wise, knowing the true nature of things; to pass judgment, to decide, pass a verdict; to judge and pass sentence; to prevent or restrain from wrongdoing or corruption; to turn someone back from wrongdoing or ignorance

This name is used in the Qur'ān. For example, see 6:114

The words hakam and hakīm both arise from the same h-k-m root, but hakam is a verbal noun which emphasizes the delivery of justice, while hakīm is a noun which indicates the essential nature of the possessor of wisdom.

Al-Adl

The Equitable, The Impartial, The Just

AL-ADL
The Just, The Equitable

The One who rectifies and sets matters straight in a fair, impartial and equitable manner. The One who always acts justly. The One who delivers absolute justice. The One whose wisdom of justice is based upon complete knowledge of past, present and future.

From the root 'a-d-l which has the following classical Arabic connotations: to act justly, fairly; to be equitable, impartial; to adjust properly, to make even; to straighten, to rectify, to establish justice; to balance, counterbalance, to make equal, uniform; to turn one away from something, rightly direct; to make comfortable with what is right

The term 'Adl is not specifically used as a Beautiful Name in the Qur'ān.

Although a situation may seem unfair to us due to our limited understanding, the Supreme Justice is absolute and unerring in fairness and equality.

Al-Latif

The Most Subtle, The Gracious, The Refined and Benevolent

AL LATEEF

The One who is most subtle and gracious. The One whose nature is gentle, affectionate, courteous and refined. The One who is kind, gracious, and understanding, with regard for the subtle details of individual circumstances. The One whose actions are so fine and subtle that they may be imperceptible, beyond our comprehension. The One whose delicate perception reveals the subtleties of all things.

From the root l-t-f which has the following classical Arabic connotations: to be thin, delicate, refined, elegant, graceful; to be gentle, gracious, courteous, kindly; to be subtle, to know the obscurities of all affairs; to treat with regard for circumstances; to be most soothing and refined in manner; to treat with kindness, goodness, gentleness, benevolence, affection

This name is used in the Qur'ān. For example, see 67:14

The names Qahhār (ever-dominating, overpowering) and Latīf (subtle, refined) are sometimes used together to honor and appreciate the opposing, yet complementary, ways of the One

Al-Khabir

The Inner-Knowing, The Knower of Reality, The Knower of Inner Truth

AL KABEER

The One who knows the internal qualities and meanings of all things. The One who has perfect knowledge and understanding of the true reality of all things. The One who knows and understands the meaning of even the most hidden secrets. The One who know the inner truth of every condition and situation. The One who knows and understands secret requests and unspoken prayers. The One who knows and understands the real condition, the inner reality, of everything.

From the root kh-b-r which has the following classical Arabic connotations: to know, or be aware of the real inner nature of something; to have understanding of the inner, intrinsic nature of something; to know the reality of something; to know the secret inner state of something; to prove, try, test by experience (resulting in inner knowledge)

This name is used in the Qur'ān. For example, see 22:63

Related names: **'Alīm** denotes knowing with certainty, especially intuitive knowing, omniscience. **Khabīr** denotes an understanding of the inner qualities, secrets and true reality.

Al-Halim

The Most Serene, The Most Kind and Gentle, The Calm Abiding

The One who is kind, gracious and serene in all situations. The One who is calm and deliberate, never hasty, even with the rebellious and wrongdoers. The One whose manner is lenient and mild. The One who gives us the opportunity and situations to learn to be kind, gracious and patient.

From the root h-l-m which has the following classical Arabic connotations: to be forbearing, mild, lenient, clement; to be forgiving, gentle, deliberate; to be leisurely in manner, not hasty; to be calm, serene; to manage one's temper; to exhibit moderation

This name is used in the Qur'ān. For example, see 22:59

Related names: **Halīm** is the patience that arises from a sense of deep serenity, lenience, calm deliberation. **Sabūr** is the patience that arises by self-restraint, enduring something without complaint.

Al-Azim

The Supreme Glory, The Mighty Splendor, The Most Grand, The Greatest

The One who is greatest, mightiest, grandest and above all. The One who is of the greatest importance. The One who is magnificent, vast and most revered. The One who is of perfect and absolute greatness.

From the root 'a-z-m which has the following classical Arabic connotations: to be great, large, big; to be vast, huge, enormous; to be great in rank, importance or dignity; to be imposing, powerful, superior; to be magnificent, honored, revered, sublime; to be immense, stupendous, lofty; to be above imperfection

This name is used in the Qur'ān. For example, see 2:255

Al-Ghafur

The Forgiving, The Forgiver of Sins and Faults, The Perfectly Forgiving, The Pardoner

AL-GHAFUR
The forgiver & Hider Of Faults

The One who completely forgives our sins and faults. The One who accepts repentance and pardons sins and faults. The One who veils or forgives our faults and sins such that they are not seen by anyone else, not even the angels. The One who is the perfection of forgiveness. The One whose forgiving demonstrates excellence, completeness and perfection of forgiveness.

From the root gh-f-r which has the following classical Arabic connotations: to cover, veil, conceal, hide; to pardon, to forgive, to set aright; to cover a thing to protect it from dirt

This name is used in the Qur'ān. For example, see 40:3

Note that the root gh-f-r has given rise to three Beautiful Names that are all used in the Qur'ān: Ghaffār, Ghafūr and Ghāfir. However, only Ghaffār and Ghafūr were included in the list of 99 Names narrated by Tirmidhi.

In Qastalānī's commentary on Bukhārī, it is said that the root gh-f-r means a covering or protection which is either between man and the commission of sin [protecting, or watching over], or between sin and the effects of that sin [forgiving, veiling or concealing].

In al-Nihāyah (a dictionary of hadīth), it is said that Ghāfir refers to the One who protects us from the commission of sins, and that Ghafūr refers to the One who forgives our sins and faults.

Sheikh Tosun Bayrak portrays the differences as:

al-Ghāfir, the veiler of our faults from the eyes of other men; al-Ghafūr, who keeps the knowledge of our faults even from the angels; and al-Ghaffār who relieves us from the suffering of continual remembrance of our faults.

The Arabic word astaghfirullāh (sometimes written as astghfrallāh, estagfurullāh or estaferallāh) is from this same gh-f-r root, and is an invocation of Divine Protection having a range of possible connotations that include “Allāh please forgive me”, “Allāh please hide away my faults”, “Allāh please watch over me and protect me from faults”.

The Arabic lexicon and commentary Tāj al-'Arūs reminds us that truly asking for forgiveness must be by both word and deed, not by the tongue alone.

The names Ghafūr, Ghaffār and Ghāfir denote forgiving or protecting, while 'Afūw indicates complete removal or obliteration of the condition.

Ash-Shakur

The Most Grateful, The Most Appreciative, The Rewarder of Good Works

AL - SHAKUR
The Rewarder Of Thankfulness

The One who is most thankful for righteousness and bestows great rewards for good deeds. The One who gratefully gives large rewards, even for a small amount of good work. The One who acknowledges and bountifully rewards all acts of goodness, thankfulness and praise. The One who frequently and greatly approves, rewards and forgives.

From the root sh-k-r which has the following classical Arabic connotations: to praise or commend for a benefit or benefits; to acknowledge beneficence; to offer thanks, acknowledgement; to be thankful, grateful; to produce, supply, give forth bountifully

This name is used in the Qur'ān. For example, see 35:30

Al-Ali

The Exalted, The Most High

AL-ALI
The Highest

The One Who is above and exceeds all others. The Most High, above whom there is nothing higher. The One whose rank and station are the Most High. The One who is above and surpasses all that has ever been, all that there now is, and all that shall ever be.

From the root 'a-l-w which has the following classical Arabic connotations: to be high, elevated, lofty; to be exalted, to rise up, to ascend; to be higher, to exceed, surpass; to overcome, overwhelm; to advance, promote, rise above; to mount, be overtop, eminent

This name is used in the Qur'ān. For example, see 2:255

Al-Kabir

The Most Great, The Greatest, The Perfection of Greatness

The One whose essence is the perfection of greatness. The One who is incomparably great. The One whose greatness is beyond measure. The One whose nature is Greatness. The One whose own essence is unimaginably great perfection.

From the root k-b-r which has the following classical Arabic connotations: to be great in rank, dignity, nobility, majesty; to be great in size, vast, formidable; to be great in age, oldest; to be great in learning, most knowing; to have rights above all others

AL-KABIR
The Greatest

This name is used in the Qur'ān. For example, see 22:62

Kabīr is a less intensive form which honors the One as being the essence of greatness.

Related names: **Jalīl** is considered to be greatness in attributes.

Azīm is greatness in both attributes and self.

Mutakabbir is an empathic form which denotes actively using rights, privileges, rank and attributes that are above and beyond the rights of everyone else.

The phrase Allāhu Akbar, uses this same k-b-r root and means Allāh is the greatest

---

Al-Hafiz

The Preserver, The Protector, The Guardian

AL-HAFIZ
The Preserver

The One whose power preserves the heavens and the earth. The One who is the guardian and preserver of all the worlds. The One who protects and preserves all of creation from perishing. The One who is vigilantly guarding every detail of all that has been created. The One who remembers and preserves all that has ever been and all that is, while keeping under Divine protection the knowledge of all that shall be.

From the root h-f-z which has the following classical Arabic connotations: to preserve, guard, protect; to keep, retain, take care of, tend; to prevent from perishing or becoming lost; to be watchful, mindful, attentive, vigilant

This name is used in the Qur'ān. For example, see 11:57

Al-Muqit

AL-MUQIT
The Nourisher

The Sustainer, The Nourisher, The Preserver, The Maintainer, The Guardian

The One who has the ability to nourish all of creation. The One who maintains all that exists. The One who oversees all things. The One who guards and preserves. The One who is the sustainer of all, the seen and the unseen, the outer and the inner.

From the root q-w-t which has the following classical Arabic connotations: to feed, nourish; to supply, sustain; to keep, preserve, guard; to witness, observe, watch over

This name is used in the Qur'ān. For example, see 4:85

Sustenance includes not only a supply of food for the body, but also an endless supply of loving-kindness for the heart.

Al-Hasib

The Reckoner, The Accountant, The Sufficient

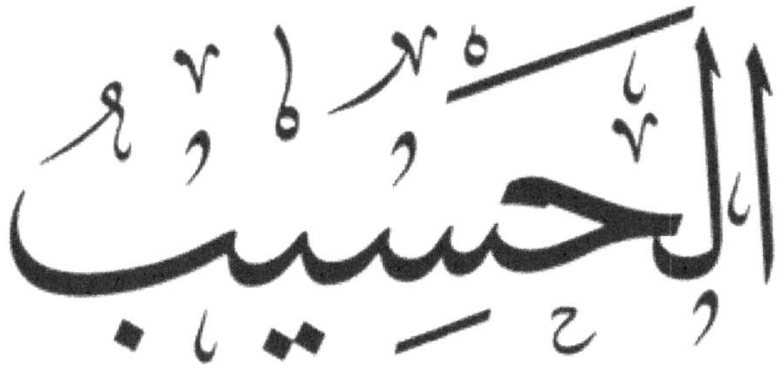

AL HASEEB

The One who takes account of all actions and reckons them. The One who is the measurer and accountant of every deed. The One who is sufficient to meet all needs. The One who gives what is sufficient and necessary in every situation.

From the root h-s-b which has the following classical Arabic connotations: to reckon, number, count, calculate, compute, think; to give without sparing or scanting; to give without the receiver's expectation; to suffice, to be sufficient, or without measure

This name is used in the Qur'ān. For example, see 4:86

Al-Jalil

The Glorious, The Majestic, The Independent, The Sublime, The Resplendent

AL JALEEL

The One who is majestic, glorious, sublime. The One who is great and above all in rank and dignity. The One who is above all, superior, independent. The One who is the owner and the source of all attributes of greatness and majesty. The One whose greatness and majesty are immeasurable and cannot be comprehended by the senses. The One whose glorious nature is indicated by the great things that are created.

From the root j-l-l which has the following classical Arabic connotations: to be supremely great; to be glorious, majestic; to be sublime; to be high, lofty, far above, independent

The term Jalīl is not specifically used as a Beautiful Name in the Qur'ān.

The word Jalāl comes from this same root and is translated as greatness, loftiness, sublimity, majesty.

Al-Karim

The Most Generous, The Most Bountiful, The Most Esteemed, The Beneficent

AL KAREEM

The One who is the most generous, both physically and spiritually. The One who is continually giving forth the grandest and most precious bounty. The One whose kind, noble and generous essence is most esteemed, valued and honored. The One who endlessly gives all manner of precious gifts, including support and refuge. The One who is eternally giving, even unto those who may not seem (to us) to be deserving.

From the root k-r-m which has the following classical Arabic connotations: to be noble, grand, high minded; to be generous, giving, beneficent; to be highly esteemed, honored, prized, valued; to be excellent, precious, valuable, rare; to be productive, fruitful

This name is used in the Qur'ān. For example, see 82:6

Ar-Raqib

The Watcher, The All-Observing, The Witness, The Watchful

AR-RAQIB
The Watchful One

The One who watches all things. The One who is the ever vigilant witness. The One from whose observation nothing is hidden. The One who observes all thoughts, deeds and feelings.

From the root r-q-b which has the following classical Arabic connotations: to look, watch, be vigilant; to expect, anticipate, await; to keep an eye on, detect, observe; to be mindful of; to be a spy, scout, observer; to regard, hold in consideration, respect

This name is used in the Qur'ān. For example, see 4:1

Al-Mujib

The Fullfiller of Prayers, The Answerer of Prayers, The Responsive One

The One who answers prayers. The One who responds to needs. The One who penetrates through every obstacle in order to respond. The One who responds to an invitation. The One who responds to requests, prayers and praise by means of gifts and acceptance.

AL-MUJIB
The Responder To Prayer

From the root j-w-b which has the following classical Arabic connotations: to answer, reply, respond, accept; to cut, pierce, penetrate; to have a dialog or conference; to comply with a desire when invited to do so

This name is used in the Qur'ān. For example, see 11:61

Mankind's share of this name, to respond when we are called upon, is described in the Qur'ān (2:186):

"When my servants ask thee concerning Me I am indeed close (to them); I listen to the prayer of every supplicant when he calleth on Me; let them also with a will listen to My call and believe in Me; that they may walk in the right way."

Al-Wasi

The All-Embracing, The All-Sufficient, The All-Pervading, The Boundless

Al-Wasi
The All-Comprehending

The One whose expansive essence holds and embraces all of creation. The One who is vast without limit. The One of limitless capacity and abundance. The One who is ample-giving, all-embracing and all-pervading. The One whose power, knowledge, mercy and generosity are boundless.

From the root w-s-' which has the following classical Arabic connotations: to be sufficient in capacity or size, wide, spacious; to be ample, plentiful, bountiful, rich; to comprehend, embrace, include, take in, pervade

This name is used in the Qur'ān. For example, see 2:115

Al-Hakim

The Most Wise, The Most Judicious

AL HAKEEM

The One who is Most Knowing. The One who possesses the quality of discrimination between right and wrong and who is free from error or misunderstanding. The One who has perfect wisdom. The One whose wisdom turns mankind back from wrongdoing. The One who is qualified to judge the worth of all things.

From the root h-k-m which has the following classical Arabic connotations: to prevent or restrain from wrongdoing or corruption; to turn someone back from wrongdoing or ignorance; to be wise, knowing the true nature of things; to pass judgment, to decide, pass a verdict; to judge and pass sentence

This name is used in the Qur'ān. For example, see 2:32

The words hakam and hakīm both arise from the same h-k-m root, but hakam is a verbal noun which emphasizes the delivery of justice, while hakīm is a noun which indicates the essential nature of the possessor of wisdom.

Al-Wadud

The Most Loving, The Most Affectionate, The Beloved, The Loving-Kindness

AL-WADUD
The Loving One

The One who loves. The One who is the source of all love and loving-kindness. The One Love. The One who is most affectionate. The Beloved. The One who is deserving of all love and affection. The One who is the goal of the highest love.

From the root w-d-d which has the following classical Arabic connotations: to love; to be affectionate; to long for, to desire, to wish for

This name is used in the Qur'ān. For example, see 85:14

Al-Majid

The All-Glorious, The Glorious and Majestic, The Most Honorable and Praiseworthy

AL MAAJID

The One who is glorious, dignified, majestic, bountiful and exceedingly generous. The One whose essence is the perfection of majesty and glory, abounding in goodness. The One whose majesty, glory and generosity deserve all praise and honor.

From the root m-j-d which has the following classical Arabic connotations: to be glorious, dignified, majestic, noble, honorable; to be lauded, exalted, sublime; to be liberal, bountiful, exceedingly generous

This name is used in the Qur'ān. For example, see 11:73

Al-Majīd indicates the One whose essential nature is glorious, dignified, noble and honorable, and whose essential nature is to give liberally and bountifully.

Al-Mājid denotes the One who is praised for the existence of the specific deeds and attributes of great glory, dignity, nobility, honor, and exceeding generosity.

That is, the name al-Majīd denotes the glorious essential nature of the One, while the name al-Mājid honors specific deeds performed by the One.

Abū Hāmid al-Ghazālī says that the name Al-Majīd expresses the combined meanings of al-Jalīl (the majestic), al-Wahhāb (the bestower) and al-Karīm (the generous).

Al-Baith

The Awakener, The Resurrector, The Arouser, The Dispatcher

AL- BA'IS
The Resurrector

The One who chooses who shall awaken and who shall be sent forth. The One who decides who to raise up. The One who awakens the dead. The One who resurrects. The One who rouses up mankind. The One who sends Light into the worlds. The One who dispatches messengers into the world.

From the root b-'a-th which has the following classical Arabic connotations: to call forth, awaken; to raise up from sleep or death; to resurrect; to delegate, consign; to send, send out, make manifest

The term Bā'ith is not specifically used as a Beautiful Name in the Qur'ān.

Ash-Shahid

The Omniscient Witness, The Certifier, The Testifier

ASH-SHAHID
The Witness

The One who directly and ever-presently observes everything in creation. The One from whose knowledge nothing is hidden. The One who witnesses both that which is seen and that which is unseen. The One who has knowledge of all that happens everywhere at all times. The One who is the ultimate witness on judgment day.

From the root sh-h-d which has the following classical Arabic connotations: to bear witness; to offer testimony; to have knowledge of, to experience; to be present with

This name is used in the Qur'ān. For example, see 85:9

Al-Haqq

The Truth, The Reality, The Just and Correct, The Truly Existing

The One who is the truth, the real, and the truly-existing. The One whose essence is the only substance and the only reality. The One whose essence is wisdom, justice, right, rightness. The One who is just, right, proper, correct. The One whose essence is unavoidable. The One who acts in accord with the needs of every situation. The One through whom all righteousness, justice, and truth are revealed.

AL HAQQ

From the root h-q-q which has the following classical Arabic connotations: to be suitable to the requirements of wisdom, justice, truth or fact; to be in accord with the needs of the situation; to be true, right, correct, just, proper; to be genuine, authentic, real, sound, substantial; to be established, confirmed as fact; to be necessary, requisite, justified; to be unavoidable, inevitable, due; to be binding, obligatory, incumbent upon; to happen without doubt or uncertainty

This name is used in the Qur'ān. For example, see 22:62

Al-Wakil

The Trustee, The Guardian, The Disposer of Affairs, The Advocate

The One and only One who can be entrusted with the management and resolution of all affairs. The One who is the supreme trustee, guardian and administrator of all things. The One who may be trusted to do better for us that we can do for ourselves. The One who can be entrusted to provide the perfect resolution for all matters.

AL-WAKIL
The Trustee

From the root w-k-l which has the following classical Arabic connotations: to appoint or entrust for the care or management of something; to have a commissioned agent, a guardian of one's interests; to rely upon, confide in, lean upon, submit to

This name is used in the Qur'ān. For example, see 6:102

This same root w-k-l also gives rise to the word tawakkul (or tawakul), which indicates submitting to Allāh, relying upon Allāh, putting one's trust in Allāh.

One's trust in Allāh should not be allowed to breed laziness or lack of care, but rather one must always do one's own personal best, and then leave the rest to Allāh, as indicated so clearly by the Prophet Muhammad when he said: **"Tie your camel, then put your trust in Allāh."**

Al-Qawi

The Supremely Strong, The Inexhaustible Strength

The One whose strength is supreme. The One who possesses unlimited strength and endurance. The One whose vigor and strength prevail over all of creation. The One who is beyond all weakness. The One whose strength is inexhaustible.

AL-QAWI
The Possessor Of All Strength

From the root q-w-y which has the following classical Arabic connotations: to be strong, vigorous, potent; to be robust, hardy, sturdy; to have sufficient strength or power; to prevail over

This name is used in the Qur'ān. For example, see 42:19

Related names: **Qawī** - Strong - the One who is all-mighty and possesses inexhaustible strength. **Matīn** - Firm - the One whose nature it is to be firm, determined and steadfast. **Qahhār** - Dominator - the One who dominates, conquers, overpowers. **Muqtadir** - Determiner - the One who uses supreme power to enforce whatever Divine wisdom decrees or decides.

Al-Matin

The Firm, The Steadfast, The Ever-Constant

AL MATEEN

The One who is most steadfast and solid. The One whose strength produces certitude. The One who is loyal, firm and constant. The One whose nature is the utmost firmness and steadfastness. The One who can easily overcome anything through supreme firmness and strength of determination.

From the root m-t-n which has the following classical Arabic connotations: to be strong, stout, firm, hard; to be solid, robust; to be steadfast, certain, sure; to possess any quality in a strong degree; the hard outer or apparent part of something; elevated and hard ground

This name is used in the Qur'ān. For example, see 51:58

Al-Wali

The Protecting Friend, The Loving Defender, The Nearby Guardian

Al-Wali
The Protecting Friend

The One who is lover, protector and lord. The One who is lovingly supportive. The One who is the protecting friend. The One who guards and rules all of creation. The One who lovingly guides mankind to turn toward the path of righteousness.

From the root w-l-y which has the following classical Arabic connotations: to be near, close, nearby; to be a friend, helper, supporter; to defend, guard (lit. friendly dealing); to be in charge, to turn one toward something; to be the master, owner, lord

This name is used in the Qur'ān. For example, see 42:28

According to Rāghib, the root w-l-y indicates one thing taking place by the side of another in such a way that there is no distance between them, both physical and figurative. Wālī emphasizes the aspects of lordship, ownership and mastery of the One who is also friend and helper.

Walī emphasizes the nearness and loving, protective, guarding and helping aspects of the One who is also the lord and master.

Al-Hamid

The Praiseworthy, The Laudable One, The Object of all Praise

Al-Hamid
The Praised One

The One who is praised and is praiseworthy. The One who is worthy of all thankful praise. The One and only One who truly deserves all praise, honor and adoration.

The One who is exalted, praised and glorified by the very existence of creation. The One who deserves every manner of praise, exaltation and glorification, both public and private.

From the root h-m-d which has the following classical Arabic connotations: to praise, to laud with deep feelings of adoration and submission; to praise one for something done by that one's own will; to speak well of, honor, commend; to eulogize

This name is used in the Qur'ān. For example, see 22:64

The root h-m-d denotes the highest praise and honoring being offered with deep feelings of thankfulness, admiration, humility and submission.

Hamīd indicates one who is praised and praiseworthy due to his own inherent qualities, not due to any specific favor, and who does glorious works entirely of his own volition and according to his own will.

Shakūr denotes appreciation, gratitude or praise for some particular favor.

The root h-m-d is also the basis of the expression al-hamdulillāh (all praise is for Allah), as well as being the root of the names Ahmad (praiseworthy), Mahmūd (praised) and Muhammad (much praised, or repeatedly praised).

Al-Muhsi

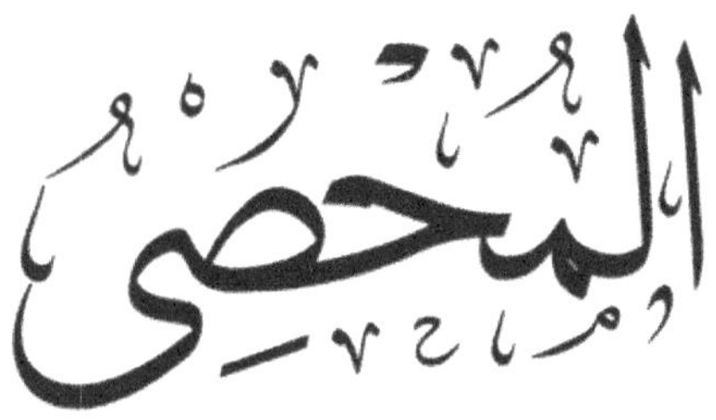
AL MUHSEE

The Reckoner, The Appraiser, The Accountant

The One who knows the details of each and every thing. The One who possesses all quantitative knowledge. The One who comprehends everything, small or great, inner or outer. The One who registers and records every thought and deed.

From the root h-s-y which has the following classical Arabic connotations: to number, count, reckon, compute; to collect in an aggregate by numbering; to register or record something; to take an account of something; to comprehend or know altogether; to possess full comprehension

The name Mushī is not specifically used as a Beautiful Name in the Qur'ān.

Al-Mubdi

The Originator, The Starter, The Beginner

AL MUBDI

The One who is the originator of all creation. The One who is the founder of creation. The One who begins all things. The One who initiates all creation.

From the root b-d-' which has the following classical Arabic connotations: to begin, create, make something new; to make something be first, have precedence; to contrive a new thing; to invent, to do first; to commence, start, at the beginning

The term Mubdi' is not specifically used as a Beautiful Name in the Qur'ān.

The terms al-Mubdi' (the Starter) and al-Mu'īd (the Restorer) are often used together in the hadith, and are also paired together by many commentators including al-Ghazālī who described them as:

al-Mubdi' (the Beginner) **al-Mu'īd** (the Restorer) - these terms mean the One who bestows existence, and when this origination is not preceded by something like it, it is called a beginning; but when it is preceded by something like it, then it is called restoration; all things began with Him and are restored to Him; began in Him and in Him are restored.

And similarly, the two attributes al-Mubdi' al-Mu'īd are defined together in the lexicon Tāj al-'Arūs as: “He who createth mankind, and who returneth them after life to death.”

In some Classical Arabic literature, the participles Mubdi' and Badī' are used interchangeably. However, in many Qur'ān commentaries, these terms are used to describe slightly different attributes, with the name Mubdi' emphasizing the initiation of creation, while Badī' emphasizes the awesome innovation of such creation.

Related names: **Mubdi'** is the One who initiates, starts or begins the production or creation of all things. **Badī'** is the One who creates in awesome, wonderful, amazingly original ways that have no precedent whatsoever. **Mu'īd** is the One who repeats, restores and revives that which had been previously invented. **Bāri'** is the way the One works with substances, often creating from existing matter, making and evolving that which is free and clear of imperfections, free and clear of any other thing. **Khāliq** is the One who continues to plan, measure out and create and who has the power to change things from one state to another, in and out of existence. **Musawwir** is the One who arranges forms and colors, and who is the shaper of beauty.

Al-Mu'id

The Restorer, The Reviver, The Renewer, The Re-Creator

AL MUEED

The One who restores and repeats all that has been created. The One who constantly renews, revives and repeats creation. The One who restores and revives the spiritual essence of every person. The One who repeatedly renews mankind's proper relationship with goodness. The One who repeatedly restores and revives creation, both physically and spiritually.

From the root '-w-d which has the following classical Arabic connotations: to return to something; to repeat, reproduce, to come back; to restore, to renew

The term Mu'īd is not specifically used as a Beautiful Name in the Qur'ān.

The terms al-Mubdi' (the Starter) and al-Mu'īd (the Restorer) are often used together in the hadith, and are also paired together by many commentators including al-Ghazālī who described them as:

al-Mubdi' (the Beginner) al-Mu'īd (the Restorer) - these terms mean the One who bestows existence, and when this origination is not preceded by something like it, it is called a beginning; but when it is preceded by something like it, then it is called restoration.... all things began with Him and are restored to Him; began in Him and in Him are restored.

And similarly, the two attributes al-Mubdi' al-Mu'īd are defined in the lexicon Tāj al-'Arūs as: "He who createth mankind, and who returneth them after life to death."

Al-Muhyi

The Bestower of Life, The Giver of Life, The Reviver

AL MUHYI

The One who created life. The One who makes all things live. The One who decides what will be vitalized and brought to life. The One, and only One, who can bring something to life. The One who brings the heart to life. The One who revives and grants wholeness, even to the spiritually dead.

From the root h-y-y which has the following classical Arabic connotations: to live, to be living; to become apparent, distinct; to animate, to revive; to vitalize, to call into being; to be whole, sound; to call, summon, invite, hasten

This name is used in the Qur'ān. For example, see 41:39

The name al-Hayy (ever-living) is also from this same h-y-y root.

The names Mumīt (the life-taker) and Muhyī (the life-giver) are opposites.

Al-Mumit

The Creator of Death, The Slayer, The Life-Taker

AL MUMEET

The One who created the inanimate world, to which all living forms return. The One who ordains what shall become lifeless. The One who creates the appearance of death, physically or spiritually.

From the root m-w-t which has the following classical Arabic connotations: to die, pass away, burn out, be lifeless; to be quiet, still, calm; to be inanimate; to be deprived of sensation; to be spiritually dead, lacking spiritual life

The name Mumīt is not specifically used as a Beautiful Name in the Qur'ān.

The names Mumīt (the life-taker) and Muhyī (the life-giver) are opposites.

The esoteric meaning of this name is well summarized by the Sufi saying that one should strive to "die before you die". In such a light, al-Mumīt is the One who has the power to kill lusts and attachments, the One who can slay the sense of separateness, the One who can quiet the ego.

Al-Hayy

The Living, The Alive, The Everlasting, The Deathless, The Ever-Living

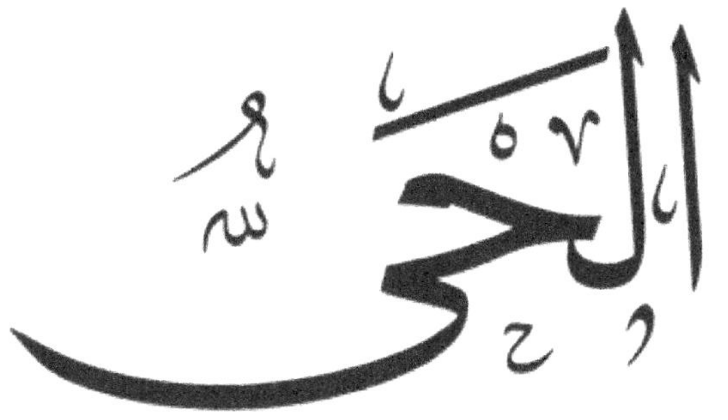

AL HAYY

The One who is undying, everlasting. The One who is eternally whole and sound. The One Life from whom all life arises. The One who calls all life into being. The One who animates all life and who makes each living thing different and distinct.

From the three letter root h-y-y, which has the following classical Arabic connotations: to live, to be living; to become apparent, distinct; to animate, to revive; to vitalize, to call into being; to be whole, sound; to call, summon, invite, hasten

This name is used in the Qur'ān. For example, see 2:255

The attributes of al-Hayy and al-Qayyūm are often used to together, with al-Hayy signifying the attribute of ever-lasting life, and al-Qayyūm signifying the attribute of self-existing life. Thus, the attributes of al-Hayy and al-Qayyūm express two aspects of the One Life.

Abu Hurairah reported that whenever the Prophet, peace be upon him, was faced with a serious difficulty, he would raise his head to the sky and supplicate, "Subhan-Allah al-'Azim (glory be to Allah, the Mighty)." And when he implored seriously and strongly, he would say "Ya Hayyu, Ya Qayyum (O Ever-Living One, O Self-Existing One)." (Tirmidhi Hadith Collection)

Al-Qayyum

The Self-Subsisting, The Self-Existing One upon Whom all others depend

AL-QAYYUM
The Sef-Existing One

The One whose nature it is to exist. The One who is free of any dependence on anything else for existence. The One through whom all things arise. The One by whom all things are eternally managed aright. The Ever-Living, Self-Existing One who is the foundation upon which all things exist.

From the root q-w-m which has the following classical Arabic connotations: to stand up, to rise up, to ascend, become high; to begin, to start, to come to pass; to arise, to set out; to be on-going, to exist; to be founded, to be built on; to undertake, to carry out, to manage; to make aright, straighten out, accurate, exact; to make righteous, upright

This name is used in the Qur'ān. For example, see 2:255

The attributes of al-Hayy and al-Qayyūm are often used to together, with al-Hayy signifying the attribute of ever-lasting life, and al-Qayyūm signifying the attribute of self-existing life. Thus, the attributes of al-Hayy and al-Qayyūm express two aspects of the One Life.

Abu Hurairah reported that whenever the Prophet, peace be upon him, was faced with a serious difficulty, he would raise his head to the sky and supplicate, "Subhan-Allah al-'Azim (glory be to Allah, the Mighty)." And when he implored seriously and strongly, he would say "Ya Hayyu, Ya Qayyum (O Ever-Living One, O Self-Existing One upon Whom we all depend)." (hadith of Tirmidhi)

The attribute of al-Qayyūm is also nicely described by the words of Acts 17:28 which say: "in Him we live and move and have our being"

The name al-Qayyūm also has much the same meaning as the Hebrew phrase in Exodus 3:14 which is written as: "I am that I am", or "I am that which I have become".

As Sri Aurobindo wrote in his commentary of the Isha Upanishad:

God is the only Being and all other existences are only His becomings.

The word mustaqīm, also from this same q-w-m root, means straight, righteous, upright, rising upwards or ascending.

Al-Wajid

The Finder, The All-Perceiving, The Wealthy, The Resourceful

AL-WAJID
The Finder

The One who has discovered and obtained everything. The One who perceives and possesses everything. The One who has no wants and who lacks nothing.

From the root w-j-d which has the following classical Arabic connotations: to find, discover, attain what was sought; to become aware of something, to perceive, to experience; to gain or possess wealth, property, resources; to be rich, to have abundance; to be without wants

The name Wājid is not specifically used as a Beautiful Name in the Qur'ān.

The ancient roots of wājid point toward an open hand holding of every manner of abundance.

Al-Majid

The Noble, The Generous, The Magnificent

The One whose deeds are glorious, dignified, noble, honorable and exceedingly generous. The One whose deeds and ways are noble, great and bountiful. The One who shows mankind the highest, most perfect example of goodness, richness, and generosity.

AL MAJEED

From the root m-j-d which has the following classical Arabic connotations: to be glorious, dignified, noble and honorable; to be lauded, exalted, sublime; to be liberal, bountiful, exceedingly generous

The name Mājid is not specifically used as a Beautiful Name in the Qur'ān.

Al-Majīd indicates the One whose essential nature is glorious, dignified, noble and honorable, and whose essential nature is to give liberally and bountifully.

Al-Mājid denotes the One who is praised for the specific deeds and attributes of great glory, dignity, nobility, honor, and exceeding generosity.

That is, the name al-Majīd denotes the glorious essential nature of the One, while the name al-Mājid honors specific deeds performed by the One.

Al-Wahid

The One, The Creator of Diversity from Unity, The Manifestation of Unity

The One unique starting point from which all else has arisen. The One source from which all of creation springs forth. The One whose unity includes all that appears as diverse, separate or individual.

From the root w-h-d which has the following classical Arabic connotations: to be one, to be made one, to be called one; to connect, join, unite; to be unique, singular; to be one apart from others

This name is used in the Qur'ān. For example, see 39:4

The ancient roots of Ahad point toward to the essential qualities which describe Unity, while the ancient roots of Wāhid point toward the manifestations which arise from that Unity.

That which is Ahad cannot be divided into parts, or any parts distinguished. That which is Wāhid has the appearance of being divisible into separate parts, or being comprised of separate parts.

Wāhid indicates the solitary Starting Point, the One Source, the First of the Many, from which all of creation has arisen as manifestations of Unity. From a human point of view, the manifestations may appear separate and diverse, but in reality they are One.

Al-Ahad

The One and Only, The Unity, The Sole One

The One who has ever been and ever remains alone. The incomparable, unequalled, indivisible One. The One who is the essence of Unity. The Sole One. The One and Only One. The One who has no second [that shares] in the lordship, nor in the essence, nor in the attributes. The One who was not begotten and has never begotten. The One who depends upon no other, and to Whom there is no likeness. The One in whom all names, attributes and relationships are united.

From the root a-h-d which has the following classical Arabic connotations:

to be one
to be the only one, one alone, sole
to unite, unify

This name is used in the Qur'ān. For example, see 112:1

The ancient roots of Ahad point toward to the essential qualities which describe Unity, while the ancient roots of Wāhid point toward the manifestations which arise from that Unity.

That which is Ahad cannot be divided into parts, or any parts distinguished. That which is Wāhid has the appearance of being divisible into separate parts, or being comprised of separate parts.

Ahad is used to refer to the One, the sole One, the One who was not begotten and who has ever been alone, the One who has no second, the Indivisible.

As-Samad

The Eternal, The Everlasting, The Satisfier of Every Need

AS SAMAD

The One who is eternal and above whom there is none. The One who is unaffected, unchanged, and without any needs. The One who is besought by all, and who is above all. The One who can satisfy every need and without whom no affair could be accomplished. The One who satisfies every need as it should be satisfied, and not necessarily as mankind might imagine. The One who is the sole recourse, the only one to turn to. The One upon whom all depend, yet who does not depend on any.

From the root s-m-d which has the following classical Arabic connotations: to endeavor to reach or attain something; to turn to, to need; to direct oneself toward or aim toward something; to set up, to erect something; to remain unaffected, unchanged; to be sublime, everlasting

This name is used in the Qur'ān. For example, see 112:2

Al-Qadir

The All-Capable, The Most Able, The All-Powerful

AL-QADIR

The All Powerfull

The One who possesses the power and the ability to measure-out anything and everything. The One who has the capability to make any decree and to determine what will be. The One whose decree determines the measure and distribution of all things. The One who does as He wills, acting or not acting in accord with whatever He decides.

From the root q-d-r which has the following classical Arabic connotations: to measure something; to make manifest the measure of something; to distribute or apportion (as though by measure), measure-out; to decree, to ordain, to decide a matter (as though measuring it to fit); to exercise thought in preparing something, to make use of reason (measuring out); to have the power to accomplish, to be rendered able, capable; to be able to prevail, to be empowered, to have control over

This name is used in the Qur'ān. For example, see 77:23, 6:37

Muqtadir is an intensive form of the root q-d-r which emphasizes the Supreme Power to enforce or enact whatever Divine wisdom decides; being omnipotent, having the ability to do everything.

Qādir is a less intensive form of the root q-d-r which describes the attribute of being able to decree, ordain, appoint, measure-out, decide.

These both involve power in the sense of power being the intention by which something comes into being according to a certain measure and a certain willful decree, as in saying 'kun' (Be!), and it is.

Al-Muqtadir

The All-Determining, The Prevailing Ordainer, The Powerful Determiner

The One whose supreme power determines and delivers the suitable measure of all things. The One whose decisions always prevail. The One who has power and ability to ordain all things. The One who is empowered to do whatever wisdom decides. The One who has the power and ability to decide the outcome of all matters. The One whose power enforces all decrees and ordains the course of all affairs. The One whose decree prevails in every situation.

AL-MUQTADIR

The Creator Of All Power

From the root q-d-r which has the following classical Arabic connotations: to measure something, know the measure of something to distribute, allot or apportion the suitable measure; to decree, to ordain, to decide a matter (as though measuring it to fit); to exercise thought in preparing something, to make use of reason; to intend or determine something; to have the power to accomplish, to be rendered able; to be able to prevail, to be empowered

This name is used in the Qur'ān. For example, see 54:55

Qādir, from this same q-d-r root, indicates the supreme ability to make a decree or ordain something, while Muqtadir points to the supreme power by which that decree is enacted.

That is, Muqtadir is an intensive form of the root q-d-r which emphasizes the use Supreme Power to actively enforce whatever Divine wisdom decides.

The Arabic prefix mu at the beginning of the word points toward the means by which something happens, or the embodiment of an action, leading to translations such as the one who is, or the one who does (similar to the suffix er in English).

Qādir is a less intensive form of the root q-d-r which describes the attribute of being able to decree, ordain, appoint or decide.

Related names: **Qawī** - Strong - the One who is all-mighty and possesses inexhaustible strength. **Matīn** - Firm - the One whose nature it is to be firm, determined and steadfast. **Qahhār** - Dominator - the One who dominates, conquers, overpowers. **Qādir** - the One whose nature it is to decree, ordain, appoint, measure-out, decide. **Muqtadir** - the One whose supreme power enforces whatever Divine wisdom decrees or decides; omnipotent, able to do everything.

Al-Muqaddim

The Promoter, The One who Brings Forward, The Expediter

AL-MUQADDIM
The Expediter

The One who moves things forward. The One who grants advancement. The One who expedites things. The One who advances or promotes.

From the root q-d-m which has the following classical Arabic connotations: to precede, to come before; to head, to lead; to offer, to bring forward; to make foremost, to put at the front; to advance, to promote; to exist without beginning

The name Muqaddim is not specifically used as a Beautiful Name in the Qur'ān.

The names Muqaddim (promoter) and Mu'akhkhir (delayer) are opposites.

Al-Mu'akhkhir

The Delayer, The Postponer

AL-MUWAKH'KHIR
The Delayer

The One who delays or postpones. The One who puts off advancement. The One who holds back or keeps something back to put it in its proper place. The One who causes something to lag behind.

From the root a-kh-r which has the following classical Arabic connotations: to cause to go back, backwards, retreat, recede; to retire, to drive back; to put behind or after; to cause to remain behind, hang back, lag behind; to postpone, put off, delay, retard

The name Mu'akhkhir is not specifically used as a Beautiful Name in the Qur'ān.

The name al-ākhir (last) also comes from this same a-kh-r root, and is the opposite of awwal (first). The name Mu'akhkhir (delayer) is the opposite of Muqaddim (promoter).

Al-Awwal

The First One, The Pre-Existing

The One who is the first, the beginning, the foremost. The Prior-Existing One who existed before all of creation. The One who was before any thing or any being. The One who is the cause of all the worlds. The One who is the beginning of every action, command or thought.

From the root a-w-l which has the following classical Arabic connotations: to be first, principle, to be before; to come back to, to return; to precede, to be the first part; to be foremost;

This name is used in the Qur'ān. For example, see 57:3

Awwal (first) and ākhir (last) are complementary attributes.

Al-Akhir

The Last, The End and The Ultimate

The One who remains after all of creation has passed away. The One who is the last, the conclusion, the ultimate. The One who is behind all of creation. The One beyond whom there is nothing.

From the root a-kh-r which has the following classical Arabic connotations: to put back, to put behind, to be latter; to postpone, to put at the end; to be last, final, ultimate

This name is used in the Qur'ān. For example, see 57:3

Awwal (first) and ākhir (last) are complementary attributes. The name al-Mu'akhkhir (the delayer) also comes from this same a-kh-r root.

Az-Zahir

The Manifest, The Conspicuous, The Evident

The One who has manifest all of creation and who is manifest in all of creation. The One whose nature and existence is demonstrated in all of creation. The One whose essence and attributes are shown throughout all of creation. The One who is above creation, yet who is made visible through creation.

From the root z-h-r which has the following classical Arabic connotations: to be visible, manifest, obvious, clear, distinct; to open, to come out, to cause to appear after being concealed; to be conspicuous, distinct; to ascend, mount, have higher status; to have the upper hand, subdue, overcome; to endorse, help, aid, support others, render superior

AZ-ZAHIR
The Manifest One

This name is used in the Qur'ān. For example, see 57:3

The ancient root of z-h-r points toward that which goes from the center and spreads out, disperses or radiates into being, which is to say that it becomes outwardly manifest.

Zāhir (manifest) and **Bātin** (hidden) are complementary attributes. Zāhir is that which is outward, manifest, apparent, visible. Bātin is that which is inward, concealed, obscured.

Al-Batin

The Hidden, The Secret One, The Inner One, The Knower of Hidden Things

The One who is veiled from our sensory perception. The One who is unseen, yet whose existence and essence are made known through signs. The One who knows the inner states, inner circumstances and inner thoughts of all of creation. The One who enters unseen into all of creation. The One who is concealed within all of creation. The One who is the secret inner companion.

Al-Batin
The Hidden One

From the root b-t-n which has the following classical Arabic connotations: to be concealed, to lie hidden; to penetrate into, to be inside

This name is used in the Qur'ān. For example, see 57:3

Bātin and Zāhir are opposites. Zāhir is that which is outward, manifest, apparent, visible. Bātin is that which is inward, concealed, obscured.

Al-Wali

AL-WALI
The Governer

The Sole Governor, The Friendly Lord, The Protective Ruler

The One who is the sole planner, implementer, governor and ruler of all things. The One who is the supportive, helpful master of all things. The One who is the friendly and protective ruler and governor of all of creation.

From the root w-l-y which has the following classical Arabic connotations: to be near, close, nearby; to be a friend, helper, supporter, maintainer; to defend, guard (lit. friendly dealing); to be in charge, to turn one toward something; to be the master, owner, lord

The name Wālī is not specifically used as a Beautiful Name in the Qur'ān.

Wālī emphasizes the aspects of lordship, ownership and mastery of the One who is also friend and helper. Walī emphasizes the nearness and protective, supportive, guarding aspects of the One who is also the lord and master.

Al-Muta'ali

The Supremely Exalted, The Most High

AL-MUTA-ALI
The Suprem One

The One who is exalted above all of creation. The One who is beyond the highest.... beyond the beyond. The One who far beyond any imagination, thought, limitation or ideal of mankind.

From the root 'a-l-w which has the following classical Arabic connotations: to be high, elevated, lofty; to be exalted, to rise up, to ascend;to be higher to exceed, surpass; to overcome, overwhelm; to advance, promote, rise above; to mount, be overtop, eminent

This name is used in the Qur'ān. For example, see 13:9

The term al-Muta'āli is an intensified form of al-'Alī (the Exalted) which further exalts the exalted One.

Al-Barr

The Kindly and Gracious Benefactor, The Righteous, The Source of Goodness

AL-BARR
The Doer Of Good

The One who is kind, gentle and ample in goodness. The One who is the doer of good, both materially and spiritually. The One who is kindly and gracious. The One from whom every good deed comes. The One who is the source of all kindness and goodness. The One who bountifully bestows the gifts of tolerance, gentleness, goodness and kindness. The One who is ever-merciful and compassionate.

From the root b-r-r which has the following classical Arabic connotations: to be devoted, affectionate, gentle; to be just and proper, honest, truthful; to have regard for the circumstances of another; to be beneficent, to bestow bountiful gifts; to reward for service, recompense; to behave courteously, to do good; to be benign, gracious, kindly; to be pious, virtuous, righteous; to be ample, extensive

This name is used in the Qur'ān. For example, see 52:28

Al-Tawwab

The Acceptor of Repentance, The Oft-Forgiving, The Acceptor of our Return

AT-TAUWAB
The Guide Of Repentance

The One who beckons for our return. The One who repeatedly turns mankind toward repentance. The One who forgives those who return to goodness. The One who restores to grace those who repent. The One who rewards good deeds. The One who forgives those who forgive others.

From the root t-w-b which has the following classical Arabic connotations: to return; to return to goodness, to repent; to be restored; to be rewarded for deeds; to be repeatedly summoned or called

This name is used in the Qur'ān. For example, see 49:12

Al-Muntaqim

The Avenger, The Disapprover, The Inflictor of Retribution

The One who disapproves of wrongdoers. The One who reminds us when our behavior is not right. The One who is the avenger (such that we need not seek any personal revenge). The One and Only One who has the right to exact vengeance.

AL MUNTAQIM

From the root n-q-m which has the following classical Arabic connotations: to dislike, disapprove, find fault; to punish, exact vengeance; to inflict retribution, avenge

The name Muntaqim is not specifically used as a Beautiful Name in the Qur'ān.

Al-Afuw

The Pardoner, The Most Forgiving, The Effacing, The Eliminator of Sins

The One who blots out and leaves no trace of any sin or fault. The One who passes over and absolves any fault. The One who can remove and obliterate all traces of wrong actions. The One who can make any sin, error or fault disappear.

From the root 'a-f-a which has the following classical Arabic connotations: to forgive, pardon;

to pass over, forgo, absolve; to obliterate all traces, efface, remove; to kill-off, allow to die; to turn away from punishing, not see, annul; to make unapparent, imperceptible; to give spontaneously, to give without constraint to give more than what is due

This name is used in the Qur'ān. For example, see 4:99

The words Ghafūr and Ghaffār denote simply forgiving or protecting, while 'Afūw indicates complete removal or obliteration of the condition.

The classical Arabic dictionary Taj al-Arūs offers a beautiful metaphor wherein 'afūw is said to be like a mighty desert wind which completely obliterates the footprints in the sand.

'Afūw and **Muntaqim** are complementary attributes. 'Afūw is the forgiver, while Muntaqim is the avenger.

Ar-Rauf

The Most Kind, The Tenderly Merciful, The Clement and Compassionate

The One who bestows boundless clemency, tenderness and affection. The One who shows the utmost compassion, pity and tender mercy. The One whose gentleness, kindness and mercy are beyond understanding.;

From the root r-a'-f which has the following classical Arabic connotations: to be kind, gentle, clement; to be merciful, compassionate; to show pity; to show tenderness

This name is used in the Qur'ān. For example, see 22:65

The term Ra'ūf indicates tender affection and is regarded as the utmost mercy and compassion, the ultimate limit of ar-Rahīm. The meaning is similar to ar-Rahīm, but focuses attention on the utmost tenderness, kindness and affection which accompanies the outpouring of mercy and compassion.

Malik al-Mulk

The Master of the Kingdom, The Owner of All Sovereignty, The Lord of Absolute Ruling Power

The One who is sole owner, possessor and ruler of all kingdoms. The One whose ruling power and authority have no limit. The One who possesses all authority to act in any manner, at any time, in any way. The One who is lord and master over all worlds, whether manifest or un-manifest. The One who has all mastery and authority to decide what shall be created, what shall be sustained and what shall be cease to be.

MALIK-UL-MULK
The Owner Of All

From the root m-l-k which has the following classical Arabic connotations: to possess, to own exclusively; to exercise authority to command; to have power over, command, reign; to have dominion over, to have ruling power; to have kingship

The name Mālik ul Mulk appears in the Qur'ān 3:26.

The name Malik signifies king, while the name the name Mālik, by virtue of the ā which intensifies the meaning, signifies something that is in some way greater than a king, and is often translated as master or lord. However, the exact differences between these names are not universally agreed upon.

By some traditions, al-Malik is considered to be the owner and king of this world, or of the beings of this world, while Mālik al-Mulk is considered to be the supreme lord and master of all worlds, the known and the unknown, the manifest and the un-manifest... and those explanations have been used in selecting the definitions given on this page.

Dhu-l-Jalali-wa-l-Ikram

Lord of Majesty and Generosity, Lord of Glory and Honor

The One who is most precious, revered and honored. The One who is the glorious and majestic lord of all generosity and bounty. The One who is the possessor of all glory and honor. The One who is the owner of every manner of blessing, perfection, honor and majesty. The One whose presence bestows majesty and generosity. The One who is the source of awesome splendor and abundance. This beautiful Arabic phrase begins with a pronoun, followed by two attributes of Allāh.

ذُوالْجَلاَلِ وَالإِكْرَامِ

Zul-Jalaali-wal-Ikram
The Possessor of Majesty and Honour

Dhū (pronounced "thoo") = Lord of, Possessor of

l = al = the

Jalāl = Majesty, Glory

wa = and

l = al = the

Ikrām = Generosity, Bounty

The attributes of Allāh in this phrase are based on the root j-l-l meaning: to be supremely great; to be glorious, majestic; to be sublime; to be high, lofty, far above, independent

and the root k-r-m which has the following classical Arabic connotations: to be noble, high minded, generous; to be highly esteemed, honored, prized, valued; to be excellent, precious, valuable, rare; to be productive, fruitful, bountiful

This name is used in the Qur'ān. For example, see 55:27

Though certain benefits and gifts may arrive through human hands, one must offer all praise and honor to the True Source from which all blessings come, the One who is the Lord, Possessor and Bestower of Majesty and Bounty.

The Beautiful Names al-Jalīl and al-Karīm are also derived from these same two roots. The words jalāl (glory) and ikrām (generosity) are verbal nouns, while jalīl (glorious) and karīm (generous) are adjectives.

The demonstrative pronoun Dhū literally means with, in, on, or of, but in this phrase from the Qur'ān it is often translated as Lord of, Owner of, or Possessor of.

Al-Muqsit

The Most Equitable, The Just

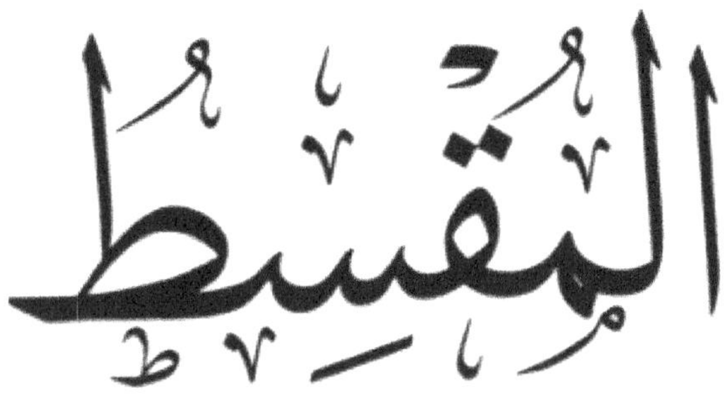
AL MUQSIT

The One who is most equitable and just. The One whose ways are balanced and just. The One who establishes justice. The One who creates harmony and balance. The One who does away with injustice. The One who leads mankind to justice and harmony.

From the root q-s-t which has the following classical Arabic connotations: to act justly, equitably; to do away with injustice; to establish an equitable balance

The name Muqsit is not specifically used as a Beautiful Name in the Qur'ān.

Al-Jami

The Gatherer, The Uniter, The Collector

AL JAAMI'

The One who reconciles and unites. The One who gathers together that which had been dispersed. The One who assembles and arranges. The One who composes, arranges and connects together.

From the root j-m-' which has the following classical Arabic connotations: to collect, gather up; to congregate, gather together; to draw together, muster; to reconcile, to connect together, combine; to form a connection between, union
to compose, arrange, resolve or settle something

This name is used in the Qur'ān. For example, see 3:9

Al-Ghani

The Self-Sufficient, The Wealthy, The Independent One

The One who is self-sufficient. The One without need of anything. The One who transcends all needs. The One who is completely satisfied. The One who is free from any wants. The One who is free from any dependence. The One who flourishes without help or aid of any sort, yet who is needed by all. The One upon whose wealth and riches all others depend.

AL GHANIYY

From the root gh-n-y which has the following classical Arabic connotations: to be free from wants or needs; to be self-sufficient, independent; to be able to do without help from others; to be content, satisfied; to be rich, wealthy, flourishing

This name is used in the Qur'ān. For example, see 6:133

Ghanī denotes the One whose essential nature is independence, self-sufficiency and supreme wealth.

Mughnī is from this same gh-n-y root and denotes specific deeds done by the One in bestowing wealth.

Al-Mughni

The Enricher, The Bestower of Wealth, The Fulfiller of Needs

AL MUGHNI

The One who gives wealth abundantly. The One who provides all that is needed. The One whose wealth fulfills all needs. The One who enriches all of creation. The One who creates all appearances of independence or self-sufficiency. The One who bestows satisfaction and contentment. The One who bestows spiritual wealth.

From the root gh-n-y which has the following classical Arabic connotations: to be free from wants or needs; to be self-sufficient; to be able to do without help from others; to be content, satisfied; to be rich, wealthy

The name Mughnī is not specifically used as a Beautiful Name in the Qur'ān.

Ghanī , from the same gh-n-y root, denotes the One whose essential nature is independence, self-sufficiency and supreme wealth. Mughnī denotes specific deeds done by the One in bestowing wealth.

Al-Mani

The Preventer, The Protector, The Defender

AL MANI'

The One who averts harm, physical or spiritual. The One who guards from harmful situations. The One who prevents undesirable actions. The One who impedes or hinders wrongful action. The One who stops one thing from harming another.

From the root m-n-' which has the following classical Arabic connotations: to prevent, hinder, hold back, restrain, deny; to impede, resist; to forbid, refuse, prohibit; to guard, defend, protect

The name Māni' is not specifically used as a Beautiful Name in the Qur'ān.

Names related to Watching and Protecting: **Hafīz** refers to the One who remembers and preserves to keep things from being lost or forgotten. **Wakīl** refers to the One who is the trusted administrator of all matters. **Raqīb** refers to the One who watches and observes. **Māni'** refers to the One who protects and defends against harmful situations.

Ad-Darr

The Correcter, The Balancer, The Distresser, The Afflicter, The Punisher

Ad-Darr
The Creator of The Harmful

The One whose wisdom may choose to use forceful corrections. The One who creates adversity or distress in order to discourage or correct wrongful behavior. The One whose wisdom may use situations that have an outward appearance of being harmful.

From the root d-r-r which has the following classical Arabic connotations: to have an opinion that is opposing; to apply forceful correction;to do an act that is disliked; to make inconvenient, annoy, distress; to cause adversity, afflict; to harm, injure, hurt

Nāfi' (creator of good) is the opposite of Dārr (distresser)

The names Dārr and Nāfi' are often used together to acknowledge the way that balance and harmony are established and maintained. These opposing attributes are often inseparable, since that which is the sweetest nectar to one person may be bitter poison to another.

Such opposites help to make one aware that every action accomplishes some purpose and is, in the grand scheme of things, subservient to the all-knowing hand of Allāh, through whom balance and harmony are created and maintained... even if we don't understand.

Abū Hāmid al-Ghazālī wrote:

Do not suppose that poison kills or harms by itself.... or that kings or men or satan, or any creature, are capable of good or evil, benefit or harm, by themselves. For all of these are subservient causes from which nothing proceeds except that for which they were utilized.

There is a grand intelligence who has a plan that is beyond our understanding, and these pairs of opposites serve to remind us to constantly focus our attention on the glory of the One, regardless of whether the situation is smooth and easy or rough and difficult. There is only one virtue and one sin for a soul on the path: virtue when he is conscious of God and sin when he is not.

-Abu Hashim Madani

The phrase ad-Dārr un Nāfi' is is often recited to honor these two complementary attributes.

An-Nafi

The Creator of Good, The Benefiter, The Propitious, The Auspicious

The One who helps and who grants all advantages. The One who creates all that produces benefit and usefulness. The One who grants all favorable circumstances. The One who confers all benefits. The One who is continually blessing all of creation with goodness and all that is useful. The One through whom all needs are fulfilled.

An-Nafi`
The Creator of Good

From the root n-f-' which has the following classical Arabic connotations: to profit, to be of use; to be beneficial, useful; to have the use of something

The name Nāfi' is not specifically used as a Beautiful Name in the Qur'ān.

Nāfi' (creator of good) is the opposite of Dārr (distresser).

The names Dārr and Nāfi' are often used together to acknowledge the way that balance and harmony are established and maintained. These opposing attributes are often inseparable, since that which is the sweetest nectar to one person may be bitter poison to another.

Such opposites help to make one aware that every action accomplishes some purpose and is, in the grand scheme of things, subservient to the all-knowing hand of Allāh, through whom balance and harmony are created and maintained... even if we don't understand.

An-Nur

The Light, The Illuminator, The One who Reveals

The One who is the divine light of all the worlds. The One whose light who illuminates the heart.

The One who is the light of wisdom and guidance. The One whose light clarifies, manifests and reveals. The One light by which the obscure is made clear. The One who clears away all darkness and directs aright.

From the root n-w-r which has the following classical Arabic connotations: to give light, to illuminate, to fill with light; to clarify, to reveal, to make visible; to blossom, to be in bloom (revealed); to be flaming, blazing and apparent to the senses; to enlighten, give counsel, give advice

This name is used in the Qur'ān. For example, see 24:35

AN-NOOR
The Light

Surah an-Nur (24:35) has a beautiful, mystical passage from the Qur'ān describing the Light: "Allāh is the light of the heavens and the earth. A likeness of His light is as a pillar on which is a lamp; the lamp is in a glass, the glass is as it were a brightly shining star - lit from a blessed olive-tree, neither eastern nor western, the oil whereof gives light, though fire touch it not - light upon light. Allāh guides to His light whom He pleases. And Allāh sets forth parables for men, and Allāh is Knower of all things." (Muhammad Ali Translation)

Al-Hadi

The Guide, The Leader, The Guide of the Right Path

AL HAADI

The One who continually shows the right way. The One who kindly guides aright. The One who sends prophets and messengers to guide mankind. The One who guides hearts to a knowledge of the Divine essence. The One who is the source of all guidance. The One who faithfully continues to guide aright until the goal is finally attained.

From the root h-d-y which has the following classical Arabic connotations: to guide rightly; to show with kindness the proper path; to guide on the right path until reaching the goal; to guide aright; to lead the right way

This name is used in the Qur'ān. For example, see 25:31

Rashīd refers primarily to being directed to, or set upon, the appointed right path with supreme certainty of the intended outcome, while Hādī refers primarily to the continuing guidance, leadership and direction that is kindly provided to reach the path and also along the path until the goal is achieved.

Al-Badi

The Wonderful Originator, The Unprecedented and Incomparable Inventor, The Absolute Cause

The marvelous One who originates, commences, invents and creates all that exists, without any model or material. The One whose incomparable will-power first brings into existence all of the unique and amazing creation without any similarity to anything else that has ever existed. The One who creates in wonderful, awesome, amazingly original ways that have no precedent whatsoever.

AL-BADI
The Originator

From the root b-d-'a which has the following classical Arabic connotations: to introduce, originate, start, innovate; to do for the first time, and not after the similitude of anything pre-existing; to cause to exist, to bring into existence; to devise, to uniquely contrive; to be amazing, outstanding, marvelous, superlative, incomparable

This name is used in the Qur'ān. For example, see 2:117

In honoring the One Creator, it has been said that mankind does not truly create, but rather merely discovers that which Allāh has already created.

The ancient Semitic roots of b-d-' point toward everything which is blossoming into existence and becoming apparent or exposed, with a sense of separation and individuality.

The expression al-Badī' refers to the Creator as well as that which is created.

In some Classical Arabic literature, the participles Mubdi' and Badī' are used interchangeably. However, in many Qur'ān commentaries, these terms are used to describe slightly different attributes, with the name Mubdi' emphasizing the initiation of creation, while Badī' emphasizes the awesome innovation of such creation.

Al-Baqi

The Everlasting, The Eternal, The Ever-Enduring, The Ever-Present

AL-BAQI
The Everlasting One

The One who has always existed and who will never cease to be. The One whose existence has neither beginning nor end. The One whose existence is beyond the realm of time. The One who existed before all of creation, and who will remain after all of this creation has come and gone. The One who is everlasting, perpetual, beginning-less, endless. The One whose existence is eternal. The One who remains forever, unaffected by time.

From the root b-q-y which has the following classical Arabic connotations: to remain, continue, endure; to be permanent, everlasting, constant; to survive forever; to be incessant, continuous, endless

The term Bāqī is not specifically used as a Beautiful Name in the Qur'ān.

The term Abqā, also from the b-q-y root, is used in the Qur'ān (20:73) where it is commonly translated as the Most Lasting, Ever Lasting or Most Abiding.

The term baqiyyah is used in the Qur'ān (11:116) to describe persons of excellence, those who possess spiritual understanding and inner discrimination, those who possess a quality of attending to that which is eternal.

The related term baqā', which is from the same b-q-y root, is often translated as eternal life. In the state of baqā' bi-llāh there is a return from the ephemeral to the eternal, a shift from the egocentric to the Divine, where all that remains is the eternal Thou. The return to the Everlasting, the return from one's worldly preoccupation with the ephemeral, the shift away from one's own ego being treated as the center of life, is often called fanā' which literally means to fade away, dwindle, recede or come to an end.

yā bāqī anta al-bāqī is a powerful wazīfa which can be translated as o' Everlasting One, Thou art The Everlasting One.

Al-Wartih

The Inheritor, The Supreme Heir

Al-Warith
The Inheritor of All

The One who remains after all of creation has perished. The One to whom all returns. The One who has everlasting ownership of all that has ever been and that will ever be. The One to whom all possessions return when the possessor is gone. The One who inherits all that we have done.

From the root w-r-th which has the following classical Arabic connotations: to inherit; to be an heir, survivor; to be the owner or sustainer after someone

This name is used in the Qur'ān. For example, see 15:23

After all greed, lust, misunderstanding and selfishness have been laid to rest, the One who remains is al-Wārith. When one surrenders, and lets go of all worldly things, the One who remains is al-Wārith. All that we possess, even our bodies, are only on loan for a moment.

Ar-Rashid

The Director to the Right Way, The Appointer of the Right Path, The Unerring Director

The Guide to Path of Rectitude

The One who unerringly decrees, appoints or ordains the right way. The One who is the supreme director to the right path and right belief. The One who perfectly and righteously directs all matters toward their proper conclusion. The One who needs no aid to direct all affairs rightly.

From the root r-sh-d which has the following classical Arabic connotations: to be directed aright; to be caused to follow the right course; to be directed to take the right way; to be caused to hold a right belief; to adopt the right path

The name Rashīd is not specifically used as a Beautiful Name in the Qur'ān.

The name al-Rashīd, according to the dictionary Lisān al-'Arab by al-Mukarram, denotes:

The One who is the Director to the right way, and the One whose regulations are conducted to the attainment of their ultimate objects in the right way, without anyone's aiding in directing their course aright.

Rashīd refers primarily to being directed to, or set upon, the appointed right path with supreme certainty of the intended outcome, while Hādī refers primarily to the continuing guidance, leadership and direction that is kindly provided to reach the path and also along the path until the goal is achieved.

The word murshid, meaning a director to the right path, is also derived from this same r-sh-d root.

As-Sabur

The Most Patient, The Patiently-Enduring

AS-SABUR
The Patient One

The One who is most patient, steadfast, and enduring. The One who is not moved by haste to carry out any action before it's proper time. The One who patiently endures and does everything in its proper time and proper manner, no matter how long that may take. The One who patiently accomplishes each thing in its proper time, in the way it needs to be and according to what it requires.

From the root s-b-r which has the following classical Arabic connotations: to be patient, to be enduring; to endure trial or affliction with good manner; to be contented in trial or affliction without show of complaint; to make no distinction between comfort and affliction; to bear calmly, to persevere cheerfully; to be steadfast, constant; to restrain, confine, restrain, withhold from something

The name Sabūr is not specifically used as a Beautiful Name in the Qur'ān.

Mankind's share of this attribute is the bountiful reward bestowed upon those who patiently persevere in overcoming the trials, lusts and errors of this world.

Sheikh Tosun Bayrak writes of al-Sabūr:

The meaning of Islam is submission; to forego one's appetites, desires and will in the favor of the will of Allāh. To be able to submit, one has to be patient. In Islam, patience is a sign of faith.

Related names: **Halīm** is the patience that arises from a sense of deep serenity, lenience, calm deliberation. **Sabūr** is the patience that arises by self-restraint, enduring something without complaint.

Islamic Expressions Glossary

As Presented by Christine Benlafquih for Islam 101

Muslims around the world use Islamic expressions in Arabic. Arabic is the language of revelation for the Qur'an, and it is the language used by Muslims around the world to recite their five daily prayers. In addition, Muslims of all backgrounds and cultures use Islamic expressions in Arabic. Following is a list of Islamic expressions with Arabic transliterations from A to Z. The English translations are sometimes used by English-speaking Muslims.

Alayhi Salam
Peace Be Upon Him - This invocation is said after the name of a prophet in honor of his high religious status. It's also used after the names of angels.

Alhamdulillah
Praise Be to Allah - Muslims liberally use "alhamdulillah" in the same context as "thank God" to express gratitude and to indicate that all is well. "Alhamdulillah" is also said after eating, drinking, and as a matter of etiquette after sneezing or burping.

Allahu Akbar
Allah is the Greater - Known as the *takbir,* this expression is commonly mistranslated to "God is Great." Muslims use it to praise Allah, show approval, or express surprise or awe.

Allahu 'Alim
Allah Knows Best - Muslims say "Allah knows best" to express uncertainty, or to describe a situation on which one can only speculate.

Ameen
Please Accept or May It Be So - Like the English equivalent "amen," this expression is typically recited at the end of prayers, supplications or invocations.

As-salamu Alaykum
Peace Be Upon You - "As-salamu alaykum" is the customary greeting between Muslims, with "wa alaykum salam – and upon you be peace" the reply. The greeting is sometimes shortened to "Salam" or lengthened to "As-salamu alaykum wa rahmatullahi wa barakatuh – Peace be upon you as well as the mercy and blessings of Allah".

Astafighurallah
I Seek Forgiveness from Allah - Muslims typically express this after doing something sinful. In Islamic etiquette, "astafighurallah" is also said after burping.

Atqaa Allah
Fear Allah - This expression is used to advise someone who is engaging in sinful behavior, and remind him that he will be accountable for his actions.

Audhu Billahi Min Ash Shaytani Ar Rajim
I Seek Protection in Allah from the Accursed Satan - Muslims invoke Allah with this expression when confronted with something unpleasant or contradictory to Islam,. Or before reading or reciting Qur'an. A shortened version, "audhu billah – I seek refuge in Allah," is also sometimes used.

Barak Allahu Feek
May the Blessings of Allah Be Upon You - In place of saying "thank you," a Muslim frequently shows appreciation by invoking Allah's blessings for someone.

Bismillah
In the Name of Allah (God) - Muslims remember Allah by saying "bismillah" many times throughout the day, particularly before beginning something. This includes before eating, drinking, cooking, working, studying, entering or leaving a home, and more.
Bismillahi Rahmani Rahim
In the Name of Allah, the Most Gracious, the Most Merciful - These are the opening words of the Qur'an, repeated by Muslims when reciting Qur'an and when making their five daily prayers. The expression is also used to commence writing, speaking, and other acts.
Fi Amanallah
In Allah's Protection - Muslims frequently use this expression when parting company.
Fi Sabilillah
In the Way of Allah - This Arabic expression might also be interpreted as "for the cause of Allah." It's used when seeking or making a charitable act.
Hasbi Allah
Allah Will Suffice Me - When they find themselves in a difficult situation, Muslims use this expression to show trust in Allah.
Inna Lillaahi Wa Inna Ilayhi Rajiun
To Allah We Belong and to Allah We Return - Muslims pronounce this upon learning of the death of someone. It's also used when a Muslim suffers from a serious affliction or trial.
Insha Allah
If Allah Wills - The English equivalent is "God willing." Muslims use this expression whenever mentioning an intended act or future event.
Jazak Allahu Khayran
May Allah Reward You for the Good - This invocation is said in gratitude to someone who has done a kind act, provided help, or given a gift. Such expressions of appreciation are preferable to simply saying "thank you."
La Hawla Wala Quwata Illa Billah
There Is No Power Nor Strength Except Allah - Muslims frequently acknowledge that all matters are ultimately controlled and decreed by Allah. This expression is particularly used at times of calamity, trouble or difficulty.
La Ilaha Ill-Allah
There Is No God Other Than Allah - The declaration that Allah is One God with no partners is the most important phrase in Islam. Belief in the oneness of Allah is the foundation of a Muslim's faith.
Ma Salama
With Peace - Some Muslims use this casual expression when parting, ending phone conversations, or when closing a letter.
Masha Allah
What Allah Wills - Muslims use this expression to show appreciation when hearing or seeing something nice, or when acknowledging compliments.
Radiyallahu Anhu (RA)
May Allah Be Pleased with Him - This invocation is made upon hearing, saying or writing the name of a companion of the Prophet Muhammad (peace be upon him). The expression changes to "radiyallahu anha" for a woman, and "radiyallahu anhum" for several people.
Rahimahullah

May Allah Have Mercy on Him - Whenever a deceased Muslim is mentioned, Muslims use this expression to ask for Allah's mercy on his soul. A variation, "rahmah Allah" might be used to ask Allah to have mercy on someone who is in distress.

Sallalahu Alayhi Wa Sallam (SAW)

May the Peace and Blessings of Allah Be Upon Him - Muslims say this whenever speaking, hearing, writing, or reading the name of the Prophet Muhammad (peace and blessings be upon him).

Subhan Allah

Glory Be to Allah - Muslims frequently praise Allah and His creation with this expression, or they use it to express joy and relief.

Subhanahu Wa Ta'ala (SWT)

Highly Praised and Glorified - This expression often follows a mentioning of Allah, signifying His Greatness and His Oneness.

Tabarak Allah

Blessed Is Allah - Upon learning of someone's accomplishments or hearing good news, Muslims will say this expression.

Tawkkalna Alay Allah

We Have Put Our Trust in Allah - Muslims use this expression while waiting patiently for a problem to be solved. A variation, "Tawakkaltu Allah – Trust in Allah," is said when advising or comforting someone who has a difficulty.

Ya Allah

O Allah (O God) - Muslims call on Allah with this expression when upset, in distress, or in pain.

Yarhamuk Allah

May Allah Bless You - A Muslim says "yarhamuk Allah" in response to another Muslim who has sneezed and said, "alhamdulillah."

These are only some of the Islamic expressions Muslims use regularly. Although many Muslims use the actual Arabic, it's acceptable for Muslims to use their native language instead. Only the five daily prayers in Islam must be recited in Arabic.

Duas

"Surely prayer keeps (one) away from indecency and evil; and certainly the remembrance of Allah is the greatest (force). And Allah knows what you do."
-Surah 29:45

Duas or short prayers prescribed by the Most Honorable Elijah Muhammad in the book Message to the Blackman in America.

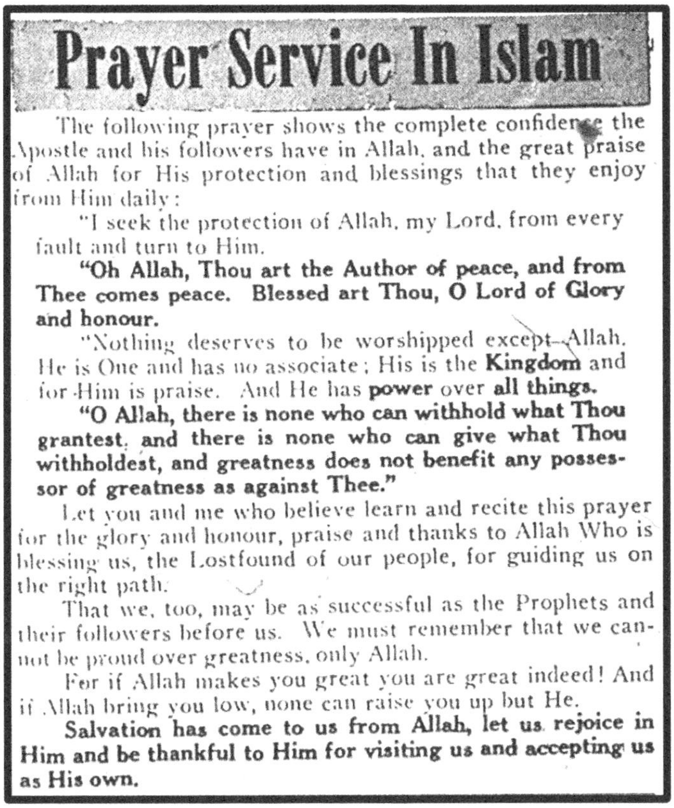

Prayer Service In Islam

The following prayer shows the complete confidence the Apostle and his followers have in Allah, and the great praise of Allah for His protection and blessings that they enjoy from Him daily:

"I seek the protection of Allah, my Lord, from every fault and turn to Him.

"Oh Allah, Thou art the Author of peace, and from Thee comes peace. Blessed art Thou, O Lord of Glory and honour.

"Nothing deserves to be worshipped except Allah. He is One and has no associate; His is the **Kingdom** and for Him is praise. And He has **power** over **all things.**

"O Allah, there is none who can withhold what Thou grantest, and there is none who can give what Thou withholdest, and greatness does not benefit any possessor of greatness as against Thee."

Let you and me who believe learn and recite this prayer for the glory and honour, praise and thanks to Allah Who is blessing us, the Lostfound of our people, for guiding us on the right path.

That we, too, may be as successful as the Prophets and their followers before us. We must remember that we cannot be proud over greatness, only Allah.

For if Allah makes you great you are great indeed! And if Allah bring you low, none can raise you up but He.

Salvation has come to us from Allah, let us rejoice in Him and be thankful to Him for visiting us and accepting us as His own.

"O Allah! I seek Thy refuge from anxiety and grief and I seek Thy refuge from lack of strength and laziness and I seek Thy refuge from cowardice and niggardliness and I seek Thy refuge from being overpowered by debt and the oppression of men. O Allah! Suffice Thou me with what is lawful to keep me away from what is prohibited and with Thy grace make me free from want of what is besides Thee."

"O Allah, we beseech Thy help and ask Thy protection and believe in Thee, and trust in Thee, and we laud Thee in the best manner and we thank Thee, and we are not ungrateful to Thee, and we cast off and forsake him who disobeys Thee."

"O Allah, we beseech Thy help and ask Thy protection. We believe in Thee and trust in Thee. We worship Thee in the best manner and we thank Thee. We are not ungrateful to Thee and we cast off and forsake him who disobeys Thee. O Allah, Thee do we serve and to Thee do we pray and make obeisance. To Thee do we flee, and we are quick. We hope for Thy mercy and we fear Thy chastisement, for surely Thy chastisement overtakes the unbelievers."

"I seek the protection of Allah, my Lord, from every fault, and turn to Him. Oh Allah, Thou art the author of peace and from Thee comes peace. Blessed art Thou, O Lord of Glory and honor."

"Nothing deserves to be worshiped except Allah. He is One and has no associate; His is the Kingdom and for Him is praise. And He has power over all things."

"O Allah, there is none who can withhold what Thou grantest and there is none who can give what Thou withholdest and greatness does not benefit any possessor of greatness as against Thee."

"O Allah, guide me among those whom Thou hast guided aright and preserve me among those whom Thou has preserved and befriended and bless me in whatever Thou doest; grant me and deliver me from the evils of what Thou has judged. Surely Thou judgest and none can judge against Thee and He whom Thou befriendest is not disgraced."

Oh Allah grant us security, grant us sustenance and exalt us; and set aright all our affairs

Below: Duas or short prayers extracted directly from the English translation of Holy Qur'an. Any and all of these short prayers may be committed to memory & recited and meditated upon by believers as powerful ways to invite the presence of Allah into our hearts and minds as we struggle for balance, success in life and the victory of the Apostle.

2:286 Our Lord, do not punish us if we forget or make a mistake. Our Lord do not lay on us a burden as You did lay on those before us. Our Lord do not impose on us (afflictions) which we have not the strength to bear. And pardon us! And grant us protection! And have mercy on us! You are our Patron, so grant us victory over the disbelieving people.

3:8-9 Our Lord, do not make our hearts to deviate after You have guided us and grant us mercy from Yourself; surely You are the most liberal Giver. Our Lord, surely You are the Gatherer of people on a day about which there is no doubt. Surely Allah will not fail in (His) promise.

3:147-148 Our Lord, grant us protection from our sins and our extravagance in our affair, and make firm our feet and grant us victory over the disbelieving people. So Allah gave them the reward of the world and a good reward of the Hereafter. And Allah loves the doers of good (to others).

3:191-195 Our Lord, You have not created this in vain! Glory be to You! Save us from the punishment of the Fire. Our Lord, whomsoever You make enter the Fire, him You indeed bring to disgrace. And there will be no helpers for the wrongdoers. Our Lord, surely we have heard a Crier calling to the faith, saying: Believe in your Lord. So we do believe. Our Lord grant us protection from our sins and remove our evils and make us die with the righteous. Our Lord grant us what You have promised
us by Your messengers and do not disgrace us on the day of Resurrection. Surely You never fail in (Your) promise! So their Lord accepted their prayer, (saying): I will not let the work of any worker among you to be lost, whether male or female; each of you is as the other.

10:85-86 On Allah we rely; our Lord, do not make us a trial for the unjust people. And deliver us by Your mercy from the disbelieving people.

14:35-41 My Lord, make this city secure, and save me and my sons from worshipping idols. My Lord, surely they have led many people astray. Our Lord, surely You know what we hide and what we proclaim. And nothing is hidden from Allah, either in the earth or in the heaven. Surely my Lord is the Hearer of prayer. My Lord make me keep up prayer and (those) from my offspring (too), our

Lord, and accept my prayer. Our Lord grant me protection and my parents and the believers on the day when the reckoning comes to pass.

59:9-10 And those who made their abode in the City and in faith before them love those who have fled to them, and find in their hearts no need of what they are given, and prefer (them) before themselves, though poverty may afflict them. And whoever is saved from the niggardliness of his soul, these it is that are the successful. And those who come after them say: **Our Lord, forgive us and our brethren who had precedence of us in faith, and leave no spite in our hearts towards those who believe. Our Lord surely Thou art Kind, Merciful.**

60:4-5 Our Lord, on Thee do we rely, and to Thee do we turn, and to Thee is the eventual coming. Our Lord make us not a trial for those who disbelieve, and forgive us, our Lord. Surely Thou art the Mighty, the Wise.

2:201 And there are some among them who say: **Our Lord, grant us good in this world and good in the Hereafter, and save us from the chastisement of the Fire.**

2:250 And when they went out against Goliath and his forces, they said: **Our Lord, pour out patience on us and make our steps firm and help us against the disbelieving people.**

3:38 There did Zacharias pray to his Lord. He said: **My Lord, grant me from Thee goodly offspring; surely Thou art the Hearer of prayer.**

4:75 And what reason have you not to fight in the way of Allah, and of the weak among the men and the women and the children, who say: **Our Lord, take us out of this town, whose people are oppressors, and grant us from Thee a friend, and grant us from Thee a helper!**

7:23 They said: **Our Lord, we have wronged ourselves; and if Thou forgive us not, and have (not) mercy on us, we shall certainly be of the losers**.

12:101 **My Lord, Thou has given me of the kingdom and taught me of the interpretation of sayings. Originator of the heavens and the earth, Thou art my Friend in this world and the Hereafter. Make me die in submission and join me with the righteous.**

17:80 And say**: My Lord, make me enter a truthful entering, and make me go forth a truthful going forth, and grant me from Thy presence a power to help (me).**

18:10 When the youths sought refuge in the Cave, they said: **Our Lord, grant us mercy from Thyself, and provide for us a right course in our affair.**

20:25-26 He said: **My Lord, expand my breast for me: And ease my affair for me**

25:74-75 And they who say, **Our Lord, grant us in our wives and our offspring the joy of our eyes, and make us leaders for those who guard against evil.** These are rewarded with high places because they are patient, and are met therein with greetings and salutation,

28:24 So he watered (their sheep) for them, then went back to the shade, and said: **My Lord, I stand in need of whatever good Thou mayest send to me.**

71:28 **My Lord, forgive me and my parents and him who enters my house believing, and the believing men and the believing women. And increase not the wrongdoers in aught but destruction!**

26:83-84 **My Lord, grant me wisdom, and join me with the righteous, And ordain for me a goodly mention in later generations, And make me of the heirs of the Garden of bliss**, And forgive my sire, surely he is of the erring ones, **And disgrace me not on the day when they are raised**

23:97 And say: **My Lord, I seek refuge in Thee from the evil suggestions of the devils,**

25:65-66 And they who say: **Our Lord, avert from us the chastisement of hell; surely the chastisement thereof is a lasting evil:** It is surely an evil abode and resting-place!

The Prophet's Dua at Taif

"O Allah! Unto You do I complain of my weakness, of my helplessness and of my lowliness before men. O most Merciful of the merciful. O Lord of the weak and my Lord too. Into whose hands have you entrusted me? Unto some far off stranger who receives me with hostility? Or unto a foe whom you have empowered against me? I care not, so long as You are not angry with me. But Your favouring help, that were for me the broader way and the wider scope. I take refuge in the light of Your Face whereby all darkness is illuminated and all things of this world and the next are rightly ordered, lest You make descend Your anger upon me or lest Your wrath beset me. Yet it is Yours to reproach until You are well pleased. There is no power and no might except through Thee."

-Prophet Muhammad

ResearchMinister.Com
A Complete Dictionary of
The Supreme Wisdom Lessons
Who Do They Say I Am?
Hail Elijah!
"When You Get Into Trouble, Nurse From Your Holy Qur'an"
How To Police The Black Community
Invincible Truth
An Invincible Truth
Malcolm?
Manhood
History, Scripture, Current Events & The Destiny of A People

Made in United States
Orlando, FL
19 April 2023

32247985R00143